# THE COMMISSIONERS

# THE
# COMMISSIONERS

BASEBALL'S MIDLIFE CRISIS

*JEROME HOLTZMAN*

TOTAL SPORTS
NEW YORK

*The book is dedicated to*

*John Hillyer*

*Friend and sportswriter extraordinaire*

# c o n t e n t s

# THE SEARCH

The first wave of applications, dated February 23, 1993, and addressed to the Office of the Baseball Commissioner, New York City, included the following from Erica Sitkoff of Marietta, Georgia:

"I would like to apply for the position of Commissioner of Baseball. I have a genuine love and knowledge of the game. Since I will be just starting at the position I would work for free.

"I avidly read about baseball and understand the game very well. Every decision I would make would be 'in the best interests of baseball.' I think the owners would get along with me better than the past commissioners. Among my best qualities are those of leadership and organizing people.

"Every year in school I have had one of the highest grade point averages in my class. Although I am not yet old enough to attend college, last year as part of a talent research program I took the SAT's and got recognized at a statewide reception for people who did well. If I was chosen I would continue my eighth grade education by correspondence courses."

"Wonderful, isn't it?" said Bill Bartholomay, a Chicago insurance executive who is active in civic affairs, and chairman of the Atlanta Braves. Bartholomay was the chairman of the Commissioner's Search Committee, and a self-described "quintessential WASP." Exceptionally pleasant and trustworthy, he is among the few owners respected by his fellow moguls.

He has known all the previous commissioners, starting with Kenesaw Mountain Landis, baseball's first czar. Bartholomay's sportsman father was a friend of Philip K. Wrigley, the longtime owner of the Chicago Cubs, and often among the guests at the Wrigley estate in Lake Geneva, Wisconsin, usually on summer Sundays when the children played softball. He has seen a photograph of himself with Landis who was also among the visitors.

"I was in white knickers. I think there was a grass stain from a diving catch," Bartholomay recalled.

"The list of applicants grows, some come and some go off," Bartholomay explained six months after the Search Committee had been formed. "It's probably still in the thirties."

The list was much larger in the beginning, in mid-February of 1993, when the owners appointed an eight-member committee to find a successor to Fay Vincent, Jr., who had resigned under pressure the previous September. Approximately 175 unsolicited applications were received, mostly through the mail.

Vincent threw in the towel nineteen months before the expiration of his four and a half year term. The pivotal moment occurred on September 3, 1992, at the Hyatt Regency in Rosemont, a Chicago suburb. It was an emergency meeting called by the league presidents, Bill White of the National League and Dr. Bobby Brown of the American. Vincent was not in attendance. Paul Beeston, a rising young executive with the Toronto Blue Jays, presided.

As he was approaching the guarded double-doors of the meeting room, Bill Giles, president of the Philadelphia Phillies, said "I don't know if everyone has the stomach for this."

They did. Simply put, the question was "Does he work for us, or do we work for him?" Seven of the nine members of the owners' Player Relations Committee (PRC), empowered to handle labor-management disputes, favored dismissal. The full vote was 18–9, with one abstention, Marge Schott of Cincinnati. A "no confidence" resolution stated in part:

"The major league clubs do not have confidence in the ability of the present Commissioner . . . and that under his direction it is impossible for baseball to move forward effectively and constructively."

George W. Bush, the son of President George Bush, was among the nine owners who opposed. George W., then in his fourth season as a general partner of the Texas Rangers, argued that Vincent be allowed to finish his term. "Every time he makes a decision, someone is not going to like him," Bush said.

As a young man during summer vacations, Vincent, along with William H. T. "Bucky" Bush, the President's younger brother, had worked as an apprentice in the future President's oil fields, sometimes enjoying brief stays at the Bush residence. Vincent often reminisced: "The President told me we used to leave a layer of grease in his pool every time we went swimming."

Most baseball insiders employed in lower-level positions were in Vincent's corner. Bobby Bragan, a baseball lifer who in his career had touched all the bases, and had been *the* force behind the adoption of the designated-hitter rule, wired Vincent:

"Your handling of the expansion payments, realignment, problems caused by television superstations makes too much logic. The owners who are against you are a bunch of egotists. The people are behind you. Give 'em hell."

Advised of the vote against him, Vincent insisted he would not resign. He changed his mind four days later, following a weekend of contemplation at his summer retreat in Cape Cod.

"To do the job without angering an owner is impossible," Vincent said in his farewell. "I can't make all twenty-eight of my bosses happy. People have told me I'm the last commissioner. If so, it's a sad thing. I hope they [the owners] learn this lesson before too much damage is done."

In a speech at Harvard University a month later, Vincent mused, "Baseball and humor are twins. What makes baseball special is that it deals openly with human frailty. What other sport acknowledges errors in the box score?"

The leaders in the movement to oust him were members of what was later called "The Great Lakes Gang":

• Bud Selig, president of the Milwaukee Brewers;

• Jerry Reinsdorf, chairman of the Chicago White Sox;

• Stanton Cook, head of the Tribune Co., which owned the Chicago Cubs;

• Carl Pohlad, chief of the Minnesota Twins;

• Peter O'Malley, the longtime majority owner of the Los Angeles Dodgers (surprisingly).

The principal complaint of O'Malley, who never before or since had joined the Selig-Reinsdorf coalition, was Vincent's stance on revenue sharing. The Dodgers had been baseball's most profitable club, a gold mine since 1958 when Peter's father, Walter, uprooted the prospering Brooklyn franchise and moved it just a few miles from downtown Los Angeles.

The younger O'Malley was among the eight or nine big-market operators resistant to the level of revenue sharing that the small-market owners thought was fair. Revenue sharing was first proposed by Bill Veeck forty years earlier when he owned the debt-ridden

St. Louis Browns. At league meetings and in public statements, Veeck contended the Browns, when in New York, were entitled to 50 percent of the Yankees' local television take. "We're half the show," Veeck said. "They can't play the game without us."

Revenue sharing was the litmus test of the '90s. In essence, it was a welfare formula in which the more profitable teams distributed funds to the less fortunate in an attempt to help equalize the widely disparate revenue streams that flow to the big-market teams. If adopted, the small-market franchises, would supposedly remain competitive.

The *local* broadcasting income of George Steinbrenner's Yankees was almost ten times that of many of the clubs in less populated areas. According to the March 15, 1993 issue of *Broadcasting* magazine, the New York Yankees' television and radio income was $47 million. The Boston Red Sox were second at $22 million, the Cubs and Atlanta next at $20 million. At the bottom were Cleveland and Minnesota, $4.5 million; Kansas City and Seattle, $5 million, and Milwaukee, $5.5 million.

"I'm a charitable guy," said Steinbrenner, who was among Peter O'Malley's allies. It was true. Steinbrenner routinely opened his purse to dozens of needy causes. "But I don't like the idea of a social-ist state. The Yankees shouldn't be punished for their success. Some of the middle- and small-market clubs have payrolls similar to ours."

The catalogue against Vincent had been growing. Many of the owners were also upset when he intervened in labor-management negotiations. It had been the private preserve of the PRC, founded in 1967 as a separate corporation for the specific purpose of excluding the commissioner from the bargaining table.

Prior to Vincent, several commissioners, most notably Bowie Kuhn, had interfered, to the dismay of the owners. Vincent's immediate predecessor, the scholarly Bart Giamatti, had remained aloof with the accurate observation that the commissioner's powers in labor matters were limited. The commissioner had suasion over only one side. He could order the owners to submit, as Kuhn had done, but he had no power over the players in labor negotiations. Donald Fehr, the executive director of the Players Association, like Marvin Miller, his predecessor, in reality, was the commissioner of the players.

There were other grievances. The National League objected to Vincent's attempt at realignment, to move the Cubs and the St. Louis Cardinals from the East to the West Division. Bill White, president of the National League, had cautioned Vincent; this action, without league approval, would be in violation of the National League Constitution.

But like Samuel Johnson's *Rasselas*, who tried to conquer the weather for equal distribution of rain and sun, Vincent was an idealist intent on perfection. The Cubs and Cardinals, moving from East to West, and Cincinnati and Atlanta from West to East, would correct a 23-year-old geographic mistake.

The Cubs sued the Commissioner on July 17 and asked the U.S. District Court in Chicago for a preliminary injunction to prevent implementation. The injunction was granted two weeks later. Attorneys for Vincent appealed. Oral arguments were scheduled for August 30. Vincent resigned before the litigation resumed, so the Cubs dropped their suit.

In addition, the NL owners were upset because Vincent had diluted their expansion swag when the league absorbed two new teams, the Colorado Rockies and the Florida Marlins. In the past, the expanding league routinely gobbled the entrance fees. In an attempt to win support in the American League and balance the vote, Vincent decreed that the AL owners were entitled to 22 percent of the $190 million take, a judgment without precedent.

Vincent had also extended the ongoing war against the superstations that had been televising games nationally. Baseball's internal tax against WGN-TV in Chicago, owned by the Tribune Co., and WTBS in Atlanta, affiliated with the Braves, was rising. For their unwelcome intrusions—435 games combined—the Braves paid $12 million annually; the Cubs, who had a lesser audience, $6 million. These fees went into baseball's Central Fund, distributed equally among the twenty-eight clubs. Both invaders had litigated against the Commissioner's office, without relief.

"If P. K. Wrigley were alive and still owned the Cubs he would have voted for the change," Vincent said. "He voted many times for things not good for the Cubs, but good for baseball. He was that unselfish."

But Wrigley was long gone, an altruist who a half century earlier had favored adjusting the reserve system. If the reserve clause was modified, the players would no longer be held in perpetual bondage. Wrigley and Tom Yawkey, who had owned the Boston Red Sox and died in 1976, were the last sportsman owners. When Wrigley recommended what was then a revolutionary and costly concept, the owners didn't even give him the courtesy of an extended discussion.

For some of the new breed of baseball owner, franchises were initially purchased for the joy of involvement, but the thrill seldom lasted beyond two or three years. Thereafter they discovered the underside, which included unanticipated and often irresponsible press criticism. There was no escape. Even the best of them, who had arrived with good intentions, were confronted by a hostile media sooner or later. For solace, they fastened their attention to the bottom line.

Vincent had the constant comfort of the New York press which was at his doorstep, supporting him with unswerving fervor. The prestigious *New York Times*, which pretends it has an exclusive on the truth, repeatedly assaulted the "Great Lakes Gang," particularly Reinsdorf who was portrayed as a Svengali who had Selig in his grasp. Claire Smith, previously an obscure entry with *The Hartford Courant*, often took the lead. She was Vincent's champion, hoisting his banner. Whenever Vincent so much as belched, she insisted it was good for the game.

Giamatti was responsible for Vincent's baseball career. They had met at a dinner party in 1979 and discovered they had much in common: both were native New Englanders, had attended Yale, had a passion for literature, and loved sports, especially baseball. They often discussed the possibility of working together and when Giamatti was appointed Commissioner, he created the position of Deputy Commissioner for Vincent.

Giamatti had a brief reign, five months, and was the first commissioner since Judge Landis to die in office. Death came on September 1, 1989, at the age of 51, from a massive heart attack. The next day Vincent was appointed Commissioner pro tem. On September 13, the owners unanimously elected him to serve the remainder of Giamatti's five-year term. Before accepting, Vincent consulted with Giamatti's widow to make sure she thought it was appropriate for him to do so.

Though confronted with the Pete Rose dilemma, Giamatti had a free ride. During his tenure, he had at most, a nodding relationship with the Players Association, and more important, had no major issue that pitted him against the owners. As skillful and charming as Giamatti was—he was an orator without compare—it isn't likely he would have been an effective commissioner.

The first order of business for Bartholomay's Search Committee was to hire an executive head-hunting firm which would help screen and, if necessary, conduct preliminary interviews. So the process began with a search for an organization experienced in finding the best fit; eleven search companies were considered. The winner was Eastman & Beaudine, with offices in Dallas, Atlanta, and Chicago.

Eastman & Beaudine, in addition to reviewing the applicants, also contacted potential candidates who had not applied and, in many instances, conducted preliminary interviews. Only two people were not interested, General Colin Powell, the hero of the Gulf War, and George W. Bush, the President's son, who at that time was a general partner of the Texas Rangers and was considering running for governor of Texas. Said one insider: "George W. was very popular. He would have had a lot of support."

A list of the desired qualities included seventeen areas, each described in one paragraph. Among them were: "Must be a strategic thinker and problem-solver. Bright and analytical with strong market planning and implementation skills. Should be a consensus-maker, accessible, charismatic, sensitive, warm and personable with a good sense of humor." From my dealings with the owners, there was no question George W. had the best sense of humor of all of them.

Also, "Must be dynamic, self-confident, poised and commanding personal style, innovative, motivated, positive, aggressive, strong character, experienced in dealing with the media, and the ability to act decisively, when necessary, for the 'best interests of baseball.'"

As of March 2, five weeks into the search, the list had been trimmed to 105, from Ms. Iolet Ambrose to Mark A. Zotti. Still in the running were Erica Sitkoff, the eighth-grader from Marietta, Georgia; Lee Iacocca, who hid behind a third party he had authorized to submit his name; and H. Ross Perot. Neither Iacocca nor Perot was interviewed. Also in supposed consideration, at that time, were Rabbi Benjamin A. Kamin of The Temple, Cleveland's historic Reform Jewish Congregation; and Ira Glasser, executive director of the American Civil Liberties Union.

Thundered Glasser: "That job is mine. I've been preparing for it all my life."

By September there were ten finalists:

• Arnold Weber, president of Northwestern University;

• Harvey Schiller, executive director and secretary general of the U.S. Olympic Committee;

• Peter Bynoe, chairman & chief executive officer of Telemat, Ltd. Before that he had a foot in the door as the president of the Illinois Sports Facilities Authority, which had overseen construction of the new Comiskey Park;

• Paul Kirk, a Massachusetts attorney and former chairman of the Democratic National Committee;

• Senator George Mitchell of Maine;

• Dick Ebersol, president of NBC Sports;

• Don Rumsfield, former Secretary of State, and president & CEO of General Instrument;

• Lynn Martin, former Secretary of Labor, senior consultant with Deloitte and Touche, an international accounting firm;

• Dick Schultz, former executive director of the NCAA;

• Anita DeFrantz, U.S. representative on the International Olympic Committee.

Two women, Lynn Martin and Anita DeFrantz, were in the top ten. Martin, a Chicagoan, appeared to be the most confident. She told interviewers she had been a lifelong fan, was a Wrigley Field and Comiskey Park regular, and had grown up "reading about the Gas House Gang and every baseball book I could buy."

After her name had surfaced, a National League owner, speaking on the condition of anonymity, told me, "All the male chauvinists out there can relax. There is no way we're going to allow a woman to tell us what to do."

I passed the word along to Lynn Martin, via my column in the *Chicago Tribune* and wrote that she shouldn't have any delusions of grandeur. Neither she nor DeFrantz had a chance. They were window dressing, despite the comments of White Sox chairman Jerry Reinsdorf who insisted, "Man or woman, it makes no difference to me. We're looking for the best person and if she's the best person, she'll get my vote." Obviously, neither of the women was the "best person."

Whatever the owners' true feelings on the matter, the inclusion of Martin and DeFrantz was politically correct, a bow to the progress of the feminist movement. Three-quarters of a century earlier, in the 1911 *Reach Baseball Guide*, editor Francis Richter published his neanderthal opinion, then acceptable, on the dangers of a female invasion.

Under the heading "Base Ball Not For Women," Richter wrote:

"We are informed that base ball has been officially added to the list of approved [sports] for women's colleges by Athletic Instructor Edgar Fauber of Barnard, the women's department of Columbia University; and with the approval of the faculty, class teams have been organized and preliminary spring practice is already under way. One more indictment against the modern unsexing system of female education and training. With due respect to Mr. Fauber and the faculty of Columbia University, we hold, and we know that base ball is not a game for any woman, not even the most masculine of that sex. It's a strenuous game for even the most vigorous and powerful men, and that fact will soon be borne in upon such women as may attempt it through the medium of broken fingers, limbs and features. The idea of women playing base ball is not inviting from any physical viewpoint, and positively repugnant when viewed in other aspects. In athletics for women the line should be drawn at tennis. So far as such essentially masculine games as base ball and foot ball are concerned woman's only relation thereto should be as spectators."

Bartholomay, personally, conducted about thirty interviews. Constantly on the run, he made a trip to France. The day after he had returned, I asked if his search had extended to Europe.

"I was there on insurance business," Bartholomay replied. "But I did have dinner with Arnold Schwarzenegger in Cannes." Bartholomay had known Maria Shriver, Schwarzenegger's wife, from her days in Chicago. "He might be a good candidate," Bartholomay said, laughing. "He could knock some heads together."

The search was abandoned on January 18, 1994, following a joint owners' meeting in Fort Lauderdale. It was Selig's nineteenth wedding anniversary with his second wife. For approval, twenty-one of the twenty-eight votes were necessary a three-fourths majority. Bartholomay went in with two finalists, Weber of Evanston, Illinois, (Bartholomay's birthplace) who was retiring as president of Northwestern; and Schiller of the U.S. Olympic Committee.

Schiller's candidacy was well known. Weber was a surprise. Bruce Corrie, a former Northwestern athletic director, described him as "strong-willed . . . If baseball wants a passive commissioner he isn't the man."

"My wife is a neurologist and a large component of her practice is headaches," reported Northwestern provost David Cohen. "She once asked Arnie 'Don't you get headaches?' He said, 'No, I just give them.'"

The day began with a morning meeting of the ten-person Executive Council. To head off discussion of the merits of the finalists, Minnesota owner Carl Pohlad introduced a resolution for Selig to remain at his post, as Chairman of the Executive Council. Of all the owners, Pohlad, an octogenarian, looked after Selig in a fatherly way. Dissatisfied with Selig's wardrobe, Pohlad sent him suits, sport coats, shirts, and neckties.

When the joint meeting began three hours later, Minnesota Twins president Jerry Bell, at Pohlad's behest, distributed the resolution that had now been signed by eleven clubs, three more than enough to defeat any potential candidate.

The resolution, hand-written on lined yellow legal paper, stated in full:

"The following clubs prefer to delay any action on appointing a new commissioner until revenue sharing and pending labor issues are resolved."

The signers, in order, were Richard E. Jacobs, Cleveland; Pohlad, Minnesota; Russell Goldsmith, San Diego; Claude Brochu, Montreal; Wendy Selig-Prieb, Milwaukee (she was running the club during her father's absence); John Ellis, Seattle; Jerry Reinsdorf, Chicago White Sox; Drayton McLane, Jr., Houston; Mike Herman, Kansas City; Wally Haas, Jr., Oakland; and Peter Magowan, San Francisco.

Then came the hard part. "It hit me cold," recalled Bartholomay who had to wipe the egg off his face. He telephoned Schiller and Weber. According to sources, Schiller responded with grace. Enraged, Weber told Bartholomay to jump into Lake Michigan.

The next day in an explanation to the press, Bartholomay reviewed Selig's accomplishments and said, "It has become increasingly clear that we could be best led through this critical time . . . by the only person who fully understands the journey, its pitfalls and its dreams. Last night's 28–0 unanimous vote was further proof. Even more proof came last night when eleven of the clubs advised the Search Committee they could not vote for a new commissioner until the labor situation was resolved. Additional clubs have since expressed support for that position. It is for that reason that we have prevailed upon Bud Selig to continue as Chairman of the Executive Council, the titular head of Major League Baseball, fully charged to make the leadership decisions this game needs."

It was Bud Selig's 498th day as the acting Commissioner. He hadn't even reached the half-mile pole.

# JUDGE LANDIS
## PART I

Kenesaw Mountain Landis, a crusty federal judge, gave birth to
the fiction that the commissioner is a fire-belching Solomon.
During his 24-year reign, he was the first and last court of recourse.
Although fragile in appearance—he was about five-foot-six and 130
pounds—he was an intimidating presence. Players and owners
quaked when summoned to his Chicago office.

There were a few exceptions, among them Philip de Catesby Ball,
owner of the St. Louis Browns who had made his fortune in the ice
business. An aspiring ballplayer—his playing career ended when he
was knifed in a savage barroom brawl—Ball was the only owner who
refused to sign the document that brought baseball under Landis's
heel. He was also the only owner to litigate against Landis in court.
Ball lost.

The Judge played it by ear. According to Dr. Harold Seymour, baseball's foremost historian, Landis "blandly ignored the law in the interests of what he conceived to be justice." His most famous ruling from
the bench was a $29.24 million judgment against Standard Oil, a sum
that Standard Oil contended exceeded its assets. Like many of his decisions, it was reversed on appeal.

Following an unsuccessful congressional impeachment against
him, the American Bar Association renewed the assault with a resolution expressing "unqualified condemnation," describing
Landis's judicial approach and manner as "derogatory to the digni-
ty of the bench."

To the public, Landis was a shaggy white-haired symbol of justice, a "Puritan in Babylon." He was often photographed in a floppy
hat leaning over a box seat railing, arms folded under his chin, a czar
surveying his empire. Friends and foes recognized that the hat and a
cane were props. He was an amateur thespian capable of playing
Shakespeare.

Heywood Broun, a major New York columnist of the time,
observed:

"His career typifies the heights to which dramatic talent may
carry a man in America if only he has the foresight not to go on
the stage."

The Judge's vocabulary was colorful and salty. "He was one of
most profane men I ever met," Ford Frick said in a 1972 interview. A
New York sportswriter who had doubled as Babe Ruth's ghostwriter,
Frick climbed to the top of baseball's executive ladder: seventeen
years as president of the National League, fourteen seasons in the
commissioner's chair. Frick, like Landis, was raised in a small Indiana
town and had acquired secretarial skills prior to setting sail.

"[Landis's] profanity was so sublime I can't remember all the
terms," Frick recalled. "Once he was talking about his golf game—he
wasn't too good a golfer. Somebody asked him how he had done. He
said, 'I bitched my drive, boogered my mashie, fucked up my
approach shot.' I don't remember the entire sequence. But he just
kept using words, every one of them worse than the one before."

Landis was aware that Frick was a history buff. In September of
1936, the year Alf Landon, the Republican presidential candidate

who lost to Franklin Roosevelt in a landslide, Landis engaged Frick in a political discussion.

"He always called me 'Mr. Fo'd. Mr. Fo'd,'" Frick recalled. "He said, 'Mr. Fo'd, who's the lousiest president the United States ever had?'

"I said, 'A lot of people. Lots of different opinion. Harding was no bargain. And Andrew Johnson.'

"'Andrew Johnson, hell,' he roared. 'The lousiest president the United States ever had was Calvin Coolidge. Did you ever hear the man talk? Ever read anything he wrote? 'Course he was the lousiest president we ever had. And now they're calling this man Landon 'the Kansas Coolidge.' You know what I think of Landon? I think he's a beer-bellied, pinch-pennied Presbyterian sonofabitch. But I'm going to vote for him, anyway, 'cause he's the kind of man this country needs.'"

Bill Veeck, in his autobiography *Veeck—as in Wreck*, revealed his own "one bad mistake." In 1944, Veeck was planning to buy the Phillies and then sign black players. With the help of Abe Saperstein, owner and founder of the Harlem Globetrotters, and Doc Young, sports editor of the *Chicago Defender*, a Negro daily, Veeck began to recruit black stars such as Satchel Paige, Roy Campanella, Luke Easter, and Monte Irvin.

"I felt Judge Landis was entitled to prior notification of what I intended to do," Veeck wrote. "I was aware of the risk I was taking but I could not see how he could stop me. The color line was a 'gentleman's agreement.' The only way the Commissioner could bar me from using Negroes would be to rule officially and publicly, that they were 'detrimental to baseball.' With Negroes fighting in the war, such a ruling was unthinkable. Judge Landis wasn't exactly shocked but he wasn't overjoyed, either. His first reaction, in fact, was that I was kidding him." (In the end, the Phillies were sold to William Cox, instead).

That was in 1944, Landis's last summer; he died on November 25. The integration of baseball began three years later when Branch Rickey, a longtime Landis antagonist, brought Jackie Robinson to the Brooklyn Dodgers. Later in that same season Veeck signed Larry Doby to his Cleveland Indians, making Doby the American League's first black player. A year later Veeck acquired Satchel Paige, a legendary black pitcher.

While on the bench, Landis swayed with his prejudices; liberal one day, conservative the next. A so-called defender of the "common man," shameless in his pursuit of publicity, he was an unswerving moralist and an advocate of prohibition but in contradiction ordered bourbon whiskey by the case. He ladled the law by whim.

The faces and names of defendants and prosecutors were crucial. He freed an 18-year-old bank clerk accused by a Chicago brokerage firm of making off with $750,000 worth of Liberty Bonds that had been entrusted to him as a messenger. The bonds were recovered. Landis held a set of bank officials responsible for a small-salaried employee's yielding to temptation.

"I am going to set this boy free," Landis decided. "I wish I had the power to jail the men who sent him out with $750,000 in bonds."

On another occasion a young man was charged with stealing a package of jewelry.

"Here's a boy who admits to the crime, stealing jewelry out of the parcel post. And beside him is his little wife, recently a mother, heartsick over her husband's troubles. A hard case for me to decide." Then, after a theatrical pause, he asked. "Now what should I do?

"Son," he shouted. "Take your little wife and your baby and go home! I won't have that infant the child of a convict."

His hatred for radicals, socialists, and World War I pacifists was reflected in numerous harsh sentences. Presiding at the sedition trial of Big Bill Haywood, secretary-treasurer of the International

Workers of the World, Landis sent Haywood and ninety-three members of that union to prison.

Haywood retaliated in his autobiography:

"Pontius Pilate or Bloody Jeffreys never enjoyed themselves better than Landis when he was imposing those terrible sentences upon a group of working men for whom he had no feeling of humanity, no sense of justice." When President Coolidge commuted the terms of the convicted I.W.W. members (but not of Haywood, who had jumped bail and fled to Moscow), Landis denounced him.

Later, Landis sentenced Victor Berger, editor and socialist Congressman from Milwaukee, and four socialists for obstructing the nation's preparation for the war against Germany. They were all released upon appeal.

Landis was possessed of a ferocious patriotism. Administering the oath of citizenship to eighteen Chicago soldiers, he told them he hoped they would kill one or more of the Kaiser's sons. When the war ended, he expressed the bizarre notion that the former German emperor be hauled into his court. Landis insisted he would indict the Kaiser for the death of a Chicagoan who had lost his life in the 1915 sinking of the Lusitania. The Wilson administration informed Landis that treaties prevented extradition.

"The Judge was always headline news," recalled A .L. Sloan of the *Chicago Herald American*. "He was a great showman. He always had a crowd. There were no dull moments."

Jack Lait, who apprenticed in Chicago and later became a front-page Hearstling, described Landis in an obituary, as "an irascible, short-tempered, tyrannical despot. His manner of handling witnesses, lawyers—and reporters—was more arbitrary than the behavior of any jurist I have ever seen before or since. He resented what we wrote; he resented what we did, and probably what we wore. He regarded his courtroom as his private preserve and even extended his autocracy to the corridors." According to Lait, Landis once called his boss and demanded he be fired.

Landis referred to the staff of *The Sporting News* as "swine." He subjected F.C. Lane of *Baseball Magazine* to such personal abuse in the presence of others that Lane wrote him an open letter in protest. Irving Vaughan of the *Chicago Tribune*, a mild-mannered baseball lifer, recalled that in dealing with the press, Landis was "given to petty reprisals."

The popular myth, encouraged by Landis, was that he had not cultivated any of the owners when they had come calling, that they simply were desperate for judicial reform following the 1919 Black Sox scandal. There was the subsequent belief that Landis, with a mild assist from Babe Ruth, saved the game.

But Landis had not been a stranger. The Judge had rescued the owners five years earlier in his handling of a suit requesting an injunction against the American and National leagues, brought before him in January 1915 by the outlaw Federal League. Landis took the case under advisement but withheld his opinion, a crucial delay that provided the established leagues time to absorb the Federals, who folded after two seasons.

Edgar G. Brands, the eminent editor of *The Sporting News*, and the original author of the 30,000-word entry on baseball in the *Encyclopedia Britannica*, observed that during this case, Landis issued a dictum concerning the game that "lingered long" in the minds of those with a financial interest in the sport.

"Any blow at the thing called baseball would be regarded as a blow against a national institution," Landis said. The "blow," as Landis saw it, would have wounded Organized Baseball, not Federal League baseball, which had challenged the monopoly with the formation of a third major league. His trust-busting days behind him, Landis no longer was the antagonist of monopoly power as he had been during the Standard Oil hearings.

Federal League attorneys had sought to collect similar litigations in other jurisdictions and bring them into one court. The centerpiece of the suit, brought directly under the Sherman Anti-Trust Act, was the charge of restraint of trade and the legality of the reserve clause. It also charged tampering with the players by the two established major leagues, inducing them to jump back from the Federal League, and generally interfering with its operations through prosecution of suits against individual jumpers.

Recognizing the legitimacy of the charges and the severe consequences should he grant the injunction, Landis finally buried the case until the warring factions had settled. The helpful jurist was not forgotten when baseball leaders sought a chief administrator.

This was a textbook example of "justice delayed, justice denied," as Landis fully understood the inequities of the reserve rule which allowed team owners to renew a player's contract in perpetuity, or until the player was traded or sold and then became the property of his new employer, who picked up the perpetuity baton.

In fact, Landis often confided to intimates the illegality of the reserve rule, but when elected commissioner he vowed to safeguard the baseball establishment against any professional competition, which always was accompanied by salary increases and a weakening of player bondage.

If not for his father's political connections, Landis might have been a small-town attorney, a rural raconteur forgotten in the fog of time. His father, Dr. Abraham Landis, a Union surgeon during the Civil War, had his leg badly crippled while attending to a wounded soldier in the Battle of Kennesaw Mountain, Georgia, during Sherman's march on Atlanta. He was performing an amputation when a Rebel cannonball ricocheted off a tree and into his leg.

Years later, when the doctor's commanding officer, Colonel Walter Gresham, a fellow Hoosier, was appointed to Grover Cleveland's second-term cabinet as Secretary of State, Gresham took young Kenesaw with him as his private secretary.

Born on November 20, 1866, in Millville, Ohio, the fourth son of seven children of Abraham and Mary Landis, he was named Kenesaw, misspelled after that battleground. The doctor later moved the family to Logansport, Indiana. Landis dropped out of high school, but he got a job with the *Logansport Journal*, covering the local courthouse. Fascinated, he taught himself shorthand and became a circuit court stenographer.

Encouraged by Gresham, Landis enrolled at the YMCA Law School in Cincinnati. He received his law degree from the Union Law School of Chicago in 1891 and was admitted to the Illinois bar. He practiced law in Chicago for the next fourteen years, except for the 1893–95 period in Washington, D.C., as Gresham's secretary. In 1905, President Teddy Roosevelt, the trustbuster, named him federal judge in the Northern District of Illinois.

Upon ascending to baseball's highest office, Landis demanded and received absolute power. No appeals of his rulings or public criticisms of his actions by owners were permitted. In a side agreement made on January 12, 1921, two months after he assumed office, the sixteen owners submitted to a remarkable "Pledge of Loyalty":

"We, the undersigned, earnestly desirous of insuring to the public wholesome and high class baseball, and believing that we ourselves should set for the players an example of the sportsmanship which accepts the umpires' decisions without complaint, hereby pledge loyally to support the Commissioner in his important and difficult task; and we assure him that each of us will acquiesce in his decisions even when we believe them mistaken, and that we will not discredit the sport by public criticisms of him or one another."

Prior to Landis's anointment, baseball was ruled by a three-man National Commission formed in 1903. It was similar to an arbitration panel, and had final authority to interpret and adjudicate the National Agreement. This guiding legislation was drawn when the National League accepted the upstart American League as an equal, the leagues joining forces in a merger of interests.

The Commission had consisted of the two league presidents and August "Garry" Herrmann, president of the Cincinnati club, and settled disputes within the structure of Organized Baseball—between the clubs in the two major leagues and between major and minor league clubs, with the power to impose fines and suspensions. A National Leaguer, Herrmann was a "neutral" chairman, acceptable to the rival American League because he had played a leading role in bringing the 1903 peace, and because of his long friendship with the American League's president Byron Bancroft "Ban" Johnson. They had known each other since Johnson's early days as a Cincinnati sportswriter.

Prior to Judge Landis's grandiose entrance, Johnson was baseball's dominant figure. He had created the American League in 1900 with the considerable assistance of his staunch friend Charles Comiskey, owner of the Chicago White Sox. It was an alliance that was to come to a bitter and acrimonious end.

Then, as now, each owner had his agenda. Like an umpire, the Commission was under constant criticism, depending on the last call. The disputes usually centered on the various clubs' rights to ballplayers. A major dissension involved George Sisler who, when underage and without parental approval—he was not yet 18—had signed with Akron of the Class B Central League.

Sisler never reported to Akron, but his contract eventually was transferred to the Pittsburgh Pirates. Sisler's father enlisted the aid of Branch Rickey, the young man's coach at the University of Michigan. An appeal was filed with the National Commission. After several years of delay, the Commission ruled the contract invalid; that Sisler was a free agent, eligible to sign with whichever club he chose.

Barney Dreyfuss, the Pittsburgh owner, once a penniless German immigrant who had made his fortune in whiskey and baseball, offered Sisler $5,200 to play for the Pirates. Sisler accepted a larger bid from the St. Louis Browns where he was reunited with Rickey, who had joined the Browns as their field manager. Distraught over the loss of Sisler, Dreyfuss became the unrelenting foe of Herrmann, who had cast the deciding vote.

The breach widened with each passing year of Sisler's success on the field. He batted over .400 twice—.420 in 1922, still the American League record—and retired with a .340 lifetime average. Rickey had an even more spectacular career as a club executive and owner. He was the father of "chain gang" baseball, making him Judge Landis's implacable foe. A quarter of a century later, he broke baseball's color line with the signing of Jackie Robinson. The Sisler controversy was among the many that contributed to the collapse of the National Commission.

The general belief is that Landis was hired in frantic reaction to the Black Sox scandal, which wasn't confirmed until the final weeks of the 1920 season. But the Commission had been abandoned in December 1919 when the National League owners rebelled, ousting Herrmann and coming out for a neutral commissioner, preferably someone without a baseball affiliation. Baseball had operated without an overriding governing body in 1920. Decisions were made by the league presidents.

The search for a messiah was brief. On November 12, 1920, the owners met in Chicago and unanimously decided Landis was the ideal choice. A platoon of moguls piled into cabs and headed for the courtroom in the Federal Building. Historian David Voigt recreated the scene:

"The atmosphere of the judicial temple overwhelmed them. In the formidable setting of the court, Landis struck an awesome pose, with black robes lending grandeur to a spare frame and a presence manifested by a shock of gray hair, a piercing scowl and a rasping voice. These were great assets for any actor, and Landis was at his best that day.

"Landis ignored them and finished the case before him. At last Landis asked them to state their business. Although he had earlier indicated his willingness to take the job, the owners were requested to restate their offer. Then came a ceremonial refusal as Landis said, 'I am doing important work in the community and the nation.'"

Landis was soon assured he could assume both positions, federal judge and baseball czar. The owners offered him a $50,000 annual salary. Landis requested his $7,500 judicial salary be deducted from that amount. The owners agreed.

A drafting committee, headed by George Wharton Pepper, a Philadelphia attorney who represented both major leagues, was formed to forge a new National Agreement. The new document included all aspects of baseball legislation: the uniform player contract, waiver procedures, the care and feeding of minor league clubs, the hiring of umpires, disciplinary measures at the player and management levels, etc.

The owners, following the lead of league presidents Ban Johnson and John Heydler, in an attempt to retain a shred of their power, questioned the wisdom of granting Landis absolute authority, especially in regard to the fining, suspension or ejection of an owner without their approval. They attempted to resurrect the three-man tribunal; the league presidents would sit with the Judge, side by side. If they agreed on a particular issue and Landis disagreed, he would be overruled.

On January 12, 1921, in the Florentine Room at the Congress Hotel in Chicago, where the club owners had assembled for the fourth time since November 12, Landis told them he would withdraw unless given unlimited power, no questions asked. The transcript of Landis's statement follows:

"Gentlemen, you have heard this document read by the secretary. It is my duty to be very frank with you. When you came to me two months ago I got the impression from what you said, and made me believe—the belief amounting to a conviction—that you had calmly and thoroughly gone into your troubles and had a structure outlined which provided for an authority to discharge a responsibility and that part of that authority would be control over whatever and whoever had to do with baseball.

"Another impression was that there had grown up in baseball certain evils not limited to bad baseball players; that men who controlled ball clubs in the past had been guilty of various offenses and the time had come where somebody would be given authority, if I may put it brutally, to save you from yourselves. People had generally understood this conclusion and that if things went wrong they knew whose head to hit—it would be mine or my successor's.

"Now we meet again here today and this draft comes in and there has been a change. You will readily understand the embarrassment with which I discuss this matter because it relates to the powers of the Commissioner to deal with the offender in baseball whoever he might be. The amendment in this document today limits the authority of the Commissioner to deal only with a crooked ballplayer.

"There is another provision I had not seen before, that the Secretary-Treasurer may be appointed by your Commissioner but he holds office with the pleasure of the presidents of the two leagues. Now it is fundamental in this situation—and I want this constantly in mind, whether I serve you or not, because I have watched this thing for many years, and I am right about this:

"It is fundamental that the Commissioner upon whom you

devolve this authority and whom you trust and hold out to the millions of fans in this country with your plea, 'Gentlemen trust this man he is our Commissioner.' But he must have the power; and you can not put in here with Mr. Heydler and with Mr. Johnson with power that the Secretary—whom the Commissioner must trust hour after hour, upon whom he must lean and trust, that nobody can remove him but the club owners who are the source of ultimate power.

"You can't hire me—there is not enough money in America—and I mean nothing offensive by this; you are under no legal obligation to me and I acquit you of any possible moral obligation down to with any power on earth except the same power that appoints me to remove the Secretary of this Commissioner.

"Now you gentlemen build up your ball teams and I will take care of the figurehead business, if I stay here, but whereas two months ago you were of the opinion there should be a Commissioner with power to deal with evil wherever he found evil, that you have now made up your minds that you went too far and that you propose now to sign an agreement that the Commissioner can deal with evil, provided the evil is found in a ballplayer.

"Now I am going to step out of here. You are free to act now as you were on the morning of the 12th of November, and whatever you do, insofar as it affects nothing but me personally, I will love you just as much as I do now and I will fight for this thing just as hard as I have fought for it, and you may come to me with your troubles unofficially, if that is your preference."

Before leaving the room, confident the job was his, Landis asked for an expanded expense account:

"It is conceivable to me that the gentleman you are going to have as Commissioner may some day have occasion to hire somebody to go some place and do something. I would add something to that list of possible expenses in order that the Commissioner may feel at liberty—something may break loose in New York, Boston, St. Louis or some other place and the Commissioner might not want to ask Mr. Heydler or Mr. Johnson, in advance, to agree with what he is going to do. That is conceivable."

Then Landis said:

"Probably you gentlemen want to discuss this matter for two or three hours. Have I been frank with you?"

Ban Johnson was the first to capitulate: "I suggest that the original agreement be signed without a change."

William L. Veeck (president, Chicago Cubs): "I second the motion."

James C. Jones (attorney, St. Louis Cardinals): "Now I move that we get the original agreement and let us all sign it and be done with it."

Thomas B. Shibe (vice president, Philadelphia Athletics): "I second the motion."

The Agreement was ratified by fifteen of the sixteen major league clubs. Phil Ball, owner of the St. Louis Browns, refused to sign out of friendship with Ban Johnson, who from that day forward was no longer baseball's dominant figure. The owners had bowed to Landis, their new god, but acknowledged that, unlike Zeus, he was not immortal as shown in Article I, Section 6:

"Upon the expiration of the Commissioner's term, or upon his resignation or death during his term, his successor shall be chosen by a vote of the majority of the Clubs composing the two Major Leagues. In the event of failure to elect a successor within three months after the vacancy has arisen, either Major League may request the President of the United States to designate a Commissioner, and the person when thus designated shall thereupon become Commissioner, with the same effect as if named herein."

# JUDGE LANDIS
## PART II

The first challenge confronting the new commissioner was the crooked 1919 Chicago White Sox. Though they were never convicted it has been established beyond doubt that eight White Sox players, in league with gamblers, had conspired to throw the World Series to the Cincinnati Reds.

A month before the Series, there had been talk that the fix was in, that the White Sox were selling out. They should have been 3-to-1 or 4-to-1 favorites over the Reds, huge odds for baseball. On the eve of the first game, when the price dropped to even money, insiders were certain the rumors were true.

Confirmation came quickly. Previously strong defensively, the White Sox were erratic in the field and lost the first two games.

Cincinnati won the Series, five games to three—it was best-of-nine—not the customary best-of-seven. The lead of the eighth-game report in the *Chicago Tribune* by baseball writer Jim Crusin-berry follows:

"Oct. 10, 1919—The Reds beat the greatest ball team that ever went into a World Series.

"That was the first statement made by Boss Gleason of the White

Sox when the show was over at Comiskey Park yesterday. His next statement was about like this:

"But it wasn't the real White Sox. They played baseball for me only a couple or three of the eight days."

Only one baseball writer, Hugh Fullerton, repeatedly insisted the fix was in. Fullerton was one of several giants of the Chicago press box early in the century and had a larger baseball readership than Ring Lardner, his teammate at the *Chicago Tribune* who daily covered the White Sox. A so-called "dopester," Fullerton was almost always correct in his World Series forecasts. In 1921, he predicted the final scores of five of the eight games.

Fullerton later worked on several New York newspapers and was generally regarded as the most knowledgeable baseball Boswell of his time. Some of the gamblers and gangsters were so upset with his stories that, according to published reports, underworld king Arnold Rothstein threatened to "rub him out." Some baseball writers criticized Fullerton for "blackening baseball's reputation."

Novelist F. Scott Fitzgerald, in his book *The Great Gatsby*, captured the general disbelief of what Rothstein had done, in influencing the Series' outcome:

"Who's he, anyhow, an actor?"

"No."

"A dentist?"

". . . No, he's a gambler." Gatsby hesitated, then added coolly: "He's the man who fixed the World Series back in 1919."

"Fixed the World's Series?" I repeated.

The idea staggered me. I remembered, of course, that the World's Series had been fixed in 1919, but if I had thought of it all I would have thought of it as a thing that *merely* happened, the end of some inevitable chain. It never occurred to me that one man could start to play with the faith of fifty million people—with the single-mindedness of a burglar blowing a safe.

"Why isn't he in jail?" I asked.

"They can't get him, old sport. He's a smart man."

Most of the crooked players weren't nearly as clever. Indicted eleven months later, some of them babbled to a Cook County Grand Jury. The formal investigation began on September 23, 1920, six weeks before the owners had approached Judge Landis. After ascending the throne on January 12 of the following year, Landis withheld judgment despite the public objections of American League president Ban Johnson. Now a bitter foe of White Sox owner Charles Comiskey, Johnson not only had launched an American League investigation but also appropriated $10,000 of league funds to assist the State's Attorney.

Three of the crooks—pitchers Eddie Cicotte and Claude Williams, and outfielder "Shoeless Joe" Jackson—signed confessions. On August 2, after those confessions were "lost," a jury found the accused not guilty of intent to defraud the gambling public. The next day, Judge Landis banned the eight players for life.

". . . Regardless of the verdict of juries," Landis announced, "no player who throws a ball game, no player that undertakes or promises to throw a ball game, no player that sits in conference with a bunch of crooked players and gamblers where the ways and means of throwing a game are discussed and does not promptly tell his club about it, will ever play professional baseball.

"Of course, I do not know that any of these men will apply for reinstatement, but if they do the above are at least a few of the rules that will be enforced. Just keep in mind regardless of the verdict of juries, baseball is entirely competent to protect itself against the crooks both inside and outside the game."

Eliot Asinof, in his book *Eight Men Out*, describes the fix as a double-double cross. The gamblers double-crossed the players by not making full payment; and White Sox first baseman Arnold "Chick" Gandil, the treacherous ringleader and the primary corrupter, double-crossed his teammates, departing with $35,000 of the $50,000 loot. It became a triple-double cross when Landis suspended the players for life. Owner Comiskey had expected leniency.

The largest fiction was that Comiskey was unaware of the fix. From beginning to end, Comiskey feigned astonishment and offered a $10,000 reward to anyone who could furnish evidence of the sellout. One player did just that, Joe Gideon, of the St. Louis Browns. Gideon, a shaky witness, gave testimony that was not considered substantial.

Bill Veeck, in his 1965 *Hustler's Handbook*, insisted Comiskey was guilty of a coverup. Veeck came to this conclusion forty years after the fact, when he owned the White Sox. Fred Krehbiel, his nephew, while working one summer at the ballpark, found the cryptic diary of Harry Grabiner hidden in the wall of a basement storage room. Grabiner had functioned as Comiskey's general manager.

Grabiner, in his journal, revealed that a gambler acquaintance told him, after the first game, that the White Sox had been "reached." Grabiner called National League president John Heydler.

"I explained to him fully what I had heard," Grabiner wrote. "I impressed on him strongly that if anything wrong did exist regardless of whatever cost to the White Sox, I wanted it eliminated for if there was anything wrong in baseball the game was big enough to stand it being cleaned."

Grabiner's chronicle included a play-by-play of the owner intrigue surrounding the Landis appointment and how Comiskey had campaigned for the Judge. Grabiner obviously had good information. He listed the eight players involved and reported that the payoff was

$15,000 per game. There is no mention of Grabiner telling Comiskey of the fix but it can be assumed the White Sox boss was fully informed.

Neither Asinof nor Veeck had the transcript of the subsequent 1924 litigation brought by Joe Jackson against the White Sox. By then, playing for $75 a week with the Americus Club, an independent team in the South Georgia League, Jackson sued for back pay and $100,000 in damages. A month later, Oscar "Happy" Felsch and Swede Risberg, also suspended by Landis, joined what was in effect a companion litigation. They asked for an aggregate $400,000 for injury to their reputations and $4,670 in back pay.

They were represented by Raymond Cannon, a Milwaukee attorney who was attempting to organize the players. Cannon's son, Robert, had better success in this department. He preceded Marvin Miller as the head of the Major League Baseball Players Association. A sweetheart negotiator, friendly with the owners, the younger Cannon was the original nominee of Los Angeles owner Walter O'Malley in 1969 when Bowie Kuhn was elected Commissioner.

Joe Jackson's White Sox contract, signed after the 1919 season, was extended through 1922. Remarkably, Jackson's "lost" confession reappeared and was used against him by Comiskey's attorney in the jury trial held in the circuit court of Milwaukee in January 1924. The jury found for Jackson, 11–1, recommending $18,000 in damages but was overturned by the presiding judge. Settlement was reached during the appeal, with Jackson apparently awarded $8,000: one year's salary. Felsch settled for $1,166 in back pay. Risberg's award, also for back pay, was $400.

Summoned to the stand on a court order, Comiskey acknowledged he had been told there was something wrong with his players during the Series, and that he had heard "rumors of crookedness which I could not locate." He said he hired a detective "at great expense," and the reward he offered failed to produce any tangible information.

Jackson got $5,000 for his part in the fix. The day after the Series ended, he went to tell Comiskey what he knew about the conspiracy and to ask what he should do with the $5,000. The Milwaukee transcript runs 1,696 typewritten pages. On page 72, Jackson is on the stand:

Q: What did you do when you got to Comiskey Park?

A: I got to the office there and the front office door was always locked, and they got a solid window there. For a ballplayer to talk to Grabiner or Comiskey, you have to knock on the window.

Q: And did they raise it up for you?

A: Yes, sir.

Q: Did you knock on the window this day?

A: I knocked on the window this day.

Q: Who came to the window?

A: Harry Grabiner.

Q: What did you say to Grabiner?

A: I told Grabiner I wanted to see Comiskey. He said Comiskey was busy and I couldn't see him. And I said, "It's important that I should see him—some information I got out of Lefty Williams in regard to the World Series.' Grabiner slammed the window down in my face and said, 'Go home. We know what you want."

Obviously, Comiskey knew, but it's apparent he didn't want anybody to know he knew. Had Comiskey confronted the fixers during the World Series, he would have wrecked his team and suffered an enormous financial loss in excess of $300,000. The players were his property. The coverup included an interesting footnote. Seven of the conspirators were given new contracts, at sizable increases, prior to the 1920 season; all but Gandil, who didn't return. The unanswered question: Was Comiskey's sudden beneficence a shamed acknowledgment that the fixers had been underpaid? Or a plea for silence?

The Landis decision was irrefutable evidence that baseball had
been cleansed. The Judge had done his duty and was hailed for his
jurisprudence—everywhere except in Washington, D.C., where
Congressman Benjamin Welty of Ohio had risen in the House of
Representatives and announced:

"I impeach Kenesaw M. Landis as District Judge of the United
States for the Northern District of Illinois."

There were five counts in the arraignment, but the centerpiece
related to a conflict of interest: Landis had become baseball's high
priest without yielding his judicial assignment. Welty quoted from
legislation passed on March 3, 1917, by the 65th Congress which in
part provides that:

"No government official or employee shall receive any salary in
connection with his services as such official or employee from any
source other than the Government of the United States."

When the controversy died down, Landis discarded his judicial
robes with the explanation, "There are not enough hours in the day
for all my activities, therefore I have forwarded my resignation."
There was no financial loss. Landis's original $50,000 baseball wage
was restored.

Landis's suspended list continued to grow. Number nine was Hal
Chase, a brilliant first baseman who had a long history of crooked
play. The Avenging Angel also barred Joe Gideon, a minor league
infielder; pitcher Claude Hendrix, Cubs; outfielder Sherry Magee,
Cincinnati; and third baseman Heinie Zimmerman of the Giants; all
accused of fixing or general wrongdoing.

Benny Kauff, a talented outfielder with the New York Giants, was
next. Kauff had been acquitted in a New York court for alleged car
theft, an incident unrelated to baseball, but in a capricious decision
was added to the blacklist. Kauff sued. Two judges of the New York
Supreme Court and John Tener, a former president of the National

League, went to bat for Kauff. They struck out. Landis now had a 100-mph Nolan Ryan fastball. His players had to be above reproach.

"Shuffling Phil" Douglas, a pitcher also with the Giants, was suspended after he wrote a letter to outfielder Leslie Mann of the Cardinals to the effect that if Mann and his teammates would make it worthwhile, he would quit the Giants, thus enabling the Cardinals to win the 1924 National League pennant.

Douglas's letter:

"I want to leave here. I don't want to see this guy [manager John McGraw] win the pennant. You know I can pitch and I am afraid that if I stay I will win the pennant for them. Talk this over with the boys, and if it is all right, send the goods to my house at night and I will go to the fishing camp. Let me know if you all want me to do this and I will go home on the next train."

Douglas, characterized as "a physical giant with the mentality of a child," said he was drunk when he wrote the letter. Once he realized the consequence he wired Mann and asked him to destroy it. Douglas was placed in a sanitarium for several days to recover from his debauch at the insistence of McGraw who was disposed to give him another chance. The Great Umpire refused to grant clemency.

After four years in office, Landis had sent nineteen players up the river. In the seventy years since, only one player, Pete Rose, has been given a lifetime sentence. Bart Giamatti, baseball's seventh czar, banned Rose, manager of the Cincinnati Reds, in 1989 for betting on his team.

Emboldened by his success, the Judge jousted with Babe Ruth. In 1925, when the Yankees slapped the Babe with an unprecedented $5,000 fine for misconduct, Landis upheld it as proper. Four years earlier, Ruth had violated the rule forbidding players who had appeared in the World Series to barnstorm; the assumption was that performing in small towns for a few hundred dollars after the Series had a cheapening effect.

Advised he was courting trouble, Ruth said, "Let the old guy jump in the lake. I guess I'm going to have show somebody who is running this game."

Landis held up Ruth's World Series purse and suspended him for the first thirty-nine days of the following season. The Yankees' colonels, Jake Ruppert and Tillinghast L'Hommidieu Huston, contended their investment was jeopardized and sent their attorney to Chicago to plead their case. Ruth was the Yankees' principal drawing card. They would suffer at the gate if he were forced to sit out one-fourth of the season. A fan petition with thousands of signatures was sent to Landis asking him to pardon the Babe.

Landis refused. "He gets away with a lot in the American League," the czar said. "But in this office he's just another player."

But Landis was prudent enough to stay his hand when Ty Cobb and Tris Speaker, two of the greatest names in baseball, were accused of betting on games. The information surfaced in December 1926, seven years after the fact. By this time they were approaching retirement: Cobb was 39; Speaker, 38. They were both managing American League clubs; Cobb in Detroit and Speaker in Cleveland.

The incriminating evidence was two letters pitcher Hubert "Dutch" Leonard had received from Cobb and pitcher Smoky Joe Wood that revealed bets on a game between Detroit and Cleveland on September 25, 1919. Leonard and Cobb were then teammates at Detroit. Wood and Speaker, a player-manager, were with Cleveland. The Indians had already clinched second-place behind the pennant winning "Black Sox" but the Tigers were still battling the Yankees for third-place money.

The Wood letter, in part:

"Enclosed please find certified check for $1,630. The only bet West [Fred West, a Detroit park attendant] could get up was $600 against $420 [10-to-7]. Cobb did not get up a cent. He told us that and I believe him. If we ever have another chance like this we will know enough to get down early."

Cobb's letter, also in part:

"Wood and myself are considerably disappointed in our business proposition, as we had $2,000 to put into it and the other side quoted us $1,400, and when we finally secured that much money it was about 2 o'clock and they refused to deal with us, as they had men in Chicago to take the matter up with and they had no time, so we completely fell down and of course we felt badly over it."

When he was managing the Tigers in 1925, Cobb had openly criticized Leonard for giving up twelve runs in a game against Philadelphia. Leonard was then put on waivers and expected Speaker, a former teammate and his presumed friend, to claim him. Speaker passed. Vengeful, Leonard began shopping the letters around.

Fearful that Leonard might go public, American League attorney Henry Killilea arranged a deal whereby Leonard surrendered the letters for $20,000, an amount Leonard claimed the Detroit club owed him for cutting short his major league career. American League president Ban Johnson brought up the matter at a league meeting in Chicago after the 1926 season. To protect Cobb and Speaker from disgrace, Johnson agreed that the incriminating data would remain secret but that they should be quietly released. Cobb resigned as manager of the Tigers; a month later Speaker also resigned.

The matter was considered closed—until the evidence was turned over to Landis. Landis released the letters to the press. An angry Johnson retaliated and issued the following statement:

"I feel deeply sorry for the families of Cobb and Speaker. It is a terrible blow to them. Cobb and Speaker evidently saw the crash coming and stepped out before the scandal became a public byword. While it shocked me beyond expression, it simply goes to show that ballplayers cannot bet on ball games and escape the results that are bound to come."

Clearly, the vendetta between Johnson and Landis had escalated. In response, Landis summoned the principals to his Chicago office. Leonard refused to appear. Cobb admitted he had written the letter but insisted he had made no bet and had acted only as an intermediary, passing along information from Wood to Leonard at Wood's request.

Cobb, in righteous anger, told newsmen: "Here I am, after a lifetime of hard, honest work forced to stand accused without ever having a chance to face my accuser. It is enough to try one's faith."

At his home in California, Leonard told Damon Runyon, "I have had my revenge."

Speaker had been drawn into the web with Leonard's contention that the day before the bets were placed, after the game of September 24, he had met under the grandstand at Navin Field, the Tigers' home park, with Cobb, Speaker, and Wood. Leonard insisted Speaker told him he "didn't have to worry about tomorrow's game."

Speaker, who had two triples in the September 25 game, denied there had been such a conversation and insisted he knew nothing about any betting until Leonard's letters were made public.

The American League owners, at a meeting on January 23, 1927, passed a resolution "unanimously repudiating any and all criticism appearing in the public press as emanating from Mr. Johnson reflecting in any way upon Judge Landis on his handling of the several investigations concerning the integrity of ballplayers in the American League," and "commended Judge Landis for his efforts in clearing baseball of any insinuations of dishonesty."

Johnson's final humiliation came four days later when Landis exonerated Cobb and Speaker. "These players have not been, nor are they now, found guilty of fixing a ballgame," Landis announced. "By no decent system of justice could such a finding be made."

Landis rescinded the releases given Cobb and Speaker and

restored them to the active list. Disgraced, Johnson resigned six months later. Cobb and Speaker signed with the Philadelphia Athletics and played two more seasons before retiring.

It was a spectacular triumph for the Judge. More victories were ahead, including a satisfying decision over Phil Ball of the St. Louis Browns. A longtime Ban Johnson ally, Ball was Landis's match at the curmudgeon counter, the only owner who didn't sign the agreement certifying Landis's absolute power.

In 1917, Ball charged his players with lying down: "Every $1,000 I lose on the Browns this season will cost the ballplayer $100. Salaries will be cut. Because they dislike their manager is no reason why they should not put forth their best efforts." When two of his players sued him for slander, Ball denied the charges.

Once, when he arrived at old Sportsman's Park to watch the Browns play, only a handful of fans were in the stands. It was suggested the game be called off.

"*I'm* here," Ball snapped. "Let's play ball."

In the winter of 1976, when Oakland owner Charlie Finley sued Bowie Kuhn for nullifying the sale of three of his players, it was generally believed to be the first time an owner had hauled a commissioner into court. But Ball was first. He sued Landis in 1931 over the disposition of Fred Bennett, an obscure outfielder who appeared in seven games with the Browns.

To avoid placing player Bennett on the waiver list, thereby making him eligible to be claimed by any other major league club, Ball shuttled him around to five of the Browns' minor league clubs. There was nothing in the rules to prohibit a major league owner from owning minor league clubs. Bennett appealed to Landis; Ball had him bottled him up and had prevented his advance with a sequence of purchase transfers to teams within the Browns' farm system.

Landis generally opposed the major league clubs' control of an inordinate number of minor league players and declared Bennett a free agent. Ball sued, claiming he was operating within the existing code. Not only did Ball lose, but the litigation, initially heard in Milwaukee, further established Landis's autocratic powers. Ball appealed and when he lost again threatened to take his fight "all the way to the Supreme Court."

Landis summoned the American League owners to his Chicago office and demanded they put a stop to the litigation. Coming out of the meeting, Ball remarked to Cleveland owner Alva Bradley, "Did you ever see a man more stubborn than Landis?"

"Yes, I have," replied Bradley, looking Ball straight in the eye.

"You don't mean me?" asked Ball.

"I don't mean anyone else."

"Well, if I'm more stubborn than Landis, I must be the most stubborn man in the United States. If that's so, I'm going to call my lawyers and tell them to drop the appeal."

The Bennett case was only the beginning. Landis always looked with aversion on the farm system, regarding it as chain gang baseball. The judge preferred local ownership in the minor leagues. But there was a problem: Minor league clubs with a major league working agreement almost always had the stronger teams and had more success at the gate and on the field.

To prevent the stockpiling of young prospects, Landis liberated hundreds of players. In 1938 he freed seventy-three prospects controlled by the St. Louis Cardinals. The next year he freed ninety players belonging to the Detroit Tigers and their affiliated clubs. The total financial loss to the big league clubs was estimated at $600,000, big money in those days. It was perhaps Landis's most courageous decision but was without lasting consequence.

Branch Rickey, then general manager of the Cardinals, insisted the Commissioner had overstepped his bounds. But Landis, who had never liked Rickey and dismissed him as a "Sunday school teacher," held firm. Later, after assuming command in Brooklyn, Rickey rebuilt his farm system.

Among the St. Louis players emancipated were outfielder Pete Reiser, who later starred with the Brooklyn Dodgers; infielder Benny McCoy; and outfielder Roy Cullenbine, all of whom, in making new connections, received large bonuses.

Dozens of small skirmishes remained, but for all intents and purposes the major battles were now over. The Judge was the undefeated champion. In July 1944, the owners agreed that after the expiration of his third term, two years hence, his contract would be extended through 1953 when he would have been 83. He died of coronary thrombosis on November 25, 1944, at age 78, and was survived by his wife, the former Winifred Reed of Ottawa, Illinois, whom he had married in 1895, and two children.

Adhering to his request there was no funeral, no flowers, no memorial service.

# HAPPY CHANDLER
## PART I

T he baton was passed to Albert Benjamin "Happy" Chandler, who rose from an impoverished Kentucky boyhood to the United States Senate. Baseball's second Commissioner, Chandler served six and a half years. He resigned after the owners refused to renew his contract for a second seven-year term. Early on, Alva Bradley, then owner of the Cleveland Indians, advised him of the perils ahead.

"We all cheat if we have to," Bradley said of his fellow moguls. "This fellow cheats, that fellow cheats. I cheat, too. We all cheat."

"Well, Mr. Bradley," Chandler said, "I wish I'd known that before I signed on for this voyage. I didn't agree to leave the United States Senate to preside over a bunch of thieves. And if I catch you, be prepared to belly up. I won't be easy."

According to Chandler, Bradley didn't seem to be listening and told him, "You've just got to learn to wink at the rule breakers."

Chandler insisted he couldn't do that: "There are sixteen teams in this game. If I wink at one, I'll have to wink at fifteen others. That's not a wink, that's a twitch."

In his 1989 autobiography, *Heroes, Plain Folks and Skunks*, published thirty-eight years after his turbulent reign, Chandler acknowledged the accuracy of Bradley's warning.

"Many of the owners were greedy," Chandler wrote. "They were cruel to the players and umpires. They abused the fans. They tried to dominate me. But I fought them. I took charge. I handled the Mexican League raids, the threat of a player strike and other tough disputes. I banished Leo "The Lip" Durocher for a full year for besmirching the game. I just didn't sit around. For the first time players got pensions and a fair shake on rights, pay and contracts. I helped integrate baseball. The avaricious owners began to boil. They finally greased the skids and railroaded me out."

"Happy was a very good commissioner but he talked a lot," said Gabe Paul, a baseball lifer who owned and/or operated four major league clubs. "If he hadn't talked so much he wouldn't have gotten into so much trouble."

It was another big talker, "Loud Larry" MacPhail, a baseball roustabout—then co-owner of the New York Yankees—who swung Chandler's election. In later years, after several losing rounds with Chandler, MacPhail insisted he had not been Chandler's champion; his first choice was Ford Frick, then president of the National League. MacPhail insisted he didn't vote for Chandler until the sixth ballot.

Several meetings of the nominating committee were held without agreement and no successor to Judge Landis was expected to be named when the owners assembled in Cleveland on April 24, 1945. Six candidates were considered: James A. Farley, the former postmaster general who had agreed to accept only a lifetime appointment; Fred Vinson, a highly placed government official who later became the Chief Justice of the U.S. Supreme Court; Robert Patterson, Undersecretary of War; Bob Hannegan, chairman of the Democratic National Committee; Governor Frank Lausche of Ohio; and Frick.

Chandler had been contacted by several owners, including MacPhail, but was not among the original candidates. His name was added to the list on MacPhail's urging, after the Cleveland meeting had begun. MacPhail emphasized that Chandler, as U.S. Senator from Kentucky and before that governor of the state, had considerable influence in Washington, a crucial consideration because of continual congressional hostility against baseball's immunity from antitrust laws. Chandler also had a splendid social presence, was an entertaining speaker, had played semi-pro and minor league baseball, had played football, and had even coached a freshman college football team.

A three-fourths majority was required. After several unsuccessful ballots, when adjournment appeared imminent, MacPhail suggested an informal poll be taken, not binding in any way but for guidance. Possibly because of MacPhail's persuasive powers, Chandler drew eleven first-place votes and was listed on all sixteen ballots. Hannegan was second with five first-place votes. MacPhail then convinced the owners that a vote should be taken in earnest. Happy received the required twelve votes on the second ballot; a third ballot made it unanimous. MacPhail called to tell him of his election.

Chandler was installed on July 12 1945, three and a half months before expiration of his senate term. Prior to his acceptance, he insisted he enjoy the same powers as Judge Landis. The owners, seventy days after Landis's death, had changed some of the criteria. Reluctantly, they restored the Landis "loyalty pledge," assurance they would acquiesce to Chandler's decisions, mistaken or otherwise.

Two other significant adjustments were inserted. Whereas Landis's contract, for both election and *renewal* required only a simple majority, three-fourths approval was now necessary. The condition for renewal was later tightened to a three-fourths majority in both the National and American leagues. In a ten-team league, for example, only four dissenting votes—a small cabal of four angry owners from either league—was a sufficient firing squad, as Bowie Kuhn discovered thirty years later.

Warren Giles, later president of the National League but then president of the Cincinnati club, refused to concede that the club owners, under the three-fourths rule, in effect held future commissioners in hostage. But the days of Judge Landis's unfettered reign had come to an end.

In a limp explanation, Giles announced:

"The commissioner is vested with such sweeping powers that we decided it would be better to have one who is acceptable to at least three-fourths of the clubs than a mere majority. There was no thought of making it difficult for any commissioner to gain reelection. We had no idea at the time this measure was adopted who the next commissioner would be."

Chandler's contract was for seven years at $50,000 a year, a hefty boost from his annual $10,000 Senate salary. At the time it seemed the crowning feather for his Horatio Alger cap. The Chandler persona bore a likeness to Huey Long. On the stump, Chandler was warm and kindly. He lacked Long's rage but embraced the common man with similar fervor. He had a strong voice. In his youth, he had yearned for a career in opera. More often than not, his speeches were spiced with song, sentimental ballads, climaxed by "My Old Kentucky Home."

His family had been poor when he was a child. He often recalled with pride how during his 1935 campaign for governor, he told the voters 816 times, "When I entered Transylvania College, I had a red sweater, a $5 bill and a smile."

He was born on April 18, 1898, in Corydon, Kentucky, the son of a handyman-farmer. Abandoned by his mother at the age of four, Chandler took to his grave the memory of her departure:

"'Do you want to take the children?' my father asked."

She was willing to take his brother, Robert, who was two.

"My father said, 'No, if you don't want both, just leave them with me.'

"I followed mother out to the buggy, crying. Dusk was beginning to settle. She gave us two boys a quick kiss, and Robert a long, long hug. The buggy wheels crunched off toward the depot. I sat down at the gate and tears rolled down my cheeks."

His mother, the former Callie Sanders, raised in an orphanage, was "vivacious, energetic and pretty," not yet 20. Married at 15, she was ten years younger than her husband and preferred city lights, not the drudgery of a fifty-acre homestead on the edge of Corydon, population 800. His father, Joseph Sephus Chandler, was "an avid reader, with beautiful penmanship." In his memoir, Chandler described him as "a workaholic who flourished on hard labor, and that is the foremost and most satisfying characteristic I inherited from him."

An apt student, determined to know everyone "who counted," Chandler was graduated from Corydon High School in 1917, valedictorian of his class. Printed beneath his photograph in the high school annual was the prophecy:

"Work hard and study while you wait,

And you'll be governor of the state."

He enrolled at Transylvania College and threw himself into every activity. He joined the glee club and the theater club and played on the baseball, football, and basketball teams. His most memorable moment in sports was pitching Transylvania to a 10–4 victory over the University of Tennessee. He played one season of semipro baseball as a pitcher-infielder for the Lexington Rios. Earl Combs, a future Hall of Fame outfielder with the New York Yankees, was a teammate.

The next stop was Harvard Law School. He dropped out after one year and transferred to the University of Kentucky. He earned his law degree in 1925, at age 27, and began his practice in Versailles,

Kentucky, where he met his future wife, Mildred Watkins. They were in an amateur theater group; she sang soprano opposite his tenor. Divorced and the mother of a two-year-old daughter, she was teaching at a girls' school in Versailles. "Mama" Chandler, in good times and bad, was constantly at her husband's side. An extrovert, she, too, delighted in pressing the flesh. They were married for sixty-five years, a joyful union unbroken until his death in 1991.

Chandler entered public life as a Democrat and served two terms as governor of Kentucky, the first from 1935 to 1939. A baseball fan, he often journeyed to nearby Cincinnati to watch the Reds. During these years he struck up a friendship with the boisterous Larry MacPhail, then the Reds' general manager. Like Chandler, MacPhail was an entrepreneur. He had encouraged Powel Crosley to purchase the team. MacPhail then sold Powel on the idea of night baseball, and Cincinnati, in 1935, was the scene of the first major league game played under the lights.

Their friendship began to cool soon after Chandler was seated as Commissioner. Never again did MacPhail run interference for him. Few if any of MacPhail's baseball relationships had a long run. He was always on the move and operated big league clubs in Cincinnati, Brooklyn, and New York (Yankees). MacPhail's first major dispute with the new commissioner was the Leo Durocher affair. Reaching into his quiver for his most potent arrow, Chandler suspended "Leo The Lip" for one year for actions he deemed detrimental to baseball.

The first of Chandler's major decisions came on April 1, 1946, when he declared the major league players who had jumped to the Mexican League suspended for five years. Jorge Pasquel, whose family fortune was estimated at $75 million, had decided that baseball, not soccer or bullfighting, should be Mexico's national sport. The flamboyant Pasquel sometimes carried a pearl-handled revolver and had nine Cadillacs, in different colors. He owned the Vera Cruz club in the Mexican League but, in effect, supported the entire league. Down the line he envisioned it as a third major league.

Aware of the discontent of some American players, especially those with the St. Louis Cardinals and the New York Giants, which had low salary scales, Pasquel and his agents convinced eighteen major league players to jump their contracts.

Ray Gillespie, a St. Louis baseball writer, was among Pasquel's recruiters. Gillespie often vacationed in Mexico and was Pasquel's principal American contact.

"Jorge always said, 'With money I can buy anything. Every woman or man has a price,'" Gillespie recalled years later.

"Once we were in a restaurant, a ritzy place, and Pasquel said, 'See that girl?' She was a beautiful cashier. `I guarantee you for a price I'll have her tonight. One thousand dollars will be enough. Any gal will do whatever you want for a thousand dollars.' And the next night he showed up with this gal on his arm."

The American ballplayers were more expensive. The principal defectors were Max Lanier, the Cardinals' leading pitcher, who had won his first six games of the 1946 season and was expected to lead the Redbirds to a flag; Sal Maglie of the New York Giants, also an outstanding pitcher; and Mickey Owen, star catcher of the Brooklyn Dodgers, who was installed as player-manager of the Vera Cruz club. Shortstop Vern Stephens, who was among the American League's best hitters, also jumped, but played only two games before returning to the St. Louis Browns.

According to one account, Ted Williams, generally regarded as the best lefthanded hitter since Babe Ruth, was offered $500,000. In another published report, he was said to have received a blank check. Jesting, Williams asked if he would be allowed four strikes. When the answer was yes, he would be given an extra strike, he replied, "Well, I won't come anyhow."

Babe Ruth, bitter in retirement, was said to have been offered the commissionership of the outlaw league. According to baseball historian Lee Allen, Ruth had no such intentions but did spend several weeks in Mexico "being idolized by Mexican fans" and participating in batting exhibitions.

Sam Breadon, owner of the Cardinals, lost three everyday players—Lanier, pitcher Fred Martin, and second baseman Lou Klein. Fearful that Stan Musial, the National League's best player, was also about to swim the Rio Grande, Breadon hurried to Mexico to talk to Pasquel. Musial, who had been earning $13,000, was offered $130,000 for five years by Pasquel, including a $65,000 advance.

During this meeting, arranged by Gillespie, Pasquel assured Breadon he wouldn't sign any more Cardinals. Breadon's hope for secrecy was destroyed when he met Gordon Cobbledick, a vacationing Cleveland baseball writer. When Chandler discovered Breadon was acting as a "lone ranger," he ordered him to his Cincinnati office and fined him $5,000. The fine was never paid, but Breadon conceded he had made a mistake; the Mexican League problem had to be handled by the Commissioner's office, not by an ambassador-owner.

Eighteen major league players had been included in the five-year ban: pitcher Alex Carrasquel, Chicago White Sox; infielder Murray Franklin, Detroit Tigers; outfielder Roberto Estalella, Philadelphia Athletics; Owen, infielder-outfielder Roland Gladu, and outfielder Luis Olmo of the Dodgers; pitchers Maglie, Ace Adams, Harry Feldman, and Adrian Zabala, infielders George Hausmann, Napoleon Reyes, and Roy Zimmerman, and outfielder Danny Gardella of the Giants; outfielder Rene Monteagudo, Philadelphia Phillies; and Lanier, Martin, and Klein of the Cardinals.

Most of the jumpers were fringe players who have since been forgotten. One of the exceptions was Danny Gardella of the Giants. A

New York City native who was popular with the fans and sportswriters, Gardella was an incurable prankster. One morning in Cincinnati, while waiting for Nap Reyes, his roommate, Gardella left a "suicide" note on his bed. Entering their fourth-floor room, Reyes hurried to an open window. A grinning Gardella was hanging onto the window sill by his arms.

Gardella was with the Giants during the 1944 and 1945 seasons, appearing in a total of 168 games. A clumsy left fielder and a .267 hitter with occasional power, he had 18 home runs in 1945. His biggest "hit" came in 1949, after he had brought a $100,000 suit, with the expectation of treble damages.

Unlike many of the jumpers, Gardella was not under contract for 1946, but because of the reserve clause he was bound to the Giants. Gardella challenged baseball's immunity from the Sherman Antitrust Act. This exemption permitted the owners to operate as a monopoly, and to hold a player's contract in perpetuity, unless he was traded or sold; in that event the new owner held him in identical bondage.

Chandler's ban, Gardella contended, was in reality a blacklist and in violation of his rights. It was not the first, or the last player versus owner courtroom confrontation over the reserve system, which had been in effect since 1897, depressing player salaries.

Fearful of the weakness of management's position, Chandler, on June, 5, 1949, in midseason, granted the fugitives amnesty shortly after the U.S. District Court in New York denied immediate reinstatement to several petitioning ballplayers pending the outcome of their litigation against Organized Baseball.

"I feel justified in tempering justice with mercy," Chandler announced in an 800-word statement. "These players have been ineligible for three years, and nearly all of them have admitted their original mistake."

Max Lanier and Fred Martin had filed a joint suit for $2.5 million.

Fred Saigh, the new owner of the Cardinals, sweet-talked them into submission; they were back in uniform in mid-June. Saigh also convinced Maglie to abandon his plans for legal retribution and to return to the Giants. Gardella didn't budge but was unable to prove damages; his income as an "outlaw" exceeded his compensation with the Giants. In October he agreed to a $70,000 out-of-court settlement. Gardella returned to the big leagues in 1950, with Saigh's Cardinals and had one final at bat, on a cold April day in Pittsburgh. He flied to left as a pinch batter for Cloyd Boyer.

The first major crisis of Chandler's commissionership had been handled smoothly, and Shirley Povich of *The Washington Post* wrote:

"That's when Chandler solidified himself with most of the owners. He accepted the whole responsibility at a time when most of the baseball men had panicked and were glad to lay the problem in his lap. Right then and there, he earned his salary for the whole seven years."

# HAPPY CHANDLER
## PART II

C handler had handled the Mexican League threat as well as possible, without complaint from the owners. But the honeymoon had already begun to sour two years earlier when Chandler, trapped in a cross-fire between Larry MacPhail and Branch Rickey, suspended Brooklyn Dodgers manager Leo Durocher for "an accumulation of unpleasant incidents . . . detrimental to baseball." The suspension was announced on April 9, 1947, six days before the season opened. "You would have thought I had dropped the guillotine on Albert Schweitzer," Chandler recalled in a 1971 interview with John Underwood of *Sports Illustrated*.

As expected, the New York columnists, almost all hostile to Chandler, hurried to the defense of their fallen hero. *Time* magazine, in an accurate appraisal, reported: "Commissioner Chandler has done the seemingly impossible. He has made Durocher a sympathetic figure."

Durocher, in his autobiography *Nice Guys Finish Last*, a triumph of revisionist history, insisted Chandler had double-crossed him, and that they had been pals:

"Happy had been a good friend. I used to run into him at the Stork Club. When he was running for the job of commissioner—and no alderman ran harder or kissed more asses—he'd give me his 'Ah Love Baseball' routine and he'd put his arms around my shoulders and say, 'If they ever ask you, put in a word for me, willya, Leo, old boy?'"

Durocher's dossier dated from the Judge Landis era. Landis had called him on the carpet before the 1941 World Series between the Dodgers and the Yankees and warned him of the dangers and severe consequences of associating with gamblers. The judge had learned that Durocher had left four tickets in his private box for movie actor George Raft, whose film career was characterized by tough-guy and gangster roles that, some believed, were a reenactment of his private life. On that occasion, MacPhail, not Branch Rickey, was Durocher's employer. MacPhail accompanied Durocher to Landis's office.

"Landis said he had information that George Raft had won $100,000 betting on baseball and no gambler was going to sit in my box," Durocher wrote. The Lip had been living in Raft's house every winter. "I told the Judge he couldn't expect me to insult the man after that kind of hospitality. I gave the man four seats and he's going to keep the four seats.

"Landis said if I didn't get the seats back I shouldn't put on my uniform the next day. And all through it MacPhail is sitting there winking at me. As soon as we were out in the corridor MacPhail turned on me like he wanted to kill me.

"'What are you, blind or something?' MacPhail hollered. 'Couldn't you see me giving the sign to tell him yes? I'll give him four in a box as good as yours. What difference does it make to him?'"

Because of the incestuous nature of big league baseball, some background on the principal characters should be helpful:

MacPhail, when he was operating the Brooklyn franchise, had given Durocher his first managerial job. This was in 1939. MacPhail had also befriended Rickey much earlier in 1931, when he brokered the $100,000 sale of the Columbus (Ohio) franchise in the International League. Rickey, then the general manager of the St. Louis Cardinals, was the grateful buyer; the Columbus Redbirds flourished as a vital link in the Cardinals' farm system. MacPhail had two options: Rickey's offer of a $10,000 finder's fee, or hiring on as the Columbus general manager. MacPhail accepted the latter. Two years later, Rickey fired him.

Next, MacPhail persuaded millionaire Powel Crosley to purchase the Cincinnati Reds, another good buy. Like Rickey, MacPhail was an innovator: first night game, first televised game, first to install a season-ticket plan and a stadium club, first to have his team travel by air, and first to establish an employee pension program.

Following numerous squabbles with Crosley, MacPhail resigned as the president of the Reds in 1936. Two years later, on January 19, 1938, he surfaced for a four-year term as vice president and general manager (and later president) of the Brooklyn Dodgers. He was an army colonel from 1942–45. After returning to civilian life in 1945, he became a one-third owner of the Yankees. Rickey had been a player, field manager, and general manager of the Cardinals. He jumped to the Dodgers in 1942, succeeding MacPhail.

They were opposites. Forceful and explosive, MacPhail was constantly changing managers. A heavy drinker and in continual public eruption, he was once described "as subtle as a punch in the nose."

Pious and shrewd, a rare combination in baseball, Rickey preached and practiced the so-called homely virtues. Tom Meany, a New York baseball writer, dubbed Rickey "The Mahatma." Meany said the idea sprouted from John Gunther's *Inside Asia*, in which Gunther described Mahatma Gandhi as "a combination of God, your own father, and Tammany Hall."

Three managers had quit on MacPhail during the 1946 season. He then pursued Durocher, now Rickey's adopted kin across the bridge in Brooklyn. Durocher wasn't interested; he had decided to re-sign with the Dodgers, which he did three weeks later, for $50,000, the highest managerial salary to that time. Said Durocher, with his usual blarney: "I hope to manage the Brooklyn Dodgers till the day I die."

MacPhail responded by hiring Chuck Dressen, Durocher's third-base coach with the Dodgers. Dressen had two years remaining on his Brooklyn contract but Rickey had given him his release in the belief he would be bettering his position, because MacPhail had planned to install Dressen as the manager of the Yankees. Instead, MacPhail hired him as a third-base coach, a parallel appointment that opened MacPhail to tampering charges. The immediate assumption was that Dressen was Durocher's advance man, that Durocher would soon follow.

This theory exploded on November 5, 1946, when MacPhail appointed Bucky Harris as Yankees manager. Almost coincident was a statement by MacPhail that Durocher had wanted to manage the Yankees but that, he, MacPhail, had turned him down. Durocher responded by claiming MacPhail was lying.

Durocher renewed his Brooklyn contract on November 25 for less money, he said, than MacPhail had offered. Durocher then settled in for a California winter as Raft's house guest. At about this same time, Westbrook Pegler, a former sportswriter who had graduated to the role of national and (irresponsible) muckraking Hearst columnist, wrote a series of articles aimed at cleaning up sports. Pegler, in his harangue, hammered away at Durocher and his "undesirable associates." Among them were Raft, whom Pegler linked to the notorious Ownie Madden and Bugsy Siegel, later murdered. Joe Adonis, Memphis Engelberg, and Connie Immerman, high profile gamblers, were also named as Durocher associates.

Upset with the avalanche of adverse publicity, Raft asked for an audience with Chandler.

"Raft came to see me," Chandler recalled. "I liked him but saw no reason to argue with him. I said, 'George, do you have a contract in baseball?'

"He said, 'No.'

"I said, 'If Durocher plays cards for money and gambles, I have to be concerned with him but not with you. So, please, just go away.'

"He said, 'But I got a bum rap.'

"I said, 'I didn't give it you.'"

Overreacting to Pegler's unsubstantiated claims, Rickey sent his assistant, Arthur Mann, to solicit Chandler's help in convincing Durocher to break these associations. Mann had been a distinguished New York journalist, a longtime sportswriter who also wrote radio scripts and sometimes doubled as a drama critic. After Rickey hired him as his special assistant, they spent many evenings together singing old church hymns, Rickey in his deep baritone and Mann playing the piano and harmonizing.

Mann and Chandler met on November 17, 1946. In his book, *Baseball Confidential, Secret History of the War Among Chandler, Durocher and MacPhail*, Mann recreated the dialogue:

"We met in his carpeted inner office behind heavy oaken doors. The exchange of courtesies was brief. His voice was light and soft, almost a whisper, with only a hint of Dixie in it.

"'Mr. Rickey needs help,' I began. 'He has been building his team and organization toward a post-war peak, and he doesn't want to encounter any unforeseen difficulties that can be avoided now.'

"Chandler eyed me steadily, for it sounded like double-talk, and I continued: 'Somehow Leo Durocher hasn't been sufficiently impressed by the fact that all of his difficulties spring directly from his associations off the field.'

"The Commissioner wanted to know if Leo had committed any specific wrong that he should know about, and if this visit was in the nature of a complaint. He said he would call a stenographer.

"'Absolutely not,' I said emphatically. 'It's simply a confidential request for your cooperation and understanding, and the assistance of your position to help a fellow realize that his so-called friends could easily become unwitting enemies. Not even Durocher is to know of this request.'

"Convinced that nothing was wrong otherwise, Chandler put in a call for Durocher at Raft's house. Durocher had left for an afternoon rehearsal of the Jack Benny radio show. The call went to the NBC studio, where a chilly receptionist informed Chandler, 'Mister Durocher is rehearsing and cannot be disturbed.'

"'Tell him Commissioner Chandler is on the phone,' Happy barked. 'That'll disturb him. And tell him to come right out.'"

They met five days later, on November 22, for more than two hours, on a fairway of the Claremont Golf Course in Berkeley, California. Chandler reached into his breast pocket and handed Durocher a list of persons he should avoid.

Durocher submitted and then advised the Commissioner that he was in love. His new sweetheart was movie actress Laraine Day. They were to be married as soon as she was divorced from Ray Hendricks, a salaried airport employee who understood the California community-property law, whereby a spouse may claim half of the other's estate. Her grounds were extreme cruelty.

Laraine Day had had a strict Mormon upbringing. She neither smoked nor drank and didn't use anything approaching bad language, the diametric opposite of her new swain. It was a classic soap opera romance. She had first seen Durocher in a New York City night club and hadn't known who or what he was, or for that matter what the Dodgers were. When they met a second time she said she had "been in love with Leo all my life."

Durocher had been married twice before. Chandler gave Durocher his blessing. According to Tom Meany, Chandler threw his arms around Durocher and declared, "You're all right with me now, as long as you watch your step."

Still, Chandler sensed trouble ahead, aware another Durocher marriage to a glamorous film queen, fifteen years his junior, would result in negative press. Chandler was correct. The decree was granted with the condition that Day was forbidden for one year to live in California as a wedded person. The press fueled the flames with a play-by-play of Durocher's fiery romance with the beautiful screen heroine.

Simultaneously, a cloud of sports scandals was forming: Middleweight boxer Rocky Graziano failed to report a $100,000 bribe to throw a scheduled fight, later canceled, to Rueben Shanks; welterweight Sugar Ray Robinson was suspended for a month on a similar charge; two professional football players, Frank Filchock and Merle Hapes of the New York Giants, had entertained a gambler's offer to throw a playoff game; two days later, confirmation came that five crooked baseball players in the Evangeline minor league were likely to be barred for life.

The Dodgers had shifted their 1947 spring training camp to Havana, Cuba. These were peaceful days, before Castro. The club was quartered at the Nacional Hotel. A worried Durocher toed the line. Dodgers broadcaster Red Barber insisted Leo lived the monastic life. In a 1987 interview Barber said:

"Leo lived like a saint. I was at the Dodgers' training camp in Havana. Leo had his meals in his room. He wouldn't be seen with anybody. He'd come out and go to the playing field, do his work, and go up to his room and stay. Nobody was ever more faithful to his word than Durocher."

The centerpiece of the Durocher flap was a column under Durocher's name, "Durocher Says," written by Harold Parrott, an accomplished sportswriter who had joined the Dodgers as their road secretary. The column ran in the Brooklyn *Eagle* on March 3 when the Dodgers and the Yankees were in Caracas, Venezuela, for an exhibition game. The column began:

"This is a declaration of war. I want to beat the Yankees as badly as I do any team in the National League. I want to wallop them Yanks because of MacPhail and Dressen. I want to beat the Yanks because MacPhail knows in his heart I love Brooklyn. Always wanted to manage there and regard Branch Rickey as my father.

"MacPhail tried to drive a wedge between myself and all those things I hold dear. When he found I couldn't be induced to manage the Yankees he resolved to knock me and make life as hard as possible for me . . . Dressen was close to me for years but he can not deny he had agreed to Brooklyn terms for two more years."

It was nothing more than sports page fodder. But the feud was ablaze six days later, on March 9, when the Dodgers and Yankees met in a weekend exhibition series in Havana. In the Saturday game, Memphis Engelberg and Connie Immerman sat in one side of a box behind third base. On the other side of the box, partially separated by a rail, were MacPhail and his party.

Rickey exploded. "Why, my own manager can't even say hello to this actor, George what's-his-name. He won't have anything to do with these gamblers or any gamblers. But apparently there are rules for Durocher and [for] the rest of baseball."

Because of the overlapping of Yankee and Dodger assignments, a full complement of New York baseball writers and columnists was on the scene. It was a sports page bonanza. Durocher was eager to fuel the fire.

"How do you like that?" The Lip bellowed, "If I even talked to those guys, I'd be called before Commissioner Chandler and probably barred."

Thoroughly aroused, MacPhail denied Engelberg and Immerman had been his guests and insisted he had nothing whatever to do with their presence. He yelled it was none of Rickey's or Durocher's business.

MacPhail's next step was a formal protest to Chandler, requesting a hearing to determine the responsibility of the statements in Durocher's "declaration of war" column. "If false," wrote MacPhail, "their utterance and/or publication constitutes slander and libel and represents, in our opinion, conduct detrimental to baseball."

Chandler held two meetings of investigation, in Sarasota, Florida, on March 24 and in St. Petersburg fourteen days later. According to Arthur Mann, who was in attendance, MacPhail's indignation lessened as the testimony proceeded. Durocher explained the controversial column was "just another rhubarb" and said he would apologize if anything in the article had "hurt Larry's feelings." MacPhail rose and shook hands with Durocher.

Meanwhile, because of his involvement with Laraine Day, Durocher was widely pictured as a "sly and designing home wrecker, invading the privacy of an unsuspecting husband."

Vincent J. Powell, director of the Catholic Youth Organization of Brooklyn, withdrew his organization from the Dodgers' Brooklyn Knothole Club, which Rickey and his associates had nurtured. The letter of resignation said Durocher was "undermining the moral training of our youth and represents an example in complete contradiction of our moral teachings."

Rickey, who never attended Sunday games, was distraught. He was a churchgoer, a firm believer in spiritual leadership and a member of YMCA councils, college boards, and other branches of activity involving the guidance of youth. Rickey had given impetus to the Brooklyn Knothole Club; upwards of more than 150,000 boys and girls were admitted, without charge, to Ebbets Field each year. It was Rickey who had launched the Knothole Club idea in 1921 when he was in St. Louis.

There was also lingering litigation against Durocher. The complainant was John Christian, 21, of Brooklyn, a 200-pound ex-serviceman who had been wounded in the Pacific theater and was awaiting a medical discharge.

Christian was in the upper deck at Ebbets Field watching the Dodgers play the Philadelphia Phillies. After a slight second-inning dispute he began yelling at Durocher, calling him, among other things, a crook and a bum. Four innings later, Christian testified, Joseph Moore, a park security man, came to where he was sitting, told him Durocher wanted to see him and insisted on taking him to the runway between the Dodgers' dugout and clubhouse.

"You've got a mother," Durocher said. "How would you like somebody to call her those names?"

Before he could reply, Christian said, the security man knocked him down with a blunt instrument, and when he got to his feet, Durocher hit him with the same instrument, knocking him down again. Christian suffered a broken jaw and settled with the Dodgers for $6,500 but the case was transferred to a criminal court and not dismissed until the summer of 1946 when Durocher was acquitted of felonious assault.

Privately, Rickey may have lectured Durocher but, speaking at a luncheon of the Brooklyn Rotary Club, Rickey described the Dodgers as "a team of ferocious gentlemen."

Later, when Chandler assembled the combatants in Sarasota, there were indications the Commissioner would call it a draw, particularly after Durocher declared he was willing to make a public apology to MacPhail.

"We've been friends too long," Durocher told MacPhail. "I don't want you as an enemy."

According to Durocher, MacPhail "took the clipping [of the Parrott column] and ripped it into little pieces. Then he put his arm around me and gave me a bearhug and said, 'You've always been a great guy with me. Forget it, buddy, it's over.'"

Durocher went downstairs into the hotel lobby. The first person he saw was Mrs. Chandler.

"What's the matter with your old man?" Durocher asked. "Is he crazy or something?

"'Ahhh,' she said. 'A little publicity, Leo. Nothing. Forget it. You going to buy me a drink?'"

Chandler announced his decision two weeks later. Durocher was suspended for one year. The Yankees and Dodgers were fined $2,000 each. Dressen was suspended for thirty days. Parrott was fined $500.

Chandler's decision, in part:

"Leo Durocher has not measured up to the standards expected or required of managers of our baseball teams. As a result of the accumulation of unpleasant incidents in which he has been involved which the Commissioner construes as detrimental to baseball, he is hereby suspended from participating in professional baseball for the 1947 season.

"Evidence produced at the hearings shows that the alleged gamblers were not guests of MacPhail and did not sit in his box in Havana.

"Evidence clearly shows that MacPhail did not offer Durocher a job as manager of the New York Yankees for the 1947 season and that statements quoting Durocher in this regard are untrue. MacPhail admitted he delayed in signing a manager to give Durocher an opportunity to negotiate a better contract with Rickey. This could not be considered an act designed to engender friendly feelings between two major league clubs and the Commissioner will not expect its repetition in the future.

"All parties are silenced from the time this order is submitted."

"Suspended!" Durocher shouted. "For God's sake, what for?"

MacPhail exploded, surprisingly in defense of Durocher, insisting no evidence was developed in the meetings at Sarasota and St. Petersburg to suspend Durocher "for as much as five minutes." MacPhail also challenged Chandler's gag order, claiming he was in violation of freedom of speech.

Rickey seethed in silence, refusing to be quoted.

Durocher was now a martyr. Public opinion turned against the Commissioner. The even-handed Arthur Daley of *The New York Times* commented: "It's like running a red light and being given the electric chair."

*The Sporting News*, then the baseball bible and in Chandler's pocket (he had been feeding exclusive stories to publisher J.G. Taylor Spink), carried five full pages on the subject which included comments by thirty-six sportswriters, most of whom were in Spink's economic embrace.

A *Sporting News* editorial, titled "The Commissioner Gets Tough," written by Spink or one of his hirelings, included the following:

"To be sure, the decision was a drastic one in appearance, unduly harsh in complexion, and perhaps even born of animus. However, Durocher had asked for it. He had been warned once, twice and told there would be no third 'Beware.'

"Those who regard the suspension as altogether out of proportion to the diamond crimes and public relations infractions committed have failed to comprehend the factors which entered into the Commissioner's action. Chandler's 1,000 word decision makes it quite plain that his action was based on a long string of circumstances.

"The public, a large portion of the sports press, even national magazines only vicariously interested in baseball, had criticized Chandler for being too benevolent. Kicked around unmercifully, maligned and even libeled and slandered, Chandler took stock of himself:

"I have been trying to be a good guy on the Golden Rule precept. I have tried to be kind to the good and sympathetic toward the transgressor, and they don't seem to like it. Well, here's where they get a tough Commissioner."

Red Barber, the patrician broadcaster, reflecting on the suspension twenty years later in his memoir, *Rhubarb in the Catbird Seat*, said:

"You have to understand that it was a war between Rickey and MacPhail. After Landis died, the owners had to come up with a new commissioner. Rickey wanted Ford Frick, a trained baseball man. Well, if Rickey wanted Ford Frick, MacPhail was dead certain it wasn't going to be Frick. Whatever Rickey wanted, Rickey wasn't going to have. And MacPhail, a very powerful and persuasive figure, came up with Chandler.

"Leo was caught in the middle. I thought it was an injustice. He is a much maligned man. I don't think anybody in baseball thought he should have been suspended. Rickey said to Chandler, 'Happy, what you have done?' Even MacPhail, who had blown the whistle on Leo, was shocked."

Except for Durocher, Chandler outlived all the characters in the play. In his 1989 Hall of Fame induction speech, he described himself as "the last leaf on the tree." And so he had the last word. In his memoir, he wrote:

"Even Durocher's ex-wife, Grace Dozier, despite the Laraine Day scandal, came and stood in front of my box at Yankee Stadium and remonstrated with me. She was the prettiest little thing, a dressmaker from St. Louis. She was defending him, although he had divorced her to marry the Hollywood woman.

"I listened to her carefully. When she got through, I said 'Grace, I want to tell you how much I admire any woman who defends her husband. That means he's a lucky fellow. But you can't do anything to help Leo. This suspension is not against you, it's against him. And it's going to stick.

"A year later I'm at Yankee Stadium and Grace Dozier comes up and stands in front of me again. She held out her hand.

"'Commissioner,' she said, 'You knew he was a sonofabitch all the time, didn't you?'"

# HAPPY CHANDLER
## PART III

T he Durocher affair had been put to bed but the next day, on April 10, during the sixth inning of a Brooklyn-Montreal exhibition game at Ebbets Field, a one-paragraph statement was distributed in the press box:

"The Brooklyn Dodgers today purchased the contract of Jackie Roosevelt Robinson from their Montreal farm club. He will report immediately."

It was the most important event of Chandler's term and had implications far beyond the diamond, a signal of the social and legal changes ahead.

Although there has been much debate on Chandler's role in the controversies that surrounded the breaking of baseball's twentieth century color line, there is no question he acted with fair-mindedness and spoke in favor of integration. Anything less might have denied Robinson and the hundreds of black players who followed their opportunity.

Rickey's motives may not have been quite as pure. Years later he was quoted as saying, "I brought him up for one reason: to win the pennant. I'd play an elephant with pink horns if it could win the pennant."

It sounds more like Durocher than Rickey. If accurate, Rickey was caught in a cynical moment. But Red Barber, the Brooklyn broadcaster who was among Rickey's friends and admirers, conceded:

"I don't and can't know everything that goes on in another man's mind. But I can tell you this: Knowing Mr. Rickey and his intelligence and quickness of mind, once he saw Robinson's ability, and once he saw Roy Campanella's ability, and once he saw Don Newcombe's ability, he said, 'Oh, man, I'm moving into tall cotton, and I'm going to get the best of these first.'"

Larry MacPhail insisted the motive was greed. Said MacPhail: "In an attempt to glorify himself, Rickey double-crossed his associates for his own personal advantage and raided the Negro leagues without adequately compensating them. Churchill must have had Rickey in mind when he said 'There but for the grace of God goes God.'"

Rickey didn't share the laurels. In 1951, when he gave the commencement speech at Wilberforce State University, he was introduced by Chandler. It was the perfect forum to reward Chandler with an assist. But Rickey, Chandler recalled, mentioned neither he nor Robinson. The several Robinson biographies are sparing in their references to Chandler.

Jules Tygiel, author of *Baseball's Great Experiment*, an exhaustive study published in 1983, described Chandler as a bit player. "When the wisdom of Solomon was required," Tygiel said, Chandler had "the discretion of a mute."

But several years after publication Tygiel acknowledged he should have given Chandler more credit, especially after Robinson joined the Dodgers; in particular, when Ben Chapman, manager of the Philadelphia Phillies, threatened to make trouble.

Within an hour of the Dodgers' memo on April 10, Chandler sent a telegram to Chapman: "If you make trouble for him, I'll make trouble for you."

Robinson recognized Chandler's contribution when he wrote: "I will never forget your part."

Bill Veeck, who later in the 1947 season, on July 5, broke the American League color line by signing Larry Doby, also acknowledged Chandler's role. "He certainly could have opposed it and could have made it more difficult," Veeck said. "If anything, he assisted Rickey and did what he could to make Robinson's path easier."

There is no question the owners were in opposition. This was evident in the suppressed MacPhail Report, written by Larry MacPhail, under the heading "Race Question," dated August 27, 1946 and endorsed by a 15–1 majority. Rickey was the dissenter.

More than likely, the 15–1 vote, which has been disputed, was taken three weeks later, on September 16, 1947 when the owners had a one-day joint meeting at the Waldorf Astoria Hotel in New York City. Historians have been divided on dates. Upset by the Mexican League raids and the threat of a players' strike, which failed, the owners, with Chandler presiding, assembled at least five times in joint session that year: twice in July and once in late August, in Chicago; in New York in September; and again at the regularly scheduled December 5–7 Winter Meetings in Los Angeles.

But there seems to be general agreement that the MacPhail Report was signed by all six members of the committee: league presidents Ford Frick of the National and Will Harridge of the American; and owners Sam Breadon of the St. Louis Cardinals; Philip K. Wrigley of the Cubs; Tom Yawkey of the Boston Red Sox; and MacPhail of the Yankees.

Frick asked that all copies be returned to him for destruction. All were returned and burned. Except one, which Chandler put in his files, exhumed after his papers were donated to the library at the University of Kentucky.

The twenty-five-page MacPhail report, prompted by a committee on equal employment opportunity chaired by New York City mayor Fiorello LaGuardia, included:

"Those campaigning to provide a better opportunity for the thousands of Negro boys who want to play baseball are not particularly interested in improving the lot of the Negro players who are already employed. They know little about baseball, and nothing about the business end of its operation. They single out Professional Baseball for attack because it offers a good publicity medium. Signing a few Negro players for the major leagues would be a gesture but it would contribute little or nothing towards a solution of the real problem.

"There are many factors in this problem and many difficulties which must be solved before any generally satisfactory solution can be worked out. The individual action of any one Club [the Dodgers had already signed Robinson to a minor league contract] may exert tremendous pressure upon the whole structure of Professional Baseball, and could conceivably result in lessening the value of several major league franchises."

The document also quoted Sam Lacey, sports editor of the Baltimore *Afro-America*:

"I am reluctant to say that we haven't a single man in the ranks of colored baseball who could step into the major league uniform and disport himself after the fashion of a big leaguer . . . . There are those among our league players who might possibly excel in the matter of hitting or fielding or base running. But for the most part, the fellows who could hold their own in more than one of these phases of the game, are few and far between—perhaps nil."

Later, many owners denied the existence of the MacPhail Report.

"Ridiculous," insisted Bob Carpenter of the Phillies. Clark Griffith of the Washington Senators commented, "The door has always been open to those boys if they were good enough to make the big leagues." "False and inflammatory," shouted MacPhail. Chandler, Frick, and Harridge were "unavailable for comment."

Emil "Buzzie" Bavasi, a longtime baseball executive, for many years vice president and general manager of the Dodgers, acknowledged he had been aware of the MacPhail Report but insisted there was no vote.

In a letter to announcer Harry Caray, dated May 15, 1997, Bavasi wrote:

"It happened 50 years ago so I might not have the date correct, but I believe it was January 27, 1947 at the Waldorf Astoria. I was there only because Mr. Rickey had an attack of vertigo and wanted me to go along with him in case he lost his balance.

"When we arrived, Bill Veeck grabbed me for a chat. Everyone was seated when Mr. Wrigley got up and said, 'Gentlemen, if this is a meeting to discuss the Robinson matter count me out. This is a Dodger problem and not a league or baseball problem. Whatever the Dodgers do they have my approval. Horace Stoneham [of the New York Giants] was next to voice his opinion. He agreed with what Mr. Wrigley said and added that he hopes the Dodgers bring Jackie up to the majors as it would help his attendance at his ballpark which was exactly a half-mile from Harlem.

"Then, to settle the issue, Bill Veeck said, 'I just told Buzzie that I wish the Dodgers bring him up immediately because I have a player who is better than Jackie.' He was referring, of course to Larry Doby."

In a 1972 interview, Chandler seemed to waffle. He said he was a passive listener when the MacPhail Report was discussed. "For one thing, the press didn't know about it," Chandler said. "And I didn't consider that a vote was in order. It was only an expression of their sentiment."

Infuriated by both the MacPhail Report and the alleged 15–1 vote, Rickey telephoned Chandler and requested a meeting. They met at Chandler's home in Versailles, Kentucky.

Chandler, in his autobiography:

"We faced each other in my walnut log cabin in my backyard. We sat on opposite sides of the big, old desk, in the cabin's book-lined study. Logs blazed and crackled in my great stone fireplace. We needed that fire. It was a cold, raw January day.

"Rickey was as emotional as I've ever seen him. He said he didn't know if he could do this in light of the opposition of his partners.

"I said, 'Branch, that 15–1 turndown at the Waldorf meeting—I think that was supposed to be mainly for my guidance, wouldn't you say?'

"Rickey nodded.

"I told Branch, 'They'll never agree. You're all alone on this one. I know you are here asking me for help. I am the only person on earth who can approve the transfer of that contract from Montreal to Brooklyn. Nobody else. You still want to go ahead and go through with it?'

"'I'd like to, Commissioner.'

"'Can Robinson play baseball?'

"'No question about that,' Rickey said.

"'Is he a major leaguer? All I know is what I've read. I've never seen him play.'

"'Yes, sir.'"

Chandler went on to explain that as a member of the Senate Military Affairs Committee he regularly saw the casualty lists and that many Blacks had fought and died for their country.

"'Branch, I'm going to have to meet my Maker some day and if He asks me why I didn't let this boy play and I say it's because he's black that might not be a satisfactory answer.

"'If the Lord made some people black and some white, and some red or yellow, He must have had a pretty good reason. It's my job to see the game is fairly played and that everybody has an equal chance. Bring him up. I'll sign the transfer.'

"And Rickey brought him up and from then on everyone made Rickey sound like God almighty."

Still another crisis that had caused considerable anxiety among the owners developed in June 1946 when Robert Murphy of Boston, 36, a former examiner for the National Labor Relations Board, attempted to organize the players into a so-called American Baseball Guild. Chandler, who, with subsequent justification, often prided himself as a players' commissioner, was not sympathetic to the players. He abandoned them completely, and with the help of several Pittsburgh players, notably pitcher Truett "Rip" Sewell, smothered Murphy in his crib.

Murphy had chosen Pittsburgh because of its strong union base, and because in Pennsylvania, the Pirates were under the umbrella of state and federal labor relations laws. Many people, sportswriters included, ridiculed the idea of a players' union with quips about "Second Baseman's Local 307" and "overtime pay for extra-inning games." President Harry Truman, a Missouri native, comforted management when he said, in supposed jest, that if the Pirates struck and it was necessary for him to intervene, he would see to it that there would be two strong teams in St. Louis.

It was the first time the major league owners were confronted with a union since David Fultz's Players' Fraternity during World War I. If it had been Marvin Miller, who surfaced twenty years later, the moguls would have had ample cause to be frightened. But the noble and naive Murphy, who worked without pay, was an amateur arrayed against skillful serpents beyond his imagination. As he later admitted, "It was a one-man war against all the tanks and ammunition they had. I was undermanned."

Murphy began organizing, not in spring training as has been repeatedly reported, but in early April when the Pirates were in

Boston for a series with the Braves. Murphy was a graduate of Harvard and attended the Harvard Law School but dropped out in his second year. All accounts describe him as a Boston attorney, but he was not a lawyer.

When I interviewed him twenty-five years later, in Baltimore in 1971, he estimated that between seventy and ninety players, from a maximum of approximately 400, had enlisted in the Guild. The membership was culled from four National League clubs: Pittsburgh, St. Louis, Cincinnati, and the New York Giants. American League players were not approached.

Murphy acknowledged he had made many mistakes. The first was in April of that year, when he told Dave Egan, a Boston columnist, about his plan. "I had this idea," Murphy said, "but I didn't want him to write anything about it until I was ready to go. The next day in the Boston *Record* there was a full-page column about it. It upset my timing. I had to go before I wanted to."

Most of the Guild members were from the Pittsburgh club. According to Murphy, thirty-two of the thirty-four Pittsburgh eligibles had joined the Guild, all except Rip Sewell, a veteran pitcher, and Jimmy Brown, a utility infielder. Twice a 21-game winner, Sewell had a $16,000 annual salary that was among the highest in the National League.

In May, Murphy met with several Pirates officials, including president William E. Benswanger, a musician and composer whose pieces had been performed by the Pittsburgh Symphony Orchestra. He had taken over the Pirates after the death of Barney Dreyfuss, his father-in-law.

Murphy asked Benswanger to recognize the Guild as the sole bargaining agent for the players. Benswanger contacted Chandler. Immediately, Chandler dispatched his special assistant, John "Frenchy" DeMoisey to Pittsburgh to monitor the situation.

Murphy met with the Pittsburgh club executives for the last time on June 5, 1946, in the Flannery Building in Oakland, Pennsylvania. Benswanger and his attorney asked for a postponement in determining the Guild's status until after the season. Instead of the Guild, they proposed a Players' Committee that would meet with management and present grievances; in effect, it would have been a company union. Enraged, Murphy walked out.

Chandler, in hourly contact with DeMoisey, his secret agent, and aware a strike was imminent, asked, "Can they pull it off?"

Advised it was a definite possibility, Chandler told DeMoisey, "Round up any players you can. If there's a strike, field some kind of Pirate team. I won't tolerate stopping baseball."

In his book, Chandler recalled DeMoisey's reply: "I think I can do that. I know Frankie Frisch [the Pittsburgh manager] and Honus Wagner [a coach] will play. So will Rip Sewell."

On June 8, prior to a night game with the Giants, the Pittsburgh players, in raised hands, voted 21–15 to strike, a majority. But Murphy had made another mistake. He had previously agreed with the dissenters that a two-thirds approval, 24–12, was necessary for a strike.

Benswanger & Co. had recruited a team of semipros in the event of a walkout. Murphy insisted that strike-breaking players were on the field while the vote was being taken. Ralph Kiner, then a rookie who roomed with Rip Sewell, is among the few surviving players from the '46 Pirates. Kiner, in a 1993 interview, couldn't recall any semipros on the scene.

Murphy attempted to return to the clubhouse for final words of advice but was barred by club attorneys and security officers. Benswanger and farm director Bob Rice, both of whom represented management, were in attendance and expressed their views but departed before the vote.

The owners had another possibly unforeseen advantage: the absence of objective newspaper coverage. Today, such an event would have attracted a media mob. But the sportswriters of that time were occupied with the game on the field and little else. Rud Rennie of the New York *Herald Tribune*, who was covering the Giants in Forbes Field, opened his report, which was typical, with:

"Murphy's mutiny on the Monongahela having backfired, the Pirates continued with the baseball business . . . ." Not another word on the near-walkout.

Rip Sewell, in a 1968 interview with Les Biederman of the *Pittsburgh Press*:

"We held a meeting before a night game with the Giants at Forbes Field and had about 35,000 fans in the park waiting for the game to start. We couldn't make up our minds what to do. It was my turn to pitch and I finally told the players I was going out to warm up and I'd pitch even if I didn't have eight players behind me.

"When I walked out to warm up, the fans gave me a standing ovation. To me, this demonstration indicated they felt as most of us did. A union had no place in sports. This had to be my fondest memory and most rewarding."

Sewell, who according to Kiner "had a reputation for embellishment," was revising history. First, he didn't pitch against the Giants on June 8. He had worked two days before, a losing effort in a day game against the Dodgers; second, the attendance was 16,884, not 35,000. Also, according to newspaper accounts, Sewell was greeted with boos, not cheers. The American Federation of Labor and CIO in Pittsburgh had pledged Murphy their support. Union sympathizers beat up Pirates infielder Jimmy Brown as he was leaving the ballpark.

Sewell pitched in the All Star Game that year, entering in the eighth inning, mopping up in a 12–0 National League defeat. He is remembered for throwing his so-called "blooper" pitch, which came in on a high arc and parachuted downward. Ted Williams waited for the ball to descend and connected for a three-run home run.

In a 1980 interview with William Marshall for the University of Kentucky Library, Sewell told what happened when he returned to the hotel after the game.

"The owners were meeting and they called me into the room," he said. "Every major league owner was there, sitting around a big table and they said, 'We want to tell you something right now. We cannot express what you've done for baseball and we want to assure you after you quit playing you'll never want for a job in baseball as long as you live.' Well, they forgot pretty quick."

More than likely, it was an exaggeration. Owners, even if they meet the day before, seldom attend the All Star Game, and the few who do are homeward bound with the last pitch, or sooner. Later in the season, Chandler did present Sewell with a gold pocket watch inscribed, "For distinguished service to baseball." Said Chandler: "I wanted him to have a memento of his heroism and a token of my personal appreciation."

Robert Murphy didn't get a watch but did become a footnote in baseball history.

"I never received ten cents," he said. He also paid all of his expenses which he estimated between $1,800 and $2,000. He disappeared from the baseball scene after the Pittsburgh players in a formal labor election, taken on August 21, rejected the Guild by a 15–3 vote.

In retrospect, Murphy was a successful failure. The four principal aims of the Guild were:

1) Minimum annual salary of $7,500.

2) Fifty percent of purchase price to go to a player sold.

3) Arbitration.

4) Freedom of contract.

Before the 1947 season, the owners, now concerned with player

unrest, approved many significant changes. A uniform player contract was adopted with a guaranteed $5,000 minimum salary, the
first time a minimum was established (previously some players were
paid as little as $2,500); moving expenses up to $500 if traded or
sold during the season; no salary cuts from one season to another
to exceed 25 percent; full payment for the season if injured and payment of all medical and hospital expenses incurred by disability
directly resulting from injury; extension from ten to thirty days
notice to a released player; a guaranteed total World Series player
pool of at least $250,000; no doubleheaders the day after a night
game; and a $25 weekly allowance advance to cover spring training
expenses, which for many years thereafter was called "Murphy
Money."

More player bounty was ahead. The biggest benefit was a pension
plan, modest in its infancy but grew enormously; thirty years later
it exceeded the $90,000 annual federal limit. The pension plan was
MacPhail's idea. But it was Chandler who solidified the program. The
original goal was a monthly $100 payment to players with ten years
of major league service who had reached the age of 50.

In addition, in all matters concerning contracts and regulations,
the players were allowed representation on the Executive Council,
previously filled only by club owners and their appointed league
presidents. Johnny Murphy, a union activist when he was a pitcher
with the Yankees (but later, as a general manager, constantly harassed
the union) and Dixie Walker, an outfielder with the Dodgers, were
designated by the players as their representatives. They were succeeded in the inner circle by Tigers pitcher Fred Hutchinson and
Cardinals shortstop Marty Marion, who with MacPhail, drafted the
pension plan.

The pension was funded by the owners, coupled with player contributions. Now on the side of the players, Chandler negotiated the

first network television package for the World Series and All Star Game. Beginning in 1947, the Gillette Safety Razor Co., which had been sponsoring the radio broadcasts, paid $1 million a year for six years for the exclusive network television rights.

Remarkably, Chandler, with MacPhail's help, convinced the owners to extract 81 percent of the new television windfall annually from the World Series pool for the players' pension fund. Later, the owners reduced their generosity to 60 percent but this initial action assured solvency. The plan also included liberal health and life insurance benefits.

According to Red Barber, Rheingold Beer topped the Gillette offer: "But Chandler, a teetotaler, did not want baseball associated with beer. And so he sold it for less to Gillette."

Chandler said his commitment to the pension plan was spurred by what he saw as indignities encountered by the game's penniless old-timers. "I saw Dazzy Vance and Grover Cleveland Alexander pitch for the House of David teams later in life because they had no money," Chandler said. "All they knew was how to play ball."

This time there was a reversal of the Rip Sewell trophy. The players sent Chandler a sterling silver tray adorned with bats and baseballs "in appreciation of your services."

After Chandler was fired, the players asked him to represent them as their commissioner at an annual salary of $40,000. Wisely, Chandler didn't pursue the offer; the union treasury was bare.

As Chandler was embracing the players, his relations with some owners had been deteriorating. Fred Saigh, who recently had purchased the St. Louis Cardinals, was the first of the Commissioner's critics. While everyone else in baseball's executive suite cheered the $6 million deal with Gillette, Saigh found fault.

"Television is in its infancy," Saigh declared. "Rights worth $1 million today may be worth several million three or four years from now."

Forgetting that he was beholden to ownership, Chandler began investigating the unscrupulous Saigh, who later was convicted of evading $558,901 in taxes and penalties on unreported income. Saigh was fined $15,000 and served six months of a fifteen-month term in the Terre Haute (Indiana) federal penitentiary.

Saigh was furious that parts of Chandler's seventeen-page probe were leaked to the press and said that Chandler, through his Washington political connections, had triggered the federal investigation. Apparently among the charges, which were uncontested, was a hidden bank account accrued from ballclub funds, payable only to Saigh, a discovery made during a routine audit by the Commissioner's office.

The auditor, finished reviewing the Cardinals' books and returned them to a clerk who said, "Do you want to see the other account?"

Surprised, the auditor asked, "What other account?"

Saigh was friendly with Bob Hannegan, a former postmaster general and pillar of St. Louis society. Sam Breadon, the owner of the Cardinals, was eager to sell. Hannegan recommended Saigh as a potential buyer and agreed to help fund the purchase. It was a major coup for Saigh. He gained control for a down payment of only $80,000.

Breadon previously had advised club vice president William Walsingham that the Cardinals would be sold to him. Several weeks later, Breadon and Walsingham's mother were at a society dinner. Enraged, Lady Walsingham threw a bread roll at Breadon's head for welshing on her son.

Chandler also investigated Del Webb, co-owner of the Yankees. Webb allegedly had connections with Las Vegas gamblers. A carpenter as a young man, Webb had made his fortune in the construction business and was the contractor for several of the large Las Vegas hotels, all equipped with lavish casinos.

Lou Perini, also a contractor, who owned the Boston Braves was in the anti-Chandler camp. Perini complained that Chandler, on his visits to Boston, was more attentive to the rival Red Sox. William O. DeWitt and his brother, Charley, who operated the St. Louis Browns out of their hat, had borrowed $300,000 from the American League and were dependent on the goodwill of league president Will Harridge, another Chandler foe. Harridge never forgave Chandler for challenging him on the supervision and pay of umpires.

Young Chuck Comiskey, the third generation owner of the Chicago White Sox, joined the dissidents after Chandler had applied his interpretation of the so-called "high school rule." Chandler insisted that George Zoeterman, a pitcher at Chicago Christian High School whose class had not graduated and who was still a student, could not be signed to a professional contract.

Chandler fined the White Sox $500 despite the vigorous objection of Leslie O'Connor, Comiskey's general manager. O'Connor was naturally disposed against Chandler; he had been Judge Landis's secretary and assistant for twenty-four years. O'Connor claimed the rule, as originally drafted, applied only to members of the National Federation of High Schools and that Chicago Christian was not a member.

Chandler, however, was on safe ground. He had previously issued two bulletins advising the clubs that the rule would apply to all high schools in the United States and Canada. After a six-day war with the White Sox, the $500 fine was paid. To appease O'Connor, Chandler recommended him for a seat on the Executive Council. Later, when O'Connor left the White Sox, Chandler opened his jewelry box and gave O'Connor a watch for "distinguished service," which was presented by Harridge.

There were a half dozen other infractions that Chandler refused to ignore. Alva Bradley's warning that all owners cheat was growing to full fruition. The Pittsburgh Pirates, for example, were fined $2,500 and lost Danny Lynch, an outstanding prospect who had a hit a home run in his first at bat. To evade the bonus rule, the Pirates had signed Lynch's father as a scout. Investigation revealed the old man had a full-time job with a bus company and didn't have a legitimate claim to the bonus paid his son.

Boston's Perini was forced to yield Jack "Lucky" Lohrke. The Braves had optioned Lohrke three times, the maximum allowed. When they tried again, Perini contacted the other clubs and asked them to pass when Lohrke's name appeared on the waiver list. Chandler ruled that Lohrke was a free agent and in a special draft raffled him to the New York Giants, who had made the highest bid.

Chandler's seven-year contract ran to April 1952. Aware of the growing opposition, Chandler went on the offensive in December 1949, asking for reappointment. It was a mistake. The owners delayed and adopted new legislation that the renewal of a commissioner's contract could not be considered more than eighteen months prior to the expiration of his term.

The following December, in a meeting in St. Petersburg, Florida, Chandler's request for renewal was reconsidered. On a trial ballot, there were nine votes for renewal and seven against. A formal ballot followed; it was 8–8. Unconvinced, Chandler asked for still another vote. It was 9–7, same as the first ballot, and Chandler was a lame-duck czar. Because of the three-fourths rule, approval from twelve of the sixteen clubs was required.

Chandler's allies went to bat for him, among them Clark Griffith of the Washington Senators and Connie Mack of the Philadelphia Athletics. Baseball pioneers, Griffith and Mack were in their declining years and unable to rally the necessary support. But Powel Crosley of Cincinnati, who had supported Chandler, urged him to resign. In a letter dated May 31, Crosley wrote:

"You know the Cincinnati club has been behind your re-election 100 percent. I agree with you that with a majority in your favor it does seem unfair that a minority can prevent it. Now that the smoke has cleared away, I very frankly feel that it would be a hopeless cause for you to expect to be able to change the alignment of owners against you. Under the circumstances I really believe you should accept a monetary settlement in full with your resignation."

Frank Murphy, an associate justice on the U.S. Supreme Court, urged Chandler to continue the fight. "Don't let the critics bother you," Murphy wrote. "Each day you are growing stronger in public esteem because you are a man of good character."

But neither Justice Murphy nor the public had a vote. On March 12, again at Chandler's request, the owners convened at the Shoremede Hotel in Miami Beach. As Crosley predicted, there was no movement. It was a secret vote: nine for Chandler, seven against. Confident of Chandler's dismissal, the owners, twenty-four hours earlier, had appointed a screening committee to find baseball's third commissioner.

"Mama," Chandler said to his wife, "if Jesus Christ were commissioner, I'm not sure he could carry twelve votes."

Saigh, Webb, and Perini orchestrated the revolt. Also definitely opposed were Bill DeWitt, St. Louis Browns; Ellis Ryan, Cleveland; and 25-year-old Chuck Comiskey, who represented the White Sox. His mother, Grace, who owned the club, later insisted he should have supported Chandler.

The general belief was that either Philip K. Wrigley, the altruistic owner of the Chicago Cubs, or Bob Carpenter of the Philadelphia Phillies cast the seventh vote. More than likely it was Wrigley, who several times had been quoted as saying he didn't approve of Chandler's electioneering.

Chandler resigned in June 1951, effective at the close of business on July 15. He received $65,000 in severance pay, the equivalent of one year's salary. In his last act as Commissioner, before a crowd of 5,000 at the dedication of a new stadium in Reading, Pennsylvania, Chandler sang "My Old Kentucky Home."

"Believe me," Chandler recalled many years later, "There wasn't a dry eye in the stands."

# FORD FRICK

## PART I

F ord Christopher Frick, who had been in the on-deck circle prior to Chandler's arrival, was the next batter. Frick had been the National League president for seventeen years and before that a full-time New York baseball writer and part-time broadcaster. To the end he insisted he didn't want to become the commissioner.

"Good Lord, I didn't want it," Frick said in a 1972 interview, six years before his death at the age of 83. "My name had been bandied about but I wasn't interested. I saw my old friend, Frankie Graham of the *New York Journal*. We had been baseball writers together, had roomed together one year when we were covering the Giants. I got him into a corner and said, 'Do me a favor, will you?'

"He said, 'Sure.'

"I told him I wanted him to say in his column that I wasn't a candidate, that I was happy in the National League.

"Well, he wrote that. But the old sonofagun. He wound up with one line across the bottom. 'I told Ford Frick I would write this. I've written it. But my candidate for commissioner is Ford Frick.'"

According to some reports there were almost 100 candidates in the original herd. The early leader was James A. Farley, former post-master general who was also on the track during the Chandler derby. Bill Corum, another of Frick's sportswriter pals, was convinced Farley would get the nod.

"From where I sit, it appears Farley will be offered the post and will accept," Corum wrote in his *New York Journal* column. "With all respect to the many other fine men who have been mentioned as possibilities, I doubt if baseball could do better."

Farley was an early dropout. He was willing to serve but only on a lifetime basis. Some of the others who failed to make it to the half-mile pole, mostly because of disinterest, were Fred Vinson, Chief Justice of the U.S. Supreme Court; J. Edgar Hoover, director of the FBI, who had been a big Chandler supporter; and Stuart Symington, head of the federal Reconstruction Finance Corporation. Arch Ward, sports editor of the *Chicago Tribune* and father of baseball's All Star Game, was also considered.

The first meeting to narrow the field was in New York City on August 7, 1951. There were nine survivors: Frick; Warren Giles, president of the Cincinnati Reds; Generals Douglas MacArthur, Maxwell Taylor, Emmett "Rosey" O'Donnell and Dwight Eisenhower; Milton Eisenhower, the general's brother, who was the president of Pennsylvania State College; and Ohio governor Frank Lausche. Two weeks later, after another meeting, the list was trimmed to five: Frick, Giles, MacArthur, Lausche, and Milton Eisenhower.

Formal voting began when the owners reconvened at the Palmer House in Chicago on September 20. Seventeen votes were submitted on the first ballot, one more than the maximum. There were sixteen teams, not seventeen. The extra vote was from the New York Yankees.

"My Gawd, Dan, did you vote, too?" Del Webb, the Yankees

chairman, asked co-owner Dan Topping. Thereafter, Topping cast the Yankees vote.

After two ballots, the choice was narrowed to Frick and Giles. The stalemate continued through fourteen ballots. The owners then broke for dinner. During the break, Philip K. Wrigley of the Cubs advised Giles that if he dropped out he would be assured the National League presidency. Giles withdrew. Frick was elected, 14–2, on the fifteenth ballot. One of the dissidents was Spike Briggs of Detroit. For cosmetic purposes, Frick was a unanimous choice on a sixteenth ballot.

Happy Chandler, who never liked Frick, was unimpressed. "It looks to me," Chandler said, "that the office of commissioner is still vacant."

Voting were Fred Saigh of the St. Louis Cardinals; Ellis Ryan, Cleveland; Chuck Comiskey, Chicago White Sox; Bill DeWitt, St. Louis Browns; Roy Mack, Philadelphia Athletics; Calvin Griffith, Washington; Tom Yawkey, Boston Red Sox; Horace Stoneham, New York Giants; Walter O'Malley, Brooklyn; Lou Perini, Boston Braves; Bob Carpenter, Philadelphia Phillies; Branch Rickey, Pittsburgh; Wrigley, Cubs; Briggs, Detroit; Giles, Cincinnati; and Topping, Yankees.

"We want a tough commissioner," Saigh said in a remarkable turnabout. "He's got to put his foot down and make decisions without regard for whom they hurt. He must be a fellow who has the courage of his convictions."

Webb, another of Chandler's antagonists, also took the high road. Webb told reporters, "We wanted the best man, whether he was a general, politician, judge or baseball man."

A baseball lifer, Frick ascended the throne at age 55. He was born on a farm near Wawaka in northeast Indiana, the only boy in a family of five children. His parents, Jacob and the former Emma Prickett, moved to Brimfield when he was five, where he attended grade school. In 1910, he graduated from the Consolidated High School in nearby Rome City.

"We had the whole world to ourselves," Frick recalled. "Woods to play in and lakes to swim in. We skated in the winter and played baseball in the summer. We made our own recreation. I suppose by modern standards we were underprivileged. But we never thought of ourselves as underprivileged.

"It would have taken all the kids in the three neighboring villages, and a lot of equipment, to have a football team. But baseball was easy. You could go out in the cow pasture, after the hay was cut, and take four or five bricks for bases and a slab of stone for home plate. We made our own baseballs and the guy who had the best baseball was captain of the team—until that ball was lost. If you had a bat you made the team. Everybody used the same bat. We had gloves that were interchangeable."

Frick described his mother as a "very saintly person." His father, "stern but generous and honest, was a reader, and so was I but we didn't do much reading together because he was always busy. When you work a farm you start at dawn and don't quit until sunset. It was a general farm—corn, wheat, potatoes, hay, and alfalfa. We were 136 miles from Chicago and in those days that was a long trip. Lord, when you went that far you packed a trunk."

After Frick graduated from high school he decided on a newspaper career. When he was told he would have to learn how to type, he took a summer course in typing and stenography at the International Business College in Fort Wayne. During his years as a sportswriter in New York, his press box colleagues often spoke of his speed at the typewriter. Said Frick, reminiscing, "Maybe I wasn't a good writer but I was hell of a typist. I could turn out a hell of a lot of words."

He enrolled at DePauw University in Greencastle, Indiana, in 1912, and worked his way through school. He was a waiter in a student boarding house, later a stringer for the *Chicago Tribune* and newspapers in Indianapolis and Terre Haute. He earned his letter on the DePauw baseball team but repeatedly insisted he wasn't much of a ballplayer. A first baseman, he had a weak arm and had to wind-up to make the throw to third. He couldn't recall any specific accident but was convinced he had hurt his arm when he was a boy.

After college he went to Colorado Springs, where he married a local girl, Eleanor Cowling. He taught English at Colorado College, wrote copy for an advertising agency, and worked on the Colorado Springs *Gazette*. Among his pupils was Jacqueline Logan, who subsequently became a movie star.

"Ever keep her after school?" a raunchy sportswriter once asked.

"No," replied Frick, a straight arrow. "There was no reason to. She never gave me any trouble."

Frick wrote editorials, police, and sports for the newspaper, but the assignment he enjoyed most was interviewing celebrities who had made brief railroad stops in Colorado Springs en route from one coast to the other. He might have remained there if a printer hadn't clipped some of his articles and sent them to Arthur Brisbane in New York. Brisbane, a writer and editor, was the chief of the Hearst newspaper empire.

Brisbane summoned Frick to the big city. This was late in 1921, after Frick had been in Colorado for five years. Brisbane put him to work writing sports for the *American*, the Hearst morning paper. A half century later, Frick was still amused when he told how Brisbane moved him to the *Journal*, Hearst's afternoon paper.

"I was covering the Giants at the Polo Grounds," Frick recalled. "The game was rained out and I was in the office writing a rainy day story, and the office boy said, 'Mr. Brisbane wants to see you.'

"I went to Mr. Brisbane's office and he told me he had taken over the *Journal* and was switching me over. When I started to walk away, he said, 'Where are you going?'

"'I'm going back to the *American* to finish my story.' And he said, 'To hell with the *American*! You're working on the *Journal*!'

"I never did go back. As far as I'm concerned, that rainy day story on the Giants is still in the typewriter."

Brisbane was a demanding boss. "You saw him only when he wanted to see you," Frick recalled in *No Cheering in the Press Box*, an assemblage of interviews with retired sportswriters. "Brisbane would send for you and you never had the slightest idea why he was calling you in. It'd be bang! bang! bang!

"He never called me anything but 'young man.' One day I answered his summons and he said, 'Young man, how fast can an elephant run?'

"I hadn't the slightest idea.

"'How far do you mean? Do you want the speed on him for a mile? For a hundred yards?'

"I called the circus, got hold of an animal trainer, various people. The Sunday paper came out with an editorial across the top, with a guy in an automobile, a guy on horseback, a man running, a man on a bicycle, all these things, and the story featured my research on an elephant.

"Brisbane always contended that nature endowed men with two legs and a brain but shortchanged him on a hell of a lot of things. Man was puny. The automobile was first, of course, the horse was second, the elephant third. The guy running was last.

"Everybody was afraid of Brisbane except Tad, the cartoonist— Theodore Aloysuis Dorgan. Tad called him George. I never did know why. In the old days the *Journal* and the *American* were published at 230 Williams Street, in an old loft building. It was kind of a V-shaped building, and Brisbane's office was at the head of the V. Down at one end was what we called the Chamber of Horrors, where the cartoonists hung out.

"Brisbane was tough on gambling of any sort. The cartoonists and some of the sportswriters had a crap game going on down there one day, and Tad is down on the floor with the dice in his hands. Brisbane comes in the door. Everybody's frightened. Tad looks up and says, 'Hey, George, couple dollars open. Do you want to cover it?' And Brisbane turned around and walked out."

Those were Frick's happiest days. It was the golden age of sports, sportswriting included. Frick was a minor player in the gilded scene that included such press box celebrities as Ring Lardner, Grantland Rice, Damon Runyon, Heywood Broun, John Kieran, Sid Mercer, Bugs Baer, Bill Corum, and Frank Graham.

"Good Lord, I was goggle-eyed, scared to death, but it was a great experience."

A capable but pedestrian scribe, Frick was a desirable companion. He golfed with Yankees manager Miller Huggins and was among Babe Ruth's ghostwriters, the author of *Babe Ruth's Own Book of Baseball*, a worthwhile work published in 1928 and reissued in 1992. He made a brief stab at fiction but had better success with a nightly fifteen-minute radio sports show, a wrap-up of the events of the day. He graduated into a part-time baseball radio broadcaster and then jumped into the big-time as master of ceremonies of *The Chesterfield Show*, a well-received network program of classical music.

It was a rigorous schedule. During Frick's last year in radio, he was home for dinner only on Sundays. But it separated him from the newspaper pack and lifted him into national prominence. In the early days of television, two decades later, Ed Sullivan, also a former New York sportswriter without theatrical skills, had a parallel career when he hosted the television's leading variety show. Frank Graham, in a 1953 magazine piece, wrote of Frick's regimen:

"He liked long train rides because he got a lot of work done. He'd shut himself up in his compartment and beat the brains out of his typewriter. For relaxation, he played bridge with the Babe, Lou

Gehrig and Herb Pennock. Or he read verse. Edgar Guest was his favorite poet and his favorite poem was the one about it takes a heap of living to make a house a home. This was before night baseball and the boys could romp from sundown to daybreak. But that held little interest for Ford. In order to get up early, he went to bed early. He had more respect than Cinderella for the stroke of midnight."

In those days and somewhat beyond, Frick seemed to be entombed in a prolonged adolescence, an affliction commonly found in sportswriters. Often, his column included inspirational verse. A sample, which appears to be a takeoff on Grantland Rice's famous "great scorer" poem, follows:

You view the game as the thing, My Lad,
For that is the youthful way.
And you count it a sin when you fail to win
In the game that you choose to play.
But there's got to be someone to lose, My Lad,
It's sad—but it's always true.
And day by day, in the game you play,
It's sure some time to be you.

And after the years are fled, My Lad,
And you're withered and bent and gray
You'll know the truth of the soul of youth
And smile at your grief of today.
For it isn't the score that counts, My Lad,
And the years as they pass speak true,
There's a something lasts when the Game is past—
It's the thing that you make—of YOU.

Unlike Ed Sullivan, Frick never cut the umbilical cord. Baseball remained his principal occupation. He was constantly aware of the reporter's need to maintain and, equally important, enlarge his stable of sources. On his trips with the Yankees to Chicago, the club stayed at the DelPrado Hotel, a few blocks from where Judge Landis lived at the Chicago Beach Hotel.

"Many a night after dinner," Frank Graham recalled, "Ford would say, 'Let's walk over and see the Judge.' It was always pleasant. The Judge and Mrs. Landis were wonderful hosts and the Judge, while breaking out a bottle of bourbon, would say, 'It's nice of you to come over. Mother and I get a little lonesome in the evening.'"

Landis told Frick, "Give me a ring when you come to Chicago. I'm just across the park. We'll play some golf."

"The Judge was a lousy golfer but he was fun to be with," Frick said. "So we came in one time, when I was with the Yankees, and I called the Judge: 'How about a little golf tomorrow?'

"Goddammit," he said. 'Do you think I've got nothing to do but play golf with you guys? I'm a busy man. I've got work to do. Goodbye!' And he hung up.

"The next day the telephone rang. It was six in the morning. It's the Judge. He says, 'Dammit, if you're going to keep calling me all the time, I might as well play golf with you. I'll be by in thirty minutes.'

"Hell, I wasn't even dressed. I got up and grabbed a cup of coffee. We went to the South Shore Country Club, which had a gentleman's course, a nine-hole course, very easy. For the Judge it was one of those inspired days. He couldn't do anything wrong. He hit a tree and it would bounce right back in the fairway. He'd go into a trap and run right through it. We get to the ninth hole and he has a twenty-foot putt that would give him a 36. Par was about 30.

"Hell, he'd never broken 40 in his life. And here's this putt. He takes a lot of time. He hits that thing and the minute he hit it you knew it was going in. He watches it roll into the hole and I think he's going to be elated. But he threw his club and shouted, 'Goddam you, Frick! I didn't want to play in the first place. And now you've ruined my whole goddam summer. You know damn well I'll never come close to that again.'"

The equally feisty John McGraw, field manager of the New York Giants and influential in National League matters, was also cultivated. It was at McGraw's recommendation that Frick, in 1933, did the first radio re-creations of major league games involving the New York teams. McGraw also persuaded the owners to hire Frick as director of the National League's embryonic Public Service Bureau, which was primarily publicity and public relations. Frick accepted with the knowledge that league president John Heydler was approaching retirement; by assuming this assignment he would be in a strategic position when a successor was chosen.

Heydler, who had been an umpire and before that a Linotype operator in the Bureau of Engraving and Printing in Washington, D.C., joined the National League in 1895 primarily to make out the official averages. Heydler succeeded John Tener as the league president in 1918. Tener's predecessor was Harry Pulliam, who committed suicide at the age of 41, in his seventh season in office; he shot himself in the temple.

As anticipated, Heydler announced his resignation within a year of Frick's appointment to the Public Service Bureau. Frick succeeded him on November 9, 1934. Cautious, the NL owners elected him for a one-year term and increased his salary from $10,000 to $20,000. It was upward and onward thereafter for Arthur Brisbane's quietly ambitious "young man."

President Frick had no prepared statement to offer but said he was deeply flattered by the honor bestowed upon him. The *Reach Base Ball Guide* hailed his appointment and described him as "clean-cut and alert-minded."

Frick remained in the baseball establishment for the next thirty-one years, seventeen as the National League president, fourteen as Commissioner. He was retired with full honors in 1965 at the age of 71.

When reviewing his career and asked what had been his most rewarding and lasting achievement, he made no mention of his role in squelching a bigoted player revolt against Jackie Robinson or his dozens of congressional appearances in successful defense of baseball's antitrust immunity, or in keeping the game free of scandal.

Uppermost, he said, was founding the Hall of Fame in Cooperstown, the so-called diamond Valhalla where the great players and some not so great club executives are immortalized in a great hall, their likenesses cast in bronze and hung to rest. An adjacent four-story museum houses some 7,000 of the game's sacred artifacts.

"That's my baby, the thing I'm proudest of," Frick said. "I started it. This was in 1936, my second year as the National League president. Judge Landis was the commissioner. There's a big portrait of me up there which I don't like. It says I was father of the whole thing.

"Judge Landis never liked the idea, never warmed up to it, probably because he didn't think of it first. Maybe I shouldn't say that. He was a great guy but a stubborn sonofagun. He did go up there in '39, made a beautiful dedication speech. But he never went back.

"Once the Hall of Fame was established each of the two major leagues set aside a $5,000 subsidy to help run the place. Every year I'd make the motion to renew our pledge for the $5,000. And every time it came up the Judge would say `What is this goddammed Hall of Fame business?'

"Finally, I got mad and said, 'Now listen, Judge, you've been asking that for the last four or five years, and I've always answered. If you don't know by now to hell with it.'"

The idea was germinated by the discovery of the "Doubleday Baseball," found in an old trunk on the Abner Graves farm near

96969696969696969696969696969696969696969696969696969696 9696969696 FORD FRICK—PART I

Cooperstown. Stephen Clark, a historian and philanthropist, bought the ball for five dollars, had it mounted, and put it on display in the Otesaga Historical Society. A Clark aide contacted Frick and suggested the major leagues pick an all-star team and play a game in Cooperstown, a one-day midsummer celebration of baseball.

"I said, 'Hell, why do that?'" Frick recalled. "'Why not start a baseball museum—a *Hall of Fame*—and have something that will last?'"

It has grown far beyond Frick's vision and has become a mecca for the hard-core and casual fan; the annual visitor count has exceeded 500,000. The museum has expanded almost ten times its original size; in 1994, a $6 million library was opened, available to researchers. Every major, and many minor, sport has followed Frick's lead. There are seventy-five such depositories nationwide, but none comparable with Cooperstown. Yearly elections are held under the auspices of the Baseball Writers Association of America, often creating controversy accompanied by a blizzard of media attention.

But it is much more than a publicity man's dream. Frick had a higher mission. He saw it as an opportunity to link the generations. "I like to think of it as tying together yesterday and today," he explained. "It keeps the continuity and gives the oldsters a chance to discuss and relive their times. You can compare the moderns and the ancients. I always believed history is important, that we should mark what has gone before."

The founder was elected in 1970.

# FORD FRICK
## PART II

H istory has not been kind to Ford Frick. He was passive in nature and more a chairman of the board than a commissioner, which was, of course, preferable to the owners who reelected him to a second seven-year term. Frick stayed out of harm's way. He was neither a theatrical, fire-belching Landis nor possessed of Chandler's gift of exuding good cheer even when there was nothing to cheer about.

During Frick's watch, the major league map underwent considerable revision. Boston's Lou Perini, who insisted he was heading for the poorhouse, was allowed to move the Braves to Milwaukee in 1953, the first change in the landscape in a half-century. A year later, the St. Louis Browns, a perennial stepbrother to the Cardinals, were transferred to Baltimore. The following season, Philadelphia also was diminished to a one-team town. The Athletics were relocated in Kansas City.

In 1957 and 1958, the Brooklyn Dodgers and the New York Giants were transplanted to the Pacific Coast, the start of a California gold rush. Two decades later, California, previously barren of major league activity, was overloaded with five franchises. Responding to the threat of Branch Rickey's Continental League, a potential outlaw, the American and National leagues, in 1961–62, expanded from eight to ten teams. Replacement franchises were awarded to New York and Washington (whose team had moved to Minnesota) with the simultaneous birth of entries in Houston and Los Angeles; in the 1966 expansion California Angels, who had invaded the Dodgers' territory, moved to Anaheim.

In this time of enormous change, Frick seemed to be a spectator along for the ride, seldom interfering in what he regarded as "league matters." He did make a decision that upset Bill Veeck but "Barnum Bill," never in the mainstream, was in constant skirmish with the game's power brokers. It was an easy decision, a trade-off of an angry Veeck for an appeased Walter O'Malley. After O'Malley had bought off Rickey in Brooklyn, he became baseball's most influential owner.

Gabe Paul, a baseball lifer whose career paralleled Frick's, insisted Frick was an "incompetent good fellow." Said Paul, who at various times owned or operated four major league franchises: "He never did anything. All he did was show up for work."

*New York Herald Tribune* columnist Red Smith, a longtime Frick ally who seldom had a good word for Happy Chandler, acknowledged that Frick had an opposite approach.

"He was a good man but will be remembered chiefly as a reluctant leader," Smith observed in his Frick obituary. "He didn't think baseball needed a house dick and didn't consider himself one. He regarded his employers as honest men capable of making their own decisions and felt he was there only to administer the rules.

"When he did take firm action, it was not announced in a press release from the Commissioner's office. Though the press found him always accessible he shrank from personal publicity. The low-keyed tone of his administration and his concept of the commissioner's role was in sharp contrast with the previous administration."

One of the first problems Frick encountered was night baseball, which had begun in the minor leagues and was introduced in the major leagues by Larry MacPhail in Cincinnati, in 1935. Many baseball men were opposed, claiming the reduced visibility under artificial light gave the pitchers an unfair advantage. Frick examined the minor league records of the previous three seasons and discovered that the hitters hit .004 worse and fielded .007 better under the stars than under the sun.

Frick issued few press releases. "We had a lot of things that never got in the papers," he said. "There was a gambling operation in St. Louis next to the ballpark. I had a guy working for me, quietly, and he found out Gussie Busch owned the building. I called Gussie—he owned the Cardinals—and told him what was going on. He said, 'Hell, I'll tear it down. I need more parking, anyway.'

"We had to go into Chicago, to [Wrigley Field]. They were betting in the stands. I'm talking about big betting, not penny-ante stuff, hundreds of dollars. Bookies were there. And we had to clean up in Detroit and Cincinnati. I've never told this to a newspaperman before. We were always on the alert."

Frick initially was too modest to acknowledge his crucial role in suppressing a strike by a small number of St. Louis players in objection to Jackie Robinson's presence with the Brooklyn Dodgers. This was in 1947, when Frick was National League president. According to Stanley Woodward, sports editor of the *Herald Tribune* who broke and embroidered the story, Frick met with the players and, "in effect," told them:

"If you do this you will be suspended from the league. You will find that the friends you think you have in the press box will not support you, that you will be outcasts. I do not care if half the league strikes and if it wrecks the National League for five years. This is the United States of America and one citizen has as much right to play as another. The National League will go down the line with Robinson whatever the consequences."

Woodward's report, under the headline "One Strike Is Out," ran on May 9 and was the unanimous choice of three judges as the top "news story" of the year in the "Best Sports Stories" series, co-edited by Irving Marsh and Edward Ehre, both of whom worked for Woodward in the *Herald Tribune* sports department; Marsh was the assistant sports editor.

Quentin Reynolds, one of the judges, commented: "If it had not been printed, it is quite likely that antagonism toward Robinson might have flared up all over the National League. The story, read by every baseball owner, had the effect of stiffening their backbones to the point where they themselves laid down the law to their players-and from that point on everything was relatively sweetness and light."

Woodward pulled out all the stops:

"The *New York Herald Tribune* prints this story in part as a public service. It is factual and thoroughly substantiated. The St. Louis players involved unquestionably will deny it. We doubt, however, that Frick or Breadon will go that far. A return of 'no comment' from either or both will serve as confirmation. On our own authority we can say that both of them were present at long conferences with the ringleaders and that both probably now feel that the overt act has been averted."

Many insiders accused Woodward of making a grandstand play. Wendell Smith of the *Pittsburgh Courier*, the first African-American writer elected to the writers' wing of the Hall of Fame and whose persistence helped break the color line, described it as "greatly exaggerated . . . it made a better newspaper story than anything else."

Bob Broeg of the *St. Louis Post-Dispatch*, a baseball writer with an impeccable reputation who was then traveling with the Cardinals, has repeatedly charged it was "terribly distorted." Said Broeg: "Ford Frick never met with the players. Just because Stanley Woodward wrote it a lot of people think it was true. But Stanley wasn't infallible. It didn't happen, not the way he told it."

What happened, according to Broeg, was that *Herald Tribune* baseball writer Rud Rennie, in St. Louis with the Giants, attended a party for the New York press hosted by Breadon. The Cardinals had lost eleven of their first thirteen games and Breadon expressed concern that attendance would drop when Robinson and the Dodgers arrived. Doc Hyland, the Cardinals' physician, told that to Rennie and also said the St. Louis club might strike in objection to Robinson. Rennie relayed this information to Woodward.

Frick's version:

"The Jackie Robinson incident had been over two or three weeks before it hit the headlines. Rud Rennie was a great friend of Dr. Hyland's and was at the Hylands' for dinner. During the conversation Jackie Robinson was mentioned. Dr. Hyland had no intention of making a public statement. It was a dinner party, not a press conference. They were discussing it. It happened weeks before and Rennie picked up the story. Rennie didn't have the guts to write it himself. He went home and told it to Woodward."

Frick conceded "the story was practically true" but insisted "the incident [with the Cardinals] wasn't half as tough as some of the other incidents we had. There was a lot of resentment among the ballplayers.

"Sam Breadon made a special trip to my office and asked what he should do. Some of his people had told him about it. I don't think the players took a vote on it. Five or six of them had said, 'Goddammit, if Brooklyn comes in with that colored guy then we won't play.'

"And the message went back to St. Louis: 'Either you play or you're out of baseball.' That was my message. I never met with any players. I thought very little of it until the story broke. The way Woodward wrote it, you would have thought all the St. Louis players were against Robinson."

In his memoir, *Games, Asterisks and People*, Frick wrote: "I don't know how Sam delivered the message, or to whom he talked. I do know he called the league office a day or two later to report that the whole matter was settled and everything was under control. Sam said, 'It was a tempest in a teapot,' that a few of his players were upset and had popped off."

Frick emerged as the reluctant hero, a turnabout from his previous stance two years earlier when he attempted to destroy the MacPhail Report designed to maintain baseball's unspoken racist policy. Frick's swift action in defense of Robinson was greeted with hurrahs from the owners, who had a vested interest beyond fair play. Their man had upheld the integrity of the game, vital to maintaining public confidence and ballpark attendance which are one and the same. Attendance always has been their primary concern.

Otherwise there was little turmoil during Frick's 17-year tenure as National League president. The best evidence of his remarkably serene voyage is that his biggest rhubarb, gauged by the volume of newspaper clippings, was a two-week joust with Jerome Herman Dean, better known as Dizzy Dean, who wasn't dizzy. He was as smart as a fox and among the most colorful and widely-quoted players of the time.

Frick, in his third year of office, suspended Dean on June 2, 1937, for comments "detrimental to baseball" and, to his surprise, discovered he was overmatched. The suspension sprouted from a free-for-all in a May 19 game the Cardinals played against the Giants. In that game, Carl Hubbell's 22nd consecutive victory, umpire George Barr called a balk on Dean.

Seven days later, in a front-page story in the Belleville (Ill.) *Daily*

*Advocate*, Dean described Barr and Frick as "the two biggest crooks in baseball."

Frick overreacted. Not only did he plaster Dean with an indefinite suspension but twice asked him to sign an apology. The second request was made when Frick summoned Dean to his New York headquarters.

"I ain't signin' nothin'!" Dean insisted.

Emerging from his office, Frick provided newsmen with a transcript of the questions he had put to the Cardinals' star pitcher and the replies:

Frick: Mr. Dean, you are quoted in the newspapers [the story was picked up nationally] as making a statement to the effect that the balk rule was instituted by the National League as a direct slap at you and constituted persecution. Did you or did you not make that statement?

Dean: I did not.

Frick: Mr. Dean, is it true that you were notified of the enforcement of the balk rule by this office one week before the balk was called?

Dean: I was warned in Brooklyn.

Frick: Is it true that you were also notified on the day of the game by Frankie Frisch, your manager, on the day the balk was called?

Dean: I was warned by Frank Frisch.

Frick: You were quoted in the paper in Belleville of making a statement that the president of the National League and umpire George Barr were the "two biggest crooks in baseball." Did you or did you not make that statement?

Dean: I never said that.

Frick: I have here a wire from the editor of the Belleville *Daily Advocate* which says: "The article speaks for itself and contains an account of what was said at the Presbyterian Men's Club dinner." Do you deny that article is true?

Dean: I didn't say it.

Frick made no effort to hide his wrath.

"It's now strictly up to Dean as to whether his suspension lasts twenty-four hours or three months," Frick told reporters. "I've played along with him but I don't see how we can overlook his actions any longer. It's down to a question whether Dean is bigger than the National League and I don't think he is. He can settle this quickly if he admits the errors of his ways, apologizes to the league for the things he said or implied, and puts it in writing."

Back in St. Louis, Dean continued to plead innocence.

"Frick even wanted me to apologize for throwing at the Giants. How does he know I was throwin' at 'em? Can't prove it, can he? Anyhow, I'd not be popping off in a church, would I?"

Dean didn't miss a pitching turn. He was out of service for only three days. Frick relented and in a prepared statement said:

"The president of the National League was not present at the time of these occurrences and therefore he can have no definite proof. Under the circumstances he is willing to accept the statement of Mr. Dean at its face value. He considers the case closed."

Frick had better success in 1943 when Bill Cox, the owner of the Philadelphia Phillies, was thrown out of baseball for betting on his team. It was the only ejection during Frick's presidency. "I took Cox by the hand and brought him to Judge Landis," Frick recalled. "The Judge took the action."

A workaholic who earned his fortune in lumber, Cox had made the mistake of firing Bucky Harris, his field manager. Harris responded by calling Cox "an all-American jerk," and in a parting shot told reporters, "He's a fine guy to fire me—when he gambles on the games we play."

Cox readily admitted he had been betting on the Phillies but pleaded ignorance, claiming he was not aware of baseball's antigambling statute. It didn't wash. It was a sad distinction for the Phillies, the only major league club to have two of its presidents given the boot. Horace Fogel, a former newspaperman, had been banished in 1912 on seven counts of rule violations.

In a sentimental "Goodbye to Baseball" radio broadcast, Cox said, "I want to say that I looked up to, rather than at my fellow club presidents with a sincere hope that I could emulate the best of their individual deeds. I hope I have not offended them. I have endeavored to lead an exemplary life and conduct myself with the proper viewpoint to this great sport. Good luck and goodbye to everyone in baseball."

It wasn't goodbye for Ford Christopher Frick. He was in the bullpen warming up for bigger and better things. In early 1944 he made what may have been his first trip to Washington. Despite President Franklin D. Roosevelt's "green light" urging baseball to continue during World War II, many of the owners feared a shutdown.

Frick was an able ambassador and said it was just as well Judge Landis wasn't given the assignment. "The Judge hates FDR so bitterly," Frick confided to his friends, that "at the very mention of him he flies into a rage. I will not be asking for anything but guidance. But the Judge won't even ask for that. He's adamant."

# FORD FRICK
## PART III

During his first year as commissioner, according to his count, Frick appeared before seventeen congressional committees. This may have been an exaggeration; perhaps he was speaking of total appearances. Whatever, his most crucial service to ownership was in squelching the repeated attempts to remove baseball's immunity from the Sherman Antitrust Law; among other advantages, the exemption provided the umbrella that sheltered the controversial reserve system.

A 1951 Special House Subcommittee on the Study of Monopoly Power, chaired by the Honorable Emanuel Celler from Brooklyn, investigated all four of the major professional spectator sports but the thrust clearly was against baseball's antitrust exemption, a concession granted in 1922 by Oliver Wendell Holmes, Associate Justice of the U.S Supreme Court.

Though not educated in the law, Frick was a surprisingly agile witness, providing his interpretation of the commissioner's authority, a perception not always shared by his successors, notably Bowie Kuhn and Fay Vincent. Kuhn and Vincent often entered into lesser disputes, a practice which eventually led to their dismissals.

"The fundamental power of the commissioner," Frick said, "is to deal with conduct detrimental to baseball. That authority is the strongest single agent baseball has for keeping its skirts clear of crookedness, of game-throwing, of gambling and of unsportsmanlike conduct of any kind. Without it, and without the right and authority within our own organization, to keep our own house in order, public confidence and public faith would be destroyed.

"The men who own ballclubs, the men who operate leagues and the men who play are in no sense crooks, nor are they addicted to sharp practices. Rather they are men of character and integrity. Nor do I imply that the commissioner, as such, is a man of holy attributes, sitting on a golden throne and cracking a whip.

"The men who own the ballclubs, the men who operate the leagues and the men who play the game must be inherently honest. If they are not, the commissioner, alone, regardless of his power, would not be able to maintain the game's integrity. What I do say is that even among any group of honest people, there are bound to be recurrent differences but the commissioner, through his broad authority, is able to resolve those differences, to make final and lasting decisions and to enforce rules in such manner as to avoid any action that would be hurtful to baseball as a game."

Frick's many appearances before the Celler Committee (which reconvened in a second unsuccessful attempt in 1957) received cursory coverage or were virtually ignored by the press. There was little interest until Casey Stengel, the manager of the New York Yankees, was summoned. Stengel's appearance was the highlight of the hearings.

As Robert Creamer, who wrote the definitive Stengel biography, observed:

"The Stengel legend peaked on July 8, 1958, when he testified in Washington. It was the day after the All Star Game in Baltimore. Sen-

ator Estes Kefauver of Tennessee, who had made his name by conducting televised investigations of organized crime figures, didn't
feel that such a broad exemption from the antitrust laws should whip
through without at least a little discussion."

Stengel, impeccably dressed in a gray suit, white shirt, and dark
tie, was asked to give a brief review of his background and his views
in regard to baseball's exemption. And Stengel was off and running,
forty-five minutes of Stengelese. There has been nothing compara-
ble, before or since, in the history of congressional hearings:

Stengel: Well, I started in professional baseball in 1910. I have
been in professional ball, I would say for forty-eight years. I have
been employed by numerous ballclubs in the majors and in the
minor leagues.

I started in the minor leagues with Kansas City. I played as low as
Class D ball, which was at Shelbyville, Kentucky, and also Class C ball
and Class A ball, and I have advanced in baseball as a ballplayer.

I had many years that I was not so successful as a ballplayer, as it
is a game of skill. And then I was no doubt discharged by baseball
in which I had to go back to the minor leagues as a manager, and
after being in the minor leagues as a manager, I became a major
league manager in several cities and was discharged. We call it discharged because there was no question I had to leave.

And I returned to the minor leagues at Milwaukee, Kansas City,
and Oakland, California, and then returned to the major leagues. In
the last ten years, naturally, in major league baseball with the New
York Yankees; the New York Yankees have had tremendous success,
and while I am not a ballplayer who does the work, I have no doubt
worked for a ballclub that is very capable in the office.

I have been up and down the ladder. I know there are some things
in baseball, thirty-five to fifty years ago, that are better now than

they were in those days. In those days, my goodness, you could not transfer a ballclub in the minor leagues, Class D, Class C ball, Class A ball.

How could you transfer a ballclub when you did not have a highway? How could you transfer a ballclub when the railroad then would take you to a town, you got off and then you had to wait and sit up five hours to go to another ballclub?

How could you run baseball then without night ball? You had to have night ball to improve the proceeds, to pay larger salaries, and I went to work, the first year I received $35 a month. I thought that was amazing. I had to put away enough money to go to dental college. I found out it was not better in dentistry. I stayed in baseball. Any other questions you would like to ask me?

Senator Kefauver: Mr. Stengel, are you prepared to answer particularly why baseball wants this bill passed?

Stengel: Well, I would have to say at the present time, I think that baseball has advanced in this respect for the player help. That is an amazing statement for me to make because you can retire with an annuity at 50 and what organization in America allows you to retire at 50 and receive money?

I want to further state that I am not a ballplayer, that is, put into that pension fund committee. At my age, and I have been in baseball, well, I will say I am possibly the oldest man who is working in baseball. I would say that when they start an annuity for the ballplayers to better their conditions, it should have been done, and I think it has been done.

I think it should be the way they have done it, which is a very good thing. The reason they probably did not take the managers in at that time was because radio and television or the income to ballclubs was not large enough that you could have put in a pension plan.

Now I am not a member of the pension plan. You have young men here who are, who represent the ballclubs. They represent the players and since I am not a member and don't receive pension from a fund which you think, my goodness, he ought to be declared in that, too, but I would say that is a great thing for the ballplayers.

That is one thing I will say for the ballplayers, they have an advanced pension fund. I should think it was gained by radio and television or you could not have enough money to pay anything of that type.

Now the second thing about baseball that I think is very interesting to the public or to all of us that is the owners' own fault if he does not improve his club, along with the officials in the ballclub and the players.

Now what causes that?

If I am going to go on the road and we are a traveling ballclub, and you know the cost of transportation now—we travel sometimes with three Pullman coaches, the New York Yankees—and remember I am just a salaried man, and do not own stock in the New York Yankees. I found that in traveling with the New York Yankees on the road and all that it is the best, and we have broken records in Washington this year, and we have broken them in every city but New York and we have lost two clubs that have gone out of the city of New York.

Of course we have had some bad weather, I would say that they are mad at us in Chicago—we fill the parks. They have come out to see good material. I will say they are mad at us in Kansas City, but we broke their attendance record. Now on the road we only get 27 cents. I am not positive of these figures, as I am not an official.

If you go back fifteen years or so if I owned stock in the club I would give them to you.

Senator Kefauver: Mr. Stengel, I am not sure that I made my question clear.

Stengel: Yes, sir. Well, that is all right. I am not sure I am going to answer yours perfectly, either.

Senator O'Mahoney: How many minor leagues were there in baseball when you began?

Stengel: Well, there were not so many at that time because of this fact: Anybody to go into baseball at that time with the educational schools that we had were small, while you were probably thoroughly educated at school, you had to be—we only had small cities that you could put a team in and they would go defunct.

Why, I remember the first year I was at Kankakee, Illinois, and a bank offered me $550 if I would let them have a little notice. I left there and took a uniform because they owed me two weeks' pay. But I either had to quit, but I did not have enough money to go to dental college, so I had to go with the manager down to Kentucky.

What happened there was if you got by July, that was the big date. You did not play night ball and you did not play Sundays in half of the cities on account of Sunday observance, so in those days when things were tough, and all of it was, I mean to say, why they closed up July 4, and there you were sitting there in the depot. You could work someplace else but that was it. So I got out of Kankakee, Illinois.

Senator Carroll: The question Senator Kefauver asked you was what, in your honest opinion, with your forty-eight years of experience, is the need for this legislation in view of the fact that baseball has not been subject to the antitrust laws?

Stengel: No.

Senator Langer: Mr. Chairman, my final question. This is the Antimonopoly Committee sitting here.

Stengel: Yes, sir.

Senator Langer: I want to know whether you intend to keep on monopolizing the world's championship in New York City?

Stengel: Well, I will tell you. I got a little concern yesterday in the first three innings when I saw three players I had gotten rid of, and I said when I lost nine what am I going to do, and when I had a couple of my players I thought so great of that did not do so good up to the sixth inning, I was more confused but I finally had to go and call on a young man from Baltimore that we don't own and the Yankees don't own him, and he is doing pretty good, and I would actually have to tell you that I think we are more the Greta Garbo type now from success.

We are being hated, I mean, from the ownership and all, we are being hated. Every sport that gets too great or one individual—but if we made 27 cents and it pays to have a winner at home, why would you not have a good winner in your own park if you were an owner?

That is the result of baseball. An owner gets most of the money at home and it is up to him and his staff to do better or they ought to be discharged.

Senator Kefauver: Thank you very much, Mr. Stengel. We appreciate your presence here. Mr. Mickey Mantle, will you come around? . . . Mr. Mantle, do you have any observations with reference to the applicability of the antitrust laws to baseball?

Mantle: My views are just about the same as Casey's.

The baseball establishment, with Frick's help and an assist by Stengel, defeated Celler's attempt to eliminate the exemption. After hearing an estimated half million words of public testimony, the committee concluded:

"Legislation is not necessary until the reasonableness of the reserve rules has been tested by the courts. If those rules are unreasonable in some respects, it would be inappropriate to adopt legislation before baseball has had an opportunity to make such modifications as may be necessary."

Among the results of the congressional probe was the adoption of regulations governing the procedures a minor league must follow for major league status. This was in response to both Celler and a 10-year request by the Pacific Coast League which had been threatening to bolt from Organized Baseball. Frick compromised. The PCL was elevated from Triple A to an Open minor league classification and was allowed to protect more of its players from the winter major league draft.

The PCL owners were appeased but continued in the belief they could form a third major league despite comparatively meager attendance and the limited capacity of their stadiums. Even Ty Cobb, in his Celler Committee testimony, insisted it was strictly minor league territory. Cobb was not prophetic. Eventually, five of the eight Pacific Coast League cities were awarded major league franchises.

An equally significant new rule was adopted making it easier to relocate a major league club. In the case of a club transferring its franchise to a city without major league representation, only the league involved, and not both leagues, must grant approval. Unanimous approval was required in the National League, three-fourths in the American League.

On March 16, 1953, confident he had the necessary votes, Bill Veeck, who at the time had been operating the St. Louis Browns, requested permission to move the Browns to Baltimore. It was a stunning setback for Veeck when he discovered the votes were not there. His only supporters were Frank Lane of the White Sox and Hank Greenberg of the Indians. At a National League meeting two days later, Lou Perini was given unanimous approval to move the Boston Braves to Milwaukee, effective for the 1953 season. The move shattered fifty years of franchise tranquillity.

Frick didn't participate in either of these league meetings but made it clear that he was opposed to Veeck's request but not Perini's.

It was personal. Veeck had been an antagonizing and disturbing influence. On September 27, the day after the regular season ended, Veeck's bid to move was again rejected. Forty-eight hours later, after Veeck had withdrawn his financial interests, the transfer was approved.

The economic success in Milwaukee and Baltimore provided the impetus for a third move. The Philadelphia Athletics, in the American League since 1901, were sold on November 4, 1954, to Arnold Johnson, a 47-year-old Chicago industrialist, on the condition he would be allowed to transplant the Athletics to Kansas City. Permission was readily granted.

Johnson had entered the baseball scene eleven months earlier when his corporation, in a financial maneuver believed to be without precedent, purchased the Yankee Stadium real estate and Blues Stadium in Kansas City for $6.5 million; both ballparks were then leased back to the Yankees. In the succeeding years the Yankees and Kansas City appeared to have somewhat of an unholy alliance and constantly were trading players back and forth, usually to the Yankees' advantage.

Frick was in command during this period of transition and generally remained silent, except in the case of Mrs. Eleanor Engle, a 24-year-old stenographer. On June 21, 1951, the Harrisburg (Pennsylvania) club in the Interstate League announced it was planning to sign her to a contract. Mrs. Engle worked out at shortstop the next day. The upshot was a ruling by George Trautman, president of the National Association, governing body of the minor leagues, barring the signing of women as players.

This was long before the advent of the feminist movement. Neither Frick nor Trautman was hauled into court and accused of chauvinism. Trautman declared that "such travesties" would not be tolerated and would be "subject to severe penalties." Frick concurred. At that time, male dominance was acceptable; the majority of women were cosigned to the work of rearing children and other domestic duties.

Encouraged by the financial success of the transplanted franchises in Milwaukee, Baltimore, and Kansas City, the next goal became California. Walter O'Malley of the Brooklyn Dodgers began campaigning for a new ballpark to replace Ebbets Field. The Dodgers scheduled seven home games in 1956 and eight the following year in Jersey City. Confident he would be rewarded with a new stadium, O'Malley, in October 1956, sold the Ebbets Field real estate for $3 million, with an agreement to lease for the next three years.

O'Malley was gone before the lease expired. In the most significant moves, the Dodgers and New York Giants, in tandem, flew cross-country to California, the Dodgers settling in Los Angeles, the Giants in San Francisco, leaving New York with only one team, the Yankees. It was an enormous blow to the abandoned fans and to the New York media. In rebuttal, *Time* magazine, headquartered in New York City, immediately hailed professional football as "the glamour sport of the 1960s."

Commissioner Frick approved the transfers. Although Congressman Celler's Brooklyn constituency had lost its beloved Bums, there could be no complaint because baseball had complied with the trust-busters who wanted major league ball in every market. For Frick it was a peaceable ride. Not an unfriendly word—until 1960 when both the National and American leagues voted to expand to ten teams.

The National League picked up Houston and the New York Mets, the latter a replacement team for the Giants and Dodgers. The American League gave birth to the Los Angeles Angels, who invaded O'Malley's territory in Southern California; moved the Washington Senators to Minneapolis-St. Paul, where they became the Minnesota Twins; and awarded a new franchise to Washington, D.C.

Bill Veeck, frozen out seven years earlier when he was not permitted to move the St. Louis Browns to Baltimore, had returned as the owner of the Chicago White Sox. Veeck tried to seize the day. Expansion offered an opportunity for him to gain control of the ten-team American League.

The league had asked Hank Greenberg, Veeck's longtime pal, to take the franchise in Southern California. Edward Bennett Williams, then a young attorney, was Veeck's man for the new Washington team. Veeck's friend Nate Dolin owned Cleveland. Elliot Stein of St. Louis, another ally, was in the wings, ready to buy the Kansas City franchise from the estate of Arnold Johnson, who died in 1960.

Calvin Griffith had also pledged himself to Veeck—in exchange for the White Sox vote approving Griffith's transfer of the Washington Senators to the Twin Cities. Even without Griffith, Veeck had five firm votes, his own included, more than ample to block any new legislation, enough to oust Joe Cronin as the American League president and have a strong voice in the election of his successor.

Veeck's grandiose plan failed. First, Griffith defected. Then Frick delivered the fatal blow. Frick had repeatedly said Los Angeles was "open" territory, but he reversed himself and ruled that O'Malley had to be paid $350,000 for territorial damages.

Greenberg yelled foul. He had been a leading member of the American League's Expansion Committee and had been assured Southern California was his, no questions asked. There is little doubt Frick, by gunning down Greenberg, was aiming at Veeck and catering to O'Malley. Rather than pay an indemnity, Greenberg bowed out. It was a costly mistake. The Angels soon left Los Angeles for Anaheim, where they became the California Angels and are now valued at an estimated $200 million. (In 1997 when The Walt Disney Co. took over partial ownership, the team became known as the Anaheim Angels.)

The conservative forces turned it into a rout. Elwood Quesada, an air force general who had been the personal pilot of Red Sox owner Tom Yawkey, was awarded the new Washington, D.C., franchise. California went to a group headed by Bob Reynolds and Gene Autry, friends of Yankee co-owner Del Webb. The other principal investors were Kenyon Brown and Paul O'Bryan, former stockholders in the Detroit Tigers.

Veeck, in his book *Veeck—as in Wreck*, wrote:

"As we met to vote for the Los Angeles franchise, we discovered that Walter O'Malley was loaded down with objections about anybody coming into his private grazing grounds. We discovered it when Ford Frick, that erstwhile apostle of the Open City, sent word that some kind of equitable settlement had to be made with O'Malley. Los Angeles wasn't any Open City anymore; it was an Open City only to the degree Walter O'Malley wanted it to be. New York was an Open City but Los Angeles was not.

"[Greenberg] and I launched a noisy campaign to force Frick into the open. The slogan of our campaign was 'Make Him Vote.' Hank and I ran from club to club, doing everything except grabbing the owners by the neck to try to convince them that all the American League had to do was refuse to accept O'Malley's terms, and Frick would be placed in the position of having to vote, for once in his life, to break the deadlock between the leagues.

"The last thing Frick wanted to do was to vote. Frick was so anxious not to vote that he looked ill. Frick has a slogan of his own, a slogan that has served him throughout the years. It goes: 'You boys settle it among yourselves.' For that he gets paid $65,000 a year, not bad as things go these days."

The American League owners let it slide, so Frick was off the hook. The newly-minted California moguls paid the pound of flesh, and in another equally remarkable concession agreed to O'Malley's request that Kenyon Brown be eliminated from their purchase group. Somewhere down the line, Brown had crossed O'Malley, and baseball's most powerful broker had neither forgotten nor forgiven.

It was an intramural skirmish in baseball's executive suite and not of much concern to either the press or the public. Frick's part went virtually without notice. But he was in the baseball fishbowl later that season when Roger Maris and Mickey Mantle were threatening to break Babe Ruth's sacred single-season home run record.

Because of expansion, the season had been extended from 154 to 162 games. On July 18, after the Yankees had played 88 games, Maris and Mantle were ahead of Ruth's historic pace. Maris had 35 home runs, Mantle 33. Then Frick issued the following manifesto:

"A player who may hit more than 60 home runs during his team's first 154 games will be recognized as having established a new record. However, if the player does not hit more than 60 after his club has played 154 games, there would have to be some distinctive mark in the record book to show that Babe Ruth's record was set under the 154-game schedule, and that the other total was compiled while the 162-game schedule was in effect."

Frick made no mention of an "asterisk," which most fans and diamond insiders assumed would be attached to Maris's record. Dick Young of the *New York Daily News*, the most influential baseball writer since Father Chadwick, repeatedly interpreted Frick's "distinctive mark" as the equivalent of an asterisk.

A few purists sided with Frick, but the overwhelming sentiment was for Maris, who hit No. 61 on the final day of the season. Fueling the debate was that Frick was defending the record of an old comrade; in his newspaper days he had been Ruth's ghostwriter. From 1924 until 1931, he had written a thrice-weekly syndicated column under Ruth's name. Frick also readily admitted the Babe was his favorite player.

"No question about it, he was the greatest," Frick said. "The Babe had everything it takes, including a lovable personality. Hell, he was the best lefthanded pitcher when he was pitching—and he was the best hitter. If he wasn't paid to hit home runs, he could have hit .400 every year."

Frick's loyalty to Ruth almost extended to the Babe's "called shot" home run in the 1932 World Series. It is among the biggest myths in sports. Ruth didn't point. I asked Frick about it at our last meeting, at his home in Bronxville, New York.

Frick laughed. "A year or two later I said, 'Babe, did you really point to the bleachers?' And he said, 'It's in the papers.'

"'But did you really point?'"

Frick smiled at the recollection. "He said, 'Why don't you read the papers? It's all right there in the papers.'"

On September 20, Maris had 58 home runs and needed two more to tie Ruth within 154 games. Mantle, with 53, had dropped out because of injuries. Maris connected off Baltimore's Milt Pappas in the third inning for No. 59 but struck out, flied deep to right, and dubbed a roller to the mound in his final three at bats. He tied Ruth in the 159th game and broke the record in the 163rd game. Like Ruth, Maris had the advantage of an extra game because of a regular season tie.

For the next thirty-one years, the record books, under the heading "most home runs, season," had a double entry: Maris, 61, for a 162-game schedule; Ruth, 60, 154-game schedule. Ruth's line was eliminated in 1992 upon the recommendation of a Committee for Statistical Accuracy appointed and chaired by Fay Vincent, baseball's eighth commissioner.

Frick was often criticized as a do-nothing commissioner. "I got panned very frequently for saying 'This was a league matter,'" he conceded. "The owners try to throw a lot of their disputes in the commissioner's lap that were never meant for the commissioner to decide. You can't remain on a judicial level, protecting honesty and integrity and holding the confidence of the fans, if you're going to be required to roll in the dirt down at a lower level. Being criticized is part of the job. But in your heart there is a scar."

Passive to the end, he spent his final years tending his stamp collection and reading Native American folklore. He died in 1979 at the age of 83 and was survived by his wife, Eleanor, and a son, Frederick Cowing Frick.

# GENERAL WILLIAM ECKERT 10

I n 1965, Joe Durso of *The New York Times* was in Chicago writing the story when his editor called and said he wanted a sidebar, a "Man in the News" biographical piece on the new commissioner.

"Who is he?" the editor asked. "We don't have any clips on him."

"All we know is he was a lieutenant general in the Air Force," Durso replied.

Durso, who had been a fighter pilot during World War II, reached an old comrade at West Point and asked if the yearbook for the Class of 1930 was available.

Lauris Norstad, who had been the Supreme Commander of the North Atlantic Treaty forces, was the first to express surprise.

"You couldn't find a less flamboyant man," Norstad explained. "Very quiet, dignified, orderly. A man of moderation. Are you sure about this?"

"No question about it," Durso said. "He is the new baseball commissioner."

The general reaction was captured best by Larry Fox of the *New*

*York World-Telegram.* Exclaimed Fox, "My god, they've elected the Unknown Soldier."

William Dole "Spike" Eckert, age 56 when elected, had a short and not altogether unhappy reign as baseball's fourth commissioner. He was in office three years, the record for brevity until the dismissal a quarter century later of Fay Vincent.

When the owners hired Eckert, they were looking for someone with business acumen but, more important, with influence in Washington. Eckert had a good record selling surplus Air Force goods, but his Washington contacts were in the Pentagon, not on Capitol Hill. And when the General couldn't give the owners any political pull, he couldn't give them anything. He was an officer and a gentleman, and he was out of his element.

From the beginning, it was painfully apparent that millions of schoolboys knew more about baseball. At Eckert's unveiling in Chicago, a reporter asked when he had last seen a major league base-ball game. Eckert said he had seen the Dodgers play in Los Angeles a year or two earlier. But as the questioning continued, it became obvious he didn't know the Dodgers previously had played in Brooklyn.

To help Eckert through the choppy waters ahead, the owners filled the lifeboat with an unprecedented five-man "cabinet" of knowledgeable insiders. The most significant appointments were Lee MacPhail, Larry MacPhail's son, previously president and general manager of the Baltimore Orioles, who tutored Eckert at the admin-istrative level; and Joe Reichler, street-smart, formerly an Associated Press baseball writer stationed in New York City, who handled Eckert's personal appearances.

Reichler had the more difficult assignment. MacPhail had the advantage of offering instruction in the privacy of the Commissioner's office. Likewise, Eckert's relationship with the owners was hidden behind closed doors. Reichler had to coach the General in the open field, at banquets and press conferences.

Early on, Reichler supplied Eckert with cue cards, each bearing harmless responses. Often, the embarrassment was acute. At a national baseball writers' meeting, the General reached into his pocket and thanked everyone for their contribution to American aviation. He had pulled the wrong deck.

In the midst of his first tour of the Florida spring training camps, Eckert discovered similarities between baseball and the Air Force. Baseball insiders winced.

"First," he observed, "you have highly competitive units—the different teams, just as you have squadrons. Then you have rules and regulations in both, rules to be made and interpreted and changed. And third, you have franchises, like Air Force bases, being opened and moved to fill needs."

He was also remarkably naive. John McHale, who succeeded MacPhail as Eckert's special assistant, arrived at the office one morning and found him in mild distress. The General explained that he had heard on the radio that the Yankees had been sold. Eckert asked McHale if he knew the new owners.

"I couldn't believe the Yankees had been sold without our knowing about it," McHale said many years later. "I told him I'd find out in a hurry. And when I found out, I didn't know how to tell him. Bob and Ray, the comedy team, had put on a skit that morning about one of them buying the Yankees."

According to some early published reports, the owners had been confused by the similarity in names and had harnessed the wrong general in the belief they were voting for General Eugene M. Zuckert, former Secretary of the Air Force. Zuckert had a national reputation. He also was on the original list of candidates and among the ten finalists.

"I sat in on all the meetings," said Clark Griffith, then a young vice president of the Minnesota Twins. "There was never any mix-up. General Eckert was described to us perfectly."

Foolproof evidence it was not a case of mistaken identity is that Eckert was the only candidate nominated by the screening committee, which in effect was a selection committee. Two of the owners in attendance have differing memories of the occasion but concurred there had been prior agreement that the recommendation of Eckert by co-chairmen John Fetzer of Detroit and John Galbreath of Pittsburgh would be approved.

"I voted against him and so did Charlie Finley and one or two others," recalled Calvin Griffith, then majority owner of the Minnesota Twins. "We voted by paper. We never had what you would call a ballot because he was the only one voted on." Gabe Paul insists a perfunctory vote was taken *after* Eckert had been approved.

Once Eckert was in office, none of the owners were willing to claim responsibility. Even Ford Frick, the retiring commissioner, was unable to discover who had been Eckert's original sponsor.

"I have an idea but I don't really know," Frick said fifteen years later. "It may have been Fetzer. Fetzer and Eckert were using the same public relations guy in Washington. Most retired generals have them. There are books to write, big fees for speeches, that sort of thing.

"Now, I don't know whether this is true or not, but Fetzer told this guy in Washington, baseball was looking for a commissioner and he asked him for advice. And the p.r. man said, 'I've got the guy for you.'"

Fetzer, who spoke softly and had made his fortune in the broadcasting industry, was influential in American League affairs. Jim Campbell, his longtime general manager, insists Fetzer never talked about Eckert's election.

"How Eckert's name came up is something I never knew," Campbell said. "Undoubtedly, someone recommended Eckert to either Mr. Fetzer or Mr. Galbreath. It wasn't something we discussed."

Charles Finley, the outspoken owner of the Oakland A's, put the finger on Fetzer.

"Fetzer called me several weeks before the election," Finley recalled, "I had never heard of Eckert. Fetzer put the heat on me. He gave me a lot of bullshit on how good he would be."

Once Finley realized the deck was stacked in favor of Eckert, he went to Washington and met with Byron "Whizzer" White, a former All-America football player then sitting on the U.S. Supreme Court. White had also been mentioned as a possible candidate. "We had a nice meeting but he wasn't interested," Finley recalled. "He would have been a great commissioner. Instead, we wound up with a guy nobody knew, who knew nothing about sports. That's when I began to realize I was sitting with a bunch of dummies."

Eckert did his best to bone up on diamond lore. During the first year, said Lee MacPhail, Eckert's aide de camp:

"Every day after work he stayed in the office and read baseball books. He was deathly afraid someone would ask, for example, who Frankie Frisch was."

Try as he did, the General was unable to catch up. Presiding at a joint owners' meeting, he referred to the Cincinnati Cardinals. "It was so embarrassing we let it pass," recalled Gabe Paul, a longtime owner. "We didn't know if he was talking about the Cincinnati Reds or the St. Louis Cardinals."

Almost everywhere he went, Joe Reichler was at his side. "My father and the General clashed a lot," revealed Reichler's son, Paul, a Washington attorney. "He had a history of command and treated people around him like orderlies. You know how generals are, when they say something everyone is expected to agree. And he had a streak of vanity. He didn't want to admit he didn't know. After he was fired, the General realized my father was always trying to help him. They became good friends, close friends."

Born on January 29, 1908, in Freeport, Illinois, Eckert was raised in Madison, Indiana, where his father, Frank, owned an animal-feed store. Eckert played baseball on the Madison High School team. He enlisted in the Indiana National Guard at the age of 15, then made it to West Point, finishing 128th in a class of 241. He had an outstanding military career and was awarded the Distinguished Service Medal; Legion of Merit with two oak leaf clusters; Flying Cross; Bronze Star Medal; Air Medal; and by France and Luxembourg, the Croix de Guerre with palm.

He had made his mark first as a pilot between the First and Second World Wars and was one of two young fliers chosen to attend the Harvard Graduate School of Business Administration. By the time the Japanese attacked Pearl Harbor, he had become an expert in supply and logistics and was transferred to the European theater to take command of the 452nd Bomber Group.

In the yearbook of his twenty-fifth class reunion at West Point, Eckert was described as "The Great Stone Face" and as an "exceptionally versatile airman." He was the Air Force comptroller when he retired in March 1961 after a mild heart attack. He then settled in Washington and for the next four years helped manage several electronics and real estate companies. Always a "solid citizen," he also busied himself in civic affairs.

Eckert's appointment as commissioner came as a complete surprise. His name was said to be among the original 156 nominees but had never been publicly mentioned. However, it was acknowledged his name was not included when the list was pared to fifteen but subsequently was restored.

The debate centered on whether the choice should be a baseball man or some other nationally prominent person. Fetzer, Galbreath, and Frick minimized this difference of opinion and insisted experience in business was the crucial requirement.

"In the last fifteen years we've gone from the ox-cart to the jet age," Frick observed. "The problems that now confront the Commissioner are on the business side, not the baseball side. Today, the Commissioner's office deals with corporate problems—moving franchises, ownership by large corporations, laws before Congress, financial arrangements, things like that."

Cognizant of the new complexities, the owners drew an organizational chart that provided for separate divisions under the commissioner such as broadcasting, public affairs, minor leagues, and amateur baseball, an overdue restructuring championed by Fetzer. Immediately prior to the election, the screening committee was expanded to include Philip Wrigley of the Chicago Cubs and Bob Reynolds of the California Angels.

It was generally assumed a new commissioner would be chosen during the annual winter convention that was held December 1–3, 1965 in Miami Beach. But the screening committee, without public notice, called for a meeting on November 17 at the Chicago Club in Chicago. It was subsequently described as a "sneak" meeting. Responding to an inquiry by Ed Prell of the *Chicago Tribune*, moments after the announcement, Fetzer insisted he didn't know which club had proposed Eckert.

Hired for a seven-year term at an annual salary of $65,000, same as his predecessor, Eckert told his new employers: "I will call the signals as I see them. In the past I have never operated as a czar. I will not be dictatorial. Authority, to me, should be exercised with good judgment and common sense."

First on the agenda was a thorny problem: The Milwaukee Braves previously had announced the desire to relocate to Atlanta. The General was at sea. Litigation had begun during Frick's term, two years prior to Eckert's arrival. Eckert did not participate, leaving this unpleasant task to a triumvirate of attorneys, which included Bowie Kuhn, counsel for the National League; three years later Kuhn replaced Eckert on the throne.

The challenge to the transfer of the Milwaukee franchise was a difficult and lengthy litigation. For the first time since the early 1900s, a major league city was being completely abandoned. Also the Braves, having moved from Boston in 1953, had drawn well and had been the first National League club with a home gate of more than two million, a figure achieved for four successive seasons. But there had been a sudden decline. The Braves' average attendance for the three-year period from 1963 through 1965 dropped to 751,608.

Milwaukee County and the State of Wisconsin brought charges against the baseball establishment. A Milwaukee County Court eventually approved the move with the understanding that a replacement franchise would be supplied for 1967, the next season. Two of the principals, on opposing sides, were Bill Bartholomay, a Chicago insurance executive, and Alan "Bud" Selig, a Milwaukee automobile dealer.

Bartholomay was an investor in the club and fought for the move; Selig was on a committee attempting to prevent the transfer. Baseball alliances often change. Selig was to become Kuhn's confidant and principal supporter during his reign; twenty-five years later, following the premature departure of Fay Vincent, Selig was the interim commissioner while Bartholomay simultaneously chaired a Commissioner's Search Committee. "I never thought it could happen," Selig said at that time, "but Bill Bartholomay is now one of my closest friends."

Eckert plunged ahead and settled several disputes, among them a salary disagreement between Roy Hofheinz, president of the Houston club, and Paul Richards, the Houston general manager, whom Hofheinz had dismissed after the 1965 season. Richards had five years remaining on his contract, at $60,000 a year, and appealed to Eckert for relief. Eckert settled the squabble to the satisfaction of both sides.

Another dispute centered on Tom Seaver, a pitcher from the University of Southern California. Seaver, who was to have a brilliant major league career, had been signed by the Atlanta Braves for their Richmond farm club for a reported $40,000 bonus. However, since USC had already begun its intercollegiate baseball schedule, the signing was in violation of baseball's so-called college rule. Eckert imposed a $500 fine against the Richmond club and ruled that the Braves couldn't sign Seaver for three years.

Although Seaver had not received any payments, collegiate authorities declared him ineligible. In an unprecedented but wise decision, Eckert arranged a special draft for Seaver. Only organizations willing to match the terms of his Richmond contract were allowed to participate in the drawing. Three clubs agreed—the New York Mets, the Philadelphia Phillies, and the Cleveland Indians. The Mets pulled Seaver's name from a hat.

Eckert, in his first year, also soothed the troubled relations between Japanese and U.S. baseball. He effected a long-term agreement with the Japanese commissioner and Japan's sponsoring newspapers that a top major league team, every two years, would play a two-week exhibition schedule in Japan following the World Series. This agreement is still in effect, but now a team of U.S. all-star players is recruited for the occasion.

The first free agent draft of amateur players was held during Eckert's watch, followed the next year, in 1967, by the first night All Star Game. Eckert was also the first commissioner confronted by Marvin Miller, the labor leader who had been elected executive director of the Major League Players Association. Years later, Miller won enormous economic gains but his principal victories were achieved after Eckert's departure.

Eckert was in office when the Kansas City Athletics were allowed to move to Oakland and was presiding when American and National league owners began laying the groundwork for the second wave of expansion and the companion conditions that divided both leagues into two geographical divisions. In May 1968, in the last year of Eckert's administration, big league baseball crossed international frontiers. The National League, expanding to twelve teams, placed franchises in Montreal and San Diego. The American League also added two new franchises for the 1969 season—the Seattle Pilots and the Kansas City Royals, the latter filling the void left by the departure of the Athletics.

It was a time of change, but Eckert's voice was seldom heard. Baseball suffered poor press as a result of his indecision following the assassination of Dr. Martin Luther King, the civil rights leader who was slain in April 1968, and the murder two months later of Senator Robert Kennedy, a popular presidential candidate. While the country mourned, there was no directive from the Commissioner's office; baseball went on as usual.

Just as Eckert's ascension was a surprise, so was his fall. He was dismissed on December 6, 1968, with three years and eleven months remaining on his seven-year term. Even in the firing, the owners were guilty of subterfuge. They had agreed to vote him out on Thursday, the day before the end of their winter convention at the Palace Hotel in San Francisco.

"The General was asked to leave the room," recalled Lee MacPhail, who had been Eckert's original tutor but had since left to become the general manager of the Yankees. "We went into the men's room. While we were standing at the urinal, the General said, 'Does this mean anything, that we're out of the room?' I said, 'I hope not, General.' But when they called us back in, he was gone."

Late Friday afternoon, at the supposed conclusion of the five-day meeting, a Saturday morning press briefing was announced. Obviously, the owners wanted minimum coverage. No more than a dozen of the estimated fifty to sixty baseball writers stayed over and saw the ax fall. Francis Dale, the new owner of the Cincinnati Reds, with Eckert at his side, read the statement:

"General Eckert has just delivered his resignation effective with the appointment of a successor. We have decided to accede to the General's wishes. We hold him in the highest esteem, especially for the integrity and honor with which he has conducted our affairs."

And for the first time, Eckert had a sympathetic press.

Dick Young in the *New York Daily News*:

"Some reporters dashed out of the room to phones, others took crouching steps toward club owners standing nearby to ask hushed questions, and as Eckert rambled on, telling pitiably of what he had tried to do, the Lords of Baseball began chattering among themselves, ignoring him for the most part and one of them said, 'Get him off there.' It was rude, terribly rude. More than that, it was cruel. The newsmen agreed that William D. Eckert, in his darkest moment, had been the biggest man in the room."

"[Eckert] was more a victim than a failure," commented Leonard Koppett of *The New York Times*. "The office for which he was chosen was already an anachronism. The men who run baseball—the owners of the major league clubs—would have preferred no Commissioner at all but could not face the public relations consequences of abolishing the office that stood for baseball's integrity.

"Eckert had no baseball background whatever and no public image. Conscientious and sincere but totally uninformed for baseball's highest position, he was as powerless as any puppet for the years it would take him to become familiar with even the rudiments of the baseball business—and when he did involve himself in a few problems of substance, the owners considered his honest efforts to be meddling."

Despite his ramrod military posture, Eckert had the universal hunger for acceptance. This final indignity ate like acid into his soul. More than any commissioner, before or since, he was completely without theatrics, a handicap greater than his lack of baseball lore. Dedicated to caution, to going by the book, he was unable to give the illusion of vigorous leadership, the quality the owners most wanted.

Also, his naiveté was so acute it bordered on embarrassment. Bowie Kuhn, after he had succeeded him, said the General, given the empty title of consultant, continued reporting to the office.

"I told him, as gently as I could," Kuhn recalled, "it wasn't necessary for him to come in."

The General moved back to Washington and died two years later, on April 16, 1971, at the age of 62 of a heart attack while on vacation, playing tennis in the Bahamas. He was survived by his wife, the former Catharine Givens, whose father was an Air Force colonel; a son, William Douglas Eckert, now an Air Force colonel assigned to the United Nations in New York City; and a daughter, Mrs. Catharine Siglow of Redlands, California.

He was buried in Arlington National Cemetery, not far from the Tomb of the Unknown Soldier.

# BOWIE KUHN
## PART I

T he ink wasn't dry on General Eckert's walking papers before the race was on for a new czar. The jockeying for position had begun prior to Eckert's dismissal. The haste and anxiety among the owners, particularly the younger set, to choose a successor was such that there was no pause to form a Search Committee.

On the track and running were Mike Burke, president, and Lee MacPhail, general manager of the New York Yankees; Charles "Chub" Feeney, vice president of the San Francisco Giants; and John McHale, president of the expansion Montreal Expos. There was also secondary support for American League president Joe Cronin and Judge Robert Cannon of Milwaukee, the former counsel for the Players Association. Ineffective, Cannon had been dismissed two years earlier, in 1966, and replaced by Marvin Miller.

Two weeks after Eckert's departure, on December 20, 1968, at Chicago's O'Hare Inn, the selection process began with a marathon thirteen-hour meeting that opened at 4:15 PM and continued until five in the morning. It was a contest between the National and American league. A three-fourths vote in each league, nine out of twelve, was needed for election. Nineteen ballots were taken without conclusion.

Feeney came closest. He had seventeen votes, twelve from the National League, five from the American. MacPhail peaked at thirteen, nine from the American, four from the National. McHale, nominated by the influential Fetzer, was next: eleven of twelve in the American League but only scattered support in the National.

Of the three principal candidates, only McHale had experience in both leagues. A graduate of Notre Dame, McHale had a brief and undistinguished major league playing career—a .193 career batting average in 64 games in five seasons, all with Detroit. He would have been the first former player to occupy the commissioner's chair. He had been the general manager in Detroit and served in a similar capacity with the Milwaukee and Atlanta Braves, eventually resigning to serve as Eckert's deputy. In 1967, he had become president of and a minority investor in the Montreal Expos, an expansion franchise in the throes of birth.

McHale turned to Bowie Kuhn, the National League attorney, for advice and asked how he should view his commitment to Montreal. Kuhn convinced McHale to withdraw his name from consideration for commissioner: He had a moral and legal obligation to the Expos. A quarter of a century later, McHale was still wondering if he had been duped.

At the owners' next and last meeting, on February 4, in Miami, the stalemate continued, the National League backing Feeney, the American League now in support of Burke of the Yankees. A recess was called. When the owners reconvened, Bowie Kent Kuhn, 42, a Wall Street lawyer, was elected commissioner pro tem, for one year, at a salary of $100,000—$35,000 more than Eckert's wage.

Although unknown to the general public, Kuhn, while in the employ of the Willkie, Farr & Gallagher law firm, had become a baseball insider. Square-jawed and mild-mannered, he had performed legal services for the National League and some of the individual major league clubs, and was the principal attorney who successfully defended the league when the City of Milwaukee sued to prevent the Braves from moving to Atlanta. Kuhn also had sat at the management side of the bargaining table during some of the labor negotiations with the Players Association, then headed by Marvin Miller, later described by the *Encyclopedia Britannica* as the "Ralph Nader of professional sports." For the next fifteen years, he was among Kuhn's principal adversaries.

Unlike Eckert, the six-foot-six Kuhn was a dominating presence and a skillful speaker. He had also been a fan. During high school summer vacations he had worked, for a dollar a day, the scoreboard at Washington Senators home games in old Griffith Stadium. At his first major press conference, Kuhn's credentials were confirmed when he named the starting lineup of the pennant-winning 1944 St. Louis Browns.

"Every American boy dreams of being commissioner," Kuhn said, "and I'm no different. I'm honored and delighted to take over this important job."

The press response was almost completely favorable, except for Red Smith of the New York *Herald Tribune*. An angel at the typewriter, Smith was the leading sports columnist of the day. He was unimpressed and regularly railed at Kuhn, calling him a "stuffed shirt."

In his memoir, Kuhn tells of a party at Toots Shor's restaurant in New York City several weeks after his election:

"Red Smith was there and stayed late. At the end, he and I went through the revolving door together onto Fifty-second Street. Standing there in the cold February night, he said, 'Commissioner, name two catchers on the 1944 St. Louis Browns.' Smith had covered the Browns for the St. Louis *Globe-Democrat*.

"Surprised though I was I answered directly, Mancuso and Red Hayworth.

"'My god,' Red Smith replied, 'you do know something about baseball.'"

The initial impression was that Kuhn had been to the manor born. It was a half-truth. His father, Louis Charles Kuhn, was an immigrant. The son of a Bavarian farm family, he had arrived in America in 1894 with little formal education. Self-trained, he rose to head the Washington, D.C. office of the Petroleum Heat and Power Company. In 1920, Louis married Alice Waring Roberts. Among her antecedents were five governors and two Maryland senators. Frontiersman Jim Bowie, reputedly the inventor of the Bowie knife, was a distant relation.

The youngest of three children, Kuhn was born on October 28, 1926. He grew up in Washington, D.C., and, in his senior year at Theodore Roosevelt High School, was president of his class and of the honor society, and was voted "most popular" and "most likely to succeed." The only field he did not excel in was athletics.

In his 1987 autobiography, *Hardball: The Education of a Baseball Commissioner*, Kuhn recalled:

"The only varsity sport I attempted was basketball. Roosevelt's coach during my senior year was Arnold Auerbach, better known today as Red Auerbach, the Hall of Fame coach and general manager of the Boston Celtics. He stopped me in the hall one day, looked up and said, 'Son, you're the tallest boy in the school. How come you're not out for the basketball team?'

"'Because I'm a lousy player,' I replied.

"'You let me be the judge of that,' and he suited me up. A week later he took me aside and said, 'Son, you were right and I was wrong. You won't have to come back tomorrow.'"

After Kuhn graduated from high school, he entered the Navy's wartime V-12 program, an officer's training ground for college students which, in effect, delayed the necessity of active service. Kuhn attended Franklin and Marshall College, then transferred to Princeton, where he took his B.A. degree. He received his law degree from the University of Virginia and had offers from several substantial legal firms. He chose Willkie, Farr & Gallagher because the National League was among its clients. This was in 1950. Five years later he married the former Luisa Degener and the couple had four children.

Kuhn's first call as commissioner was to Marvin Miller, then in his fourth season as head of the players' union and who, as Kuhn and the baseball owners were soon to learn, was the commissioner of the players. Aware that Miller was likely to be his principal foe, Kuhn was anxious for a good working relationship:

"Marvin, if you're going to be there for a while, I'd like to drop in just so you can see how my new crown fits."

As Kuhn later said, "Unfortunately, the cordiality of that hour did not foreshadow the future."

It was an exciting season for the rookie czar: 1969 was the 100th anniversary of professional baseball, which began with the Cincinnati Red Stockings. It was also the first year of a bold realignment. With both leagues now balanced at twelve teams, each league was divided into East and West divisions. There was considerable opposition, particularly in the National League. The Americans approved this arrangement on May 28, 1968. A month later, the Nationals agreed.

Warren Giles, the 72-year-old president of the National League, a baseball purist, realized the long season would be compromised. A best-of-five pennant playoff between the first-place teams in each league would be necessary. For the first time it would be possible for the team with the lesser won-loss record to advance to the World Series.

Said Giles: "It would be like running a mile race and winning it—and then being told you have to run another 100 yards to decide the real winner."

Retorted American League president Joe Cronin: "You can't sell a 12th place team."

Giles's fears were lost in the fog of time. It wasn't until the fourth year of the playoffs that a team with the second-best record won a pennant, and by then nobody noticed.

Vowing to be "where the action is," Kuhn attended thirteen games during the first seventeen days of that championship season, including seven openers, and seventy games overall. He also helped abort a threatened players' strike and settled two controversial trades, coaxing Donn Clendenon and later Ken Harrelson out of early retirement. Convinced he was made of the right stuff, the owners rewarded him with a seven-year contract.

Kuhn's first battle with Miller, compared to what was to come, was a mere skirmish. The owners had offered to increase their annual contribution to the pension fund from $4.1 million to $5.1 million. Settlement was achieved when they raised the ante to $5.45 million. The owners agreed to other concessions, such as increasing basic retirement benefits and lowering the requirement for pension vesting from five to four years, retroactive to 1959.

Miller credited Kuhn with an assist: "The Commissioner played a constructive role by pointing out [to the owners] you can't solve a problem without meeting. It's sort of obvious but it had to be said, and he said it with authority."

Kuhn was also confronted with a pair of knotty problems when Clendenon and Harrelson were traded. In an effort to fatten their pocketbooks, which they did, both players announced their retirement. The Clendenon affair had a much longer run—two and a half months, and included a third player, outfielder Jesus Alou, packaged with Clendenon and sent by the Expos to Houston in exchange for 25-year-old Rusty Staub, a budding star.

The dispute would have been settled without acrimony if Kuhn had followed the rule: a trade is nullified when a player announces his retirement. As he was to do on several other occasions, Kuhn bent the rules and was ready to invoke his "best interests" powers. It was a courageous decision, especially for a rookie czar still adjusting his crown.

Some insiders claimed Kuhn was favoring McHale, his former client who was launching the Montreal franchise. This may have entered the equation, but beyond that, Kuhn was aware the Expos had begun pegging their preseason promotions and ticket sales on the red-haired Staub, who had been in a salary squabble with Houston general manager Spec Richardson; the Expos had since satisfied Staub with a hefty pay increase.

"To take Staub away from us now would destroy the franchise before it got off the ground," McHale said.

Judge Roy Hofheinz, the Houston owner, countered with a blast at Kuhn. It was the first criticism of the new commissioner. Said Hofheinz: "This Johnny-come-lately has done more to destroy baseball in the last six weeks than all of its enemies in the last 100 years."

Tal Smith, the Astros' director of player personnel, joined the chorus. Smith found an identical instance of a 1960 three-player deal between the Boston Red Sox and the Cleveland Indians. When one of the traded players, catcher Sammy White, refused to report to Cleveland, Ford Frick voided the deal and ordered White be put on the retired list.

A 33-year-old journeyman first baseman, Clendenon had been acquired by the Expos in the expansion draft. After expressing delight with the trade—he would be closer to his Atlanta home—

Clendenon changed his mind and on February 28 announced his retirement with the explanation that he had accepted an executive position with Scripto, Inc., an Atlanta firm.

Less than a week later, on March 5, Clendenon began waffling and said, "My door remains open." He was now willing to listen to offers from other clubs. But again Clendenon reversed his field. On March 20 he declared, "I want to finally and irrevocably set the record straight and reconfirm my retirement."

If so, Houston would have been short a front-line player. Kuhn advised the clubs to negotiate. Agreement was reached. The Expos sent pitchers Jack Billingham and Skip Guinn and an undisclosed sum of cash to Houston for the loss of Clendenon, On April 3, as the season was about to begin, Clendenon decided he wanted to play, offering the limp explanation, "I owe it to the game." In June the Expos traded him to the New York Mets who gave him a $14,000 salary increase. Clendenon hung it up three years later.

As had been feared, the Clendenon caper gave birth to another "premature" retirement. Ken "Hawk" Harrelson, an outfielder with the Boston Red Sox who had a huge New England following, was traded to Cleveland but balked with the claim that his outside interests amounted to $50,000 a year, equal his baseball pay.

Harrelson, 27, was in his prime as a hitter. With a poker face he told reporters, "It'd be a sin for me to retire. But it's a matter of business. I have four children to support. It's the father instinct that makes me leave baseball."

Harrelson's fatherly instincts paid off. Kuhn came to the rescue and within the week held a hearing at his New York office. Thirty years later Harrelson recreated the dialogue: "He told the general managers [Gabe Paul of Cleveland and Dick O'Connell of Boston], 'This is bad for baseball and it's going to be resolved today. Gentlemen, I now have to excuse myself because the Commissioner cannot be present when negotiations are taking place.'" Harrelson signed with the Indians, who doubled his salary to $100,000.

From then until the mid-June trading deadline, there was apprehension every time a deal was made, because of the possibility of another threatened retirement. Kuhn realized new legislation was required and in early November, soon after the season ended, it was agreed that "the buyer must beware—once made, a deal is a deal." If a player failed to report, for any reason, the burden was on the receiving club to persuade the player to return.

As he was throughout his reign, Kuhn was concerned with the integrity of the game. He ordered two owners, Charlie Finley of Oakland and Bill Bartholomay of Atlanta, to divest themselves of their holdings in the controversial Parvin-Dohrmann Co., which allegedly had organized-crime connections and controlled three Las Vegas casinos. Finley and Bartholomay sold.

It was a busy and highly successful first season for Kuhn who constantly bolstered baseball's sagging image as America's national game, which was being threatened by professional football. Kuhn orchestrated a remarkable public relations coup on July 22, the day before the All Star Game in Washington, with a gala White House reception hosted by President Richard Nixon.

Ford Frick, the former commissioner who had been a White House guest on several occasions, led the applause. "I don't think anything like this has ever happened before," Frick said. "The President turned the White House over to baseball."

Standing next to the President, Kuhn handled the introductions as hundreds of baseball celebrities, all of whom had received engraved invitations, passed through an hour-long receiving line. Nixon was a genuine fan. Speaking at the centennial banquet the night before, Nixon told how he first began following baseball "through the newspapers." He paid tribute to the sportswriters in attendance and, in a remark that was to be widely quoted, said, "I like the job I have now but if I had my life to live over again, I'd like to have ended up as a sportswriter."

The impish Maury Allen of the *New York Post*, after Kuhn had presented him, told the President he might be willing to switch assignments. "I'll think it over," said Allen, "but I don't like the idea of taking a cut in pay."

Commissioners Pete Rozelle of the National Football League and Walter Kennedy of the National Basketball Association telephoned Kuhn the next morning with their congratulations. It may have been the most satisfying moment of Bowie Kuhn's reign.

# BOWIE KUHN
## PART II

I t was a brief honeymoon. The next year, on January 16, 1970, Curt Flood, with the financial support of the Players Association, challenged the reserve system. A month later, on February 19, Kuhn suspended Detroit pitching star Denny McLain for his alleged involvement in a Michigan gambling ring. By September, McLain had been suspended three times, believed to be a one-season record.

Flood, 32, was an outstanding center fielder, batted over .300 six times, had won seven Gold Gloves for defensive brilliance and had helped the St. Louis Cardinals win three pennants. He was not underpaid and drew a $90,000 salary in 1969, his last season with the Cardinals. When the Cardinals traded him to the Philadelphia Phillies, without his knowledge or consent, Flood charged he was deprived of his civil liberties and filed suit for $4.1 million in the U.S.District Court in New York City. The complaint was against Kuhn and the presidents of the twenty-four major league clubs.

Prior to the litigation Flood explained his position in a letter to Kuhn:

"After 12 years in the major leagues I do not feel that I am a piece

143

of property to be bought and sold irrespective of my wishes. I believe that any system that produces that result violates my rights as a citizen and is inconsistent with the laws of the United States and of the several states.

"It is my desire to play baseball in 1970 and I am capable of playing. I have received a contract offer from the Philadelphia club but I believe I have the right to consider other offers before making any decisions. I, therefore, request that you make known to all the major league clubs my feelings in this matter and advise them of my availability."

On treacherous ground, confronted with an indefensible position, Kuhn responded with diplomacy:

"I certainly agree with you that you, as a human being, are not a piece of property to be bought and sold. That is fundamental in our society and I think obvious. However, I cannot see its applicability to the situation at hand.

"You have entered into a current playing contract with the St. Louis club which has the same assignment provision as those in your annual major league contracts since 1956. The provisions of the players' contract have been negotiated over the years between the clubs and the players, most recently when the present Basic Agreement was negotiated two years ago with the Players Association.

"If you have any specific objection to the propriety of the assignment I would appreciate your specifying the objection. Under the circumstances, and pending any further information from you, I do not see what action I can take and cannot comply with your request."

The litigation heightened the players' demands for an adjustment of the reserve clause.

Said Marvin Miller: "If I had cooked up the idea, I'd brag about it. But the credit belongs to Curt."

Judge Irving Ben Cooper, who heard the case without a jury, often used baseball clichés. At the outset, he likened himself to an umpire, "a man in blue" who would "call them as I see them." After hearing the opening arguments, he said, "You have thrown the ball to me and I hope I don't fluff it."

Flood's principal counsel was the distinguished Arthur Goldberg, a former United State Supreme Court Justice and U.S. Ambassador to the United Nations. The trial ran for three weeks, May 19 to June 10. Testimony was heard from a "Who's Who" of baseball, twenty-two persons, eleven from each side.

Judge Cooper had to decide on two basic points: Do the antitrust laws apply to baseball, despite previous Supreme Court rulings granting baseball exemption from them? And are the reserve arrangements that bind a player to a club indefinitely a "reasonable" necessity to keep the baseball industry sound?

Kuhn, in his testimony, insisted, "Baseball could not operate on a league basis without the reserve clause." He traced the history of the game, told of the chaotic conditions that threatened the game between 1871 and 1879, when there was no reserve system, and said it was necessary "to maintain the integrity of the game and honesty among clubs and players."

Judge Cooper, in a forty-seven-page opinion delivered on August 12, upheld the defense argument that the federal antitrust laws did not apply and encouraged that modification be achieved in the collective bargaining process. After the U.S. Court of Appeals for the Second Circuit reaffirmed Judge Cooper's decision, the case went to the U.S. Supreme Court, where Flood was defeated 5–3.

As he said he would, Flood sat out the entire 1970 season at a considerable financial sacrifice. The Phillies had offered him $90,000 plus $8,000 in expenses. Flood spent the summer in Denmark where he worked as a portrait painter. Low on funds, Flood decided to return to baseball. "Why not?" he said. "I'm a baseball player. I don't know anything else."

Flood met with Bob Short, owner of the Washington Senators, in New York on the weekend of October 23. Miller had advised Flood not to sign unless his contract stated his return would not prejudice his appeal. Short approved and went a step further.

According to Flood, Short told him:

"I promise that I won't trade you. And I guarantee you the full year's pay no matter what happens. And at the end of the year, if we don't agree on terms for the following season, I'll make you a free agent so you can work out a deal with another club. But I can't put any of this in writing. And if anybody says I agreed to such an arrangement, I'll deny it."

Kuhn subsequently emphasized that if Short had entered into such a clandestine agreement he was, in effect, modifying the reserve system and strengthening Flood's original position. Short had agreed to give the Phillies a player for the right to talk to Flood. Kuhn ruled against this but allowed the no-trade clause *after* Short had signed Flood for $110,000 for the 1971 season and had sent three minor league players to the Phillies in exchange.

His skills and concentration eroded, Flood retired after playing only thirteen games for the Senators.

Eight years later, at a pregame party in George Steinbrenner's Yankee Stadium office, Kuhn met Flood, then employed by the Oakland A's as a broadcaster:

"Curt came across the room, put out his hand, and said, 'I'll bet you don't know who I am.' I told him I certainly did.

"'Well, I suppose I'm not one of your real favorites,' he said with a smile. I told him there were no bad feelings, because I had never questioned his sincerity. But the old schoolteacher inside me said, 'But you were wrong to walk out on Bob Short after taking his money.'"

Though defeated in the courts, the Flood litigation was a successful failure and, in retrospect, a crucial consideration in the 1976 Messersmith decision adjudicated by Peter Seitz, an impartial arbitrator. Curt Flood's lawsuit eventually helped force modification of the reserve system.

The Denny McLain suspensions, in comparison, were an amusement, a sideshow without precedent.

Reacting to a copyrighted cover story in *Sports Illustrated*, which provided the Commissioner's office with advance galleys, Kuhn suspended the 25-year-old McLain, the Detroit pitching star, and baseball's last 30-game winner—31–6 with the Tigers in 1968.

The suspension was for McLain's alleged 1967 involvement in a national gambling operation headquartered in Flint, Michigan. The *Sports Illustrated* story, titled "Baseball's Big Scandal—Denny McLain and the Mob," was never verified. Later, Kuhn conceded 80 percent of the text was false but declined to reveal which 20 percent was true.

Four days before the story broke, on February 13, Kuhn ordered McLain to his office and asked for an explanation. McLain was back in Detroit on February 18, testifying before a United States Grand Jury investigating the bookmaking scheme. McLain's appearance was voluntary. McLain was not charged and, according to James Brickley, U.S. attorney for eastern Michigan, was "free to go as he pleases." When Brickley was told the Tigers were about to open their spring training camp, he said, "I know of no reason for him not to show up."

McLain and Kuhn met again in New York the next morning for five and a half hours. In mid-afternoon, Kuhn handed McLain the following letter:

"This is to advise you that you are herewith suspended from all Organized Baseball activities pending completion of an investigation this office is conducting regarding certain of your personal activities. You and I have discussed today the reasons which required this action."

Kuhn, in a press conference two hours later, emphasized, "The action taken today is based substantially on certain admissions made candidly to me by Mr. McLain and not on allegations contained in a recent magazine article, many of which I believe to be unfounded."

According to the allegations, "poor, dumb Denny McLain," who was in debt, put up $7,500 to back a bookmaker, George "Jigs" Gazell, who in turn was "sponsored by a Syrian mob with Costa Nostra connections." McLain admitted he had been betting on basketball games and believed he had become a partner in the operation.

"The fair inference," Kuhn said, "is that his own gullibility and avarice had committed him to become a dupe of the gamblers. But there is no evidence that McLain ever bet on a baseball game involving the Detroit Tigers or any other team; or that in 1967 or subsequently, gave less than his best effort in performing for the Detroit club."

Asked by a reporter to explain the difference in attempting to become a bookmaker, as McLain had done, and actually being one, Kuhn roamed into left field for his reply:

"I think you have to consider the difference is the same as between murder and attempted murder."

Marvin Miller, defender of the players, declared McLain had been judged guilty before all the facts were in. "McLain is the victim of self-incrimination," Miller said. "Bowie called him into his office for an informal discussion and said, in the manner of a Dutch uncle, 'Tell me all about it, Denny.' Then Denny speaks and discovers he has incriminated himself."

Kuhn began his annual tour of the spring training camps. Wherever the Commissioner went, the press followed. Kuhn said the investigation was still in progress. Red Smith, the New York columnist, after attending Kuhn's "weekly half hour of silence," said,

"Triple ax murders have been solved in less time. Kuhn is determined not to make a final ruling until he has all the facts. This is wise but the weeks go by and the delay invites public suspicion."

Expecting to be eligible for the opener, McLain engaged in mild workouts at his home in Lakeland, Florida, where the Tigers trained, but was not allowed at the ballpark. There were daily dispatches on his tangled finances. Though he had been earning $200,000 a year, his debts, according to a bankruptcy petition filed in Detroit, came to $446,069. There were eighty-six creditors, including the Tigers who had given him a 1970 salary advance of $39,386. His assets were listed at $413.

On March 13, when Kuhn made the traditional visit to the White House, the annual occasion when the President is given his baseball pass, President Nixon asked if he had reached a decision on McLain.

"Yes, I have," Kuhn replied.

On April 1, six days before the presidential opener in Washington, Kuhn announced his investigation had been completed. McLain was suspended for approximately half the season, not eligible to return until July 1.

Joe Durso of *The New York Times*, who was among the dozens of newspapermen camping on McLain's doorstep, reported:

"When he heard the news, McLain put down the phone, gave a deep sigh that sagged his chest and shoulders, caught his wife, Sharyn, in a bearhug, and like a man reprieved, exclaimed, 'Till July 1st, till July 1st.'"

Said reserve catcher Jim Price, McLain's closest friend on the club, "Most of the guys thought Denny would get one or two years, or nothing at all. Three months is as close to nothing as you can get."

Like the players, most sportswriters regarded the penalty as too lenient. Dick Young of the *New York Daily News* described Kuhn as "Bowie the Benign" and wrote:

"The fans, most of them, will boo the decision. This was Kuhn's chance to be a stern commissioner, a severe commissioner. Baseball is special in American society because it has a mystique of purity. The people know it is honest and want to keep it that way, even if it takes an occasional scalp or two."

Pete Waldmeier of *The Detroit News*, who supplied much of the material for the *Sports Illustrated* story, commented: "How do you spell travesty? Better yet, what's the definition of whitewash? Kuhn ought to have a ready answer in the wake of his slap-on-the-wrist penalty."

McLain returned on July 1, in Detroit's 72nd game. He was welcomed by a crowd of 53,863, which gave him a warm embrace and cheered him throughout. It was the Tigers' biggest home gate since 1961. The Yankees knocked him out in the sixth inning after he had given up eight hits, three of them home runs.

"I'm not an emotional man," McLain told reporters. "But I thought I was going to cry when I heard those cheers. I didn't know what to expect. I almost had to swallow my tongue to hold myself together."

He was in trouble again two months later, on August 28, when he doused two Detroit baseball writers with a bucket of ice water. He soaked them one at a time, Jim Hawkins of the *Detroit Free Press* first, then Watson Spoelstra of the *News*, a former president of the Baseball Writers Association of America. Jim Campbell, the Detroit manager, suspended McLain for a period not to exceed thirty days at $500 a day.

"I was just clowning around," McLain said. But Hawkins insisted that after the dousing McLain had told him, "I'm going to get all you guys, so don't say I didn't warn you. I'd like to throw all of you, one by one, into the whirlpool before the season is over."

The season ended for McLain less than two weeks later, on September 9 when he drew suspension No. 3. This time Kuhn sat him down for carrying a gun onto an airplane. According to Kuhn's detectives, in a Chicago restaurant the week before, McLain had removed the gun from its holster and showed it to several teammates.

McLain was traded to the Washington Senators on the eve of the World Series and played two more seasons, winning a total of ten games. In 1985, thirteen years after he retired from baseball, he was convicted for racketeering, extortion, and cocaine possession and sentenced to twenty-three years in prison. He served twenty-nine months before the 11th Circuit Court of Appeals overruled the conviction. He went on to host a popular radio talk show in Detroit. Then, in December of 1996, McLain was convicted in the U.S. District Court in Detroit of looting $3 million from the pension fund of a company he owned.

McLain has since written two books, neither of which interested Kuhn, certainly not to the extent of Jim Bouton's *Ball Four*, published in 1970. Bouton's tome, coauthored by Leonard Schecter, a New York baseball writer, was a kiss-and-tell diary, at that time a sensational exposé that revealed, among other things, the Peeping Tom activities of some of his Yankees teammates.

The baseball establishment reacted with horror. Leo Durocher, then managing the Cubs, said he wouldn't have Bouton on his club. The San Diego Padres burned the book and left the charred pages in a heap in the visitors' clubhouse for Bouton to see.

"Everyone wants their book banned in Boston," said a delighted Bouton "but the next best thing is to have someone burn it."

The strait-laced Kuhn summoned Bouton and advised him of his displeasure. Bouton and his publishers responded with glee and initiated an advertising campaign as "The Book Baseball Tried to Ban." Sales soared.

It was a minor embarrassment for the Commissioner, insignificant compared to his unsuccessful efforts the following year to prevent the relocation of the Washington franchise. The Senators were Kuhn's "home" team and had been a charter member of the American League. After seventy-one seasons of uninterrupted baseball in the nation's capital, owner Short, pleading poverty, moved the franchise to Arlington, Texas, near Dallas, and renamed the club the Texas Rangers.

Kuhn did his best to abort the transfer and searched for a buyer. It was a heroic effort. He contacted the Marriott Hotel chain, headquartered in Washington; the *Washington Post*, the *Washington Star*, and subsequently national corporations such as Chrysler, Ford, Coca Cola, Pepsico, Philip Morris, Gillette and two of the three television networks.

An absentee owner—he lived in Minneapolis—Short feigned interest. He would sell if the price was right. The best offer, reportedly, was $8.4 million from a group headed by Joseph Danzansky, the president of the Washington Board of Trade.

More than likely, Short would have been forced to sell. But Danzansky began waffling, and in an eleventh hour appearance at a league meeting, confessed he had enough cash only for an option to buy and wanted the league to underwrite a $6.6 million loan for him and his partners. To move, approval was needed from nine of the league's twelve clubs. Short made it with one vote to spare.

The Washington fans, carrying obscene banners, had their revenge on the night of September 30, the Senators' final home game. There was a roar for a "Short Stinks" sign that was yanked down by security men and an even louder cheer for a hastily printed "Short Still Stinks" sign that replaced it.

When slugger Frank Howard hit a home run in the sixth inning, the fans responded with a five-minute standing ovation. Howard, who had been frequently quoted as saying he didn't want to go to Dallas, had to be persuaded by manager Ted Williams and his teammates to leave the dugout for two curtain calls. On the first, he threw his helmet liner into the crowd; on the second, he threw a kiss.

"Men and women cried, then Howard cried," reported Merrill Whittlesey of the *Washington Star*.

Judge Landis, leaning over the rail, with Detroit manager Bucky Harris.

KENESAW LANDIS NEVER MINDED THROWING OUT
THE FIRST BALL—OR POSING FOR A CAMERA.

AT A BALL GAME, JUDGE LANDIS WAS A STUDY
IN STILL LIFE——RARELY MOVING FROM THE RAIL.

Happy Chandler did more for the players than
any of the other commissioners

FORD FRICK (LEFT)
UNDERSTOOD THE
PARAMETERS OF THE JOB.

GENERAL WILLIAM ECKERT
(BELOW), THE "UNKNOWN
SOLDIER."

BOWIE KUHN FLANKED
BY SUPERSTARS WILLIE
STARGELL (LEFT) AND
REGGIE JACKSON.

KUHN ON THE SOCIAL
SCENE (RIGHT).

PETER UEBERROTH
(TOP), MAY HAVE
DISLIKED THE
OWNERS BUT HE LED
THEM TO
ENDORSEMENT AND
MERCHANDISING
RICHES.

BART GIAMATTI
(BOTTOM), THE YALE
PROFESSOR, HAD A
BRIEF AND MOSTLY
JOYFUL REIGN.

FAY VINCENT, JR. (TOP),
THE FRIEND AND DEPUTY
WHO SUCCEEDED
GIAMATTI ON THE
THRONE.

ALLAN "BUD" SELIG
(BOTTOM), BASEBALL'S
ULTIMATE INSIDER.

The fans ran onto the field with one out to go and the Senators leading 7–5. They rushed for the bases, tore up the plate, climbed to the roof
of the bullpen and took the letters from the scoreboard. The umpires
were unable to clear the field and the game was awarded to the Yankees
by the 9–0 forfeit score, the first American League forfeit since 1954.

"It was Utopia," Howard said.

Throughout the remainder of Kuhn's reign, many influential Washington politicians threatened legislation that would strip baseball's
immunity from the antitrust laws unless the city was provided with a
replacement franchise. Kuhn had to contend with this hostility during
his many subsequent appearances before congressional committees.

This was also the season the public discovered Kuhn had been
gelded. The surgery had occurred the year before, when Marvin
Miller had negotiated his second Basic Agreement, the contract that
binds the players and owners together. Miller had made an unsuccessful attempt his first time around, in 1968, to render the Commissioner powerless. But, like a dugout manager arguing an umpire's
decision, Miller understood the umpire would not reverse himself.
He was thinking ahead, fighting for the next call.

At the bargaining table, Miller insisted Kuhn and his predecessors
were employees, selected by the clubs, paid by the clubs, and responsible only to the clubs. In May 1970, while most of the owners slept,
Miller won a crucial victory: Hereafter, player grievances would be
adjudicated by impartial arbitration, and the commissioner's "best
interests" powers would be limited to protecting the "integrity of the
game." It was the cornerstone for a sequence of stunning Players
Association victories climaxed by the Messersmith decision which
forced modification of the reserve system.

Previously, the league presidents and the commissioner had been
judge and jury. As Miller explained years later, "They could make
any ruling they wanted. They could say up is down and down is up."

With impartial arbitration, this was no longer possible. A three-man panel of Miller, John Gaherin, management's principal negotiator, and an independent third party, usurped the Commissioner's authority. Since Miller and Gaherin would automatically find for their respective sides, the third vote was decisive. Lewis Gill of Philadelphia, then the president of the National Academy of Arbitrators, was the first of what was to become a succession of impartial arbitrators. Gill's word was binding and beyond appeal.

"Most of the owners didn't understand the potential ramifications and they didn't want to," Gaherin said twenty-five years later.

As sometimes happens, the press scarcely noticed the change. The belief that the commissioner was the all-powerful, all-knowing czar wasn't shattered until a grievance was filed on behalf of Alex Johnson, an angry and troubled outfielder with the California Angels. An outstanding hitter, Johnson was lackadaisical in the field. In a game against Kansas City, he was charged with three errors, dropped a fly-ball that was scored as a hit, and played a single into a triple.

The next day, on June 26, California general manager Dick Walsh suspended Johnson without pay for failing to give his best. None of Johnson's teammates came to his defense. Said Jim Fregosi, the Angels' all-star shortstop:

"A man gets paid to play, and hustling is part of the game. If you don't hustle, you shouldn't get paid. He was given every opportunity."

"[Johnson's suspension] was an action that had to be taken," said third baseman Ken McMullen.

"I'm not implying that Alex was throwing games," observed Cedric Tallis, general manager of the Kansas City Royals, "but when you don't catch a flyball you are deliberately contributing to defeat."

Miller was aware that the heavy majority of the players were against Johnson. But Miller believed there was the possibility Johnson was emotionally disturbed. If so, he should not have been disciplined and instead should have been put on the disabled list until he recovered.

The grievance traveled through the regular channels. First, American League president Joe Cronin upheld the suspension. Commissioner Kuhn followed and ruled likewise. Lewis Gill, the impartial arbitrator, had the last say. After hearing a mountain of psychiatric testimony, Gill decided that Johnson was emotionally ill and be transferred to the disabled list. It was a landmark decision, the first time mental illness was equated with physical injury.

Catfish Hunter was the next beneficiary of the new procedure. Immediately after he had helped pitch the Oakland A's to their third consecutive World Series title, Hunter charged owner Charlie Finley with breach of contract. Hunter had signed for two years for $100,000 a year; Finley's first $100,000 player. He was to draw $50,000 in salary each year, with the checks for the remaining $50,000 deferred and sent directly by the Oakland club to a third party to be designated by Hunter and his attorneys. The money was to fund an annuity, not immediately subject to federal tax.

On September 16, Finley was advised in writing that he had missed the payment deadline but had a ten-day grace period. Finley agreed to make restitution during a meeting with Hunter and American League president Lee MacPhail on October 4, on the eve of the World Series.

"Okay, Catfish, here's a check for $50,000," Finley said. "That's the rest of the money you have coming on your 1974 contract."

"I can't take it," Hunter replied. "I've been advised by my attorney that a check must be sent directly to the Jefferson Insurance Company."

Finley responded, "Why don't you call your lawyer? Here, use this phone."

Hunter called his tax adviser, J. Carlton Cherry, a 68-year-old country lawyer in Ahoskie, North Carolina, who had driven the bus for Hunter's American Legion team. Cherry's clientele consisted mostly of peanut and soybean farmers. Cherry and Hunter spoke for several minutes. Hunter then told Finley, "I'm sorry but he said I shouldn't take it."

Dick Moss, counsel for the Players Association, filed a grievance, requesting free agency, according to Section 7A in the standard players' contract:

"The Player may terminate his contract upon written notice to the Club, if the Club shall default in the payments to the Player . . . or if the Club shall fail to perform any other obligation agreed to . . . and if the Club shall fail to remedy such a default within 10 days after the receipt by the Club of written notice of such default."

On December 13, Peter Seitz, baseball's fourth impartial arbitrator, found for Hunter.

Simultaneous with Seitz's announcement, Kuhn sent a bulletin to the clubs advising that he wanted to review the decision. Direct or indirect contact between Hunter and other clubs (Oakland excepted) was temporarily prohibited, Kuhn declared. Reminded that Seitz was beyond appeal, Kuhn submitted and on December 18, directed that all of the clubs could begin contacting Hunter and his agents.

The auction ran for thirteen days. All twenty-four clubs made contact, including Oakland. Curious, Finley asked Cherry, "How much would Jim want for a new contract?"

The average baseball salary was $35,000, the top $250,000. Finley offered $200,000.

On the afternoon of December 31, 1974, Hunter signed with the Yankees. The total package was $3.2 million for five years, $640,000 a year, a concrete example of the financial effect of free agency. Still, it was an isolated litigation based on breach of contract. Free agency for all of the players was still two years away.

# BOWIE KUHN
## PART III

A rticle 10A, the so-called renewal clause in the standard players' contract:

"If, prior to March 1, the Player and the Club have not agreed upon the term of the contract, then, on or before ten days after said March 1, the Club shall have the right by written notice to the player to renew this contract for the period of one year."

It was the centerpiece of the reserve system, in effect since 1879. Interpretation differed. Commissioner Bowie Kuhn and the baseball establishment insisted it allowed a club to control a player in perpetuity, until he was traded, sold, or released.

Marvin Miller and attorney Dick Moss of the Players Association disagreed and insisted a player who had refused to sign and played under a renewed contract had fulfilled the "period of one year" obligation. Having done so, he was a free agent, not subject to further renewal. A guinea-pig player was needed for a test case.

Miller's first prospect, catcher Ted Simmons of the St. Louis Cardinals, surfaced in 1972. Simmons batted .304 in 1971 and eventually set a National League career record for home runs by a switch hit-

157

ter. The Cardinals offered $14,000: The average salary was $34,002. Simmons asked for $30,000. In late July, the Cardinals capitulated. He signed for $30,000 for 1972 and $45,000 for 1973.

Two years later there were three candidates eligible to test the reserve clause: relief pitcher Sparky Lyle of the Yankees and out-fielders Richie Zisk of the Pittsburgh Pirates and Bobby Tolan of the San Diego Padres. None was interested in becoming a martyr.

Late in the season, when the Yankees were playing Baltimore, Bobby Grich, the Orioles' star second baseman, expressed the senti-ments of many players when he told Lyle:

"Go get 'em, Sparky! We're all with you."

"I'm not out to get anybody," Lyle replied. "I'm just looking for the best deal."

Lyle got what he wanted. On the final day of the season, the Yankees rewarded him with a two-year deal; an *ex post facto* 1974 contract for a reported $87,500, an increase of $7,500; and $92,500 for the following season.

Zisk and Tolan went through the regular season under renewal but signed prior to the National League playoffs. Tolan had slightly more staying power. On October 17, the union filed a grievance in behalf of Tolan but he surrendered six weeks later, on December 9, when the Padres satisfied him with a two-year contract almost identical to Lyle's. By this time it was obvious the owners didn't want 10A tested.

A month later, with the Tolan situation rendering the grievance moot, it was withdrawn. But there was also a secondary concern. Seitz had found for Catfish Hunter only two months before, in December 1974. Looking ahead, Miller wanted to relieve the pres-sure on the arbitrator; it was too early to win two in a row.

Finally, Miller found his man: Andy Messersmith, ace of the Los Angeles pitching staff.

Messersmith had signed a one-year contract with the Dodgers for

$90,000, in 1974. They boosted him to $115,000 for 1975 but when
he requested a no-trade provision, club president Walter O'Malley
refused and invoked the renewal clause. Messersmith had a companion. Dave McNally, previously a longtime pitching star with the
Baltimore Orioles, had been traded to the Montreal Expos. McNally
had also refused to sign.

Two months into the season, on June 8, 1975, McNally retired but
not because of his salary squabble with the Expos. He had been a
consistent winner with the Orioles—181 victories in the previous
thirteen seasons—but he didn't have similar success with the Expos.
He won his first three decisions but, troubled by a sore arm, lost his
next six. He departed with a 5.26 earned run average for the season.

After he returned home to Billings, Montana, Miller called.

"Are you coming back?" Miller asked.

"Never," said McNally.

Miller was looking for insurance, a backup grievant should
Messersmith sign.

"If you need me, I'm willing to help," McNally said.

The union filed the Messersmith-McNally grievances on October 9,
1975. Aware of the potential ramifications, the owners claimed the
scope of the reserve system was not within the ambit of the arbitration panel. In an effort to enjoin the proceedings, they filed a complaint in the U.S. District Court in Kansas City. Judge John W. Oliver
denied the injunction and instructed the parties to proceed with an
arbitration hearing with the understanding that the court would
subsequently determine the question of Seitz's jurisdiction.

Lou Hoynes, Kuhn's successor as the National League's attorney,
advised the owners to dismiss Seitz, saying that it was obvious in the
Hunter grievance that he was partial to labor. Kuhn and John
McHale of the Montreal Expos were also in favor of bouncing him.
John Gaherin, the owners' chief negotiator, was on the fence.

"Any arbitrator is a compromise," Gaherin said. "Better to go with the devil you know."

Bruce Johnson, the steel industry's chief negotiator, warned the owners against Seitz. John Helyar, in *The Lords of the Realm*, quoted Johnson as saying, "He's not an analyst, he's a poet." Another management negotiator described Seitz's decisions as "baffling . . . . We lost the decisions we should have won and won the ones we should have lost."

Kuhn made a brief speech against Seitz to the owners' Player Relations Committee, which set management's labor policy, and then left the room to take a phone call. By the time he returned, the PRC had voted 6–1 for Seitz, McHale dissenting. Surprised, Kuhn called for a second vote. Again it was 6–1.

The hearing before the Seitz tribunal was held at the Barbizon Plaza Hotel in New York beginning on November 21. Kuhn was called three days later. In his opening remarks, he acknowledged:

"This is an unusual thing for me to do. I have never appeared in a baseball arbitration before but I felt that the circumstances were such that I should take the opportunity to give you, for what it may be worth, the benefit of some thoughts I have on the situation."

Led by Hoynes, Kuhn said the Messersmith-McNally dispute affected the integrity of the game and as such was within his purview.

"When we came down to this grievance," he said, "I was troubled by it because in seeking, as it does, to eliminate the reserve system, it raises a very grave question as to whether it touches the integrity and public confidence in the game that the commissioner should use his powers to withdraw this grievance from the process.

"The reserve system is necessary to protect not only the integrity but the economic viability of the game. We have two clubs today that are insolvent. The National League is currently paying the bills or advancing the money to pay the bills of one, and an interested buyer is advancing money to pay the bills of another. I think the loss of a major league team is quite possible.

"If our players were free to play out their options, you may be sure the worst results will ensue even to the point of seeming unreasonable in terms of unbalancing competition. The strongest clubs would surely buy the best players. There is not the slightest question about it."

During and after the hearing and the subsequent appeals, Seitz several times expressed his reluctance to make a decision and urged that modification be achieved at the bargaining table. Gaherin was willing but not persuasive. When the owners continued to balk, Seitz, on December 23, held that the renewal clause was not perpetual but for only one year; after one year there was no contractual bond between player and club. Players who played out their renewal year were free to negotiate with any major league team.

Messersmith was a free agent.

"I am not a new Abraham Lincoln freeing the slaves," Seitz said in an interview with C.C. Johnson Spink, editor of *The Sporting News*. "I was striking a blow at the reserve clause. I was just interpreting the renewal clause as a lawyer and an elderly arbitrator."

Spink, in a prophetic response, predicted:

"The Seitz ruling gave the reserve clause a resounding whack and is likely to result in higher player salaries whether or not a large number of players switch to other clubs. Players can be expected to demand and obtain long-term contracts at a higher pay level than now prevails."

Stunned, the owners returned to the U.S. District Court for the Western District of Missouri. Judge Oliver upheld Seitz. Next was an appeal to the U.S. Court of Appeals for the Eighth Circuit. Again Seitz was affirmed. The only remaining appeal was to the U.S. Supreme Court. The owners acknowledged defeat and saved their money.

The triumph included an unforeseen bonus—the debut of Donald Martin Fehr (pronounced, appropriately as either *fair* or *fear*) who was employed by a small and respected Kansas City firm specializing in labor law, hired by the Players Association to assist in the Messersmith grievance.

A native of Marion, Indiana, Fehr grew up in Prairie Village, Kansas. After his graduation from Indiana University, he received a law degree from the University of Missouri in 1973 and clerked for United States District Court Judge Elmo Hunter in Kansas City. Impressed, Marvin Miller, in 1977, asked Fehr to join the union staff as general counsel.

Six years later, in 1983, Miller retired and was succeeded by Kenneth Moffett, who had been a federal mediator. Moffett was dismissed after ten months on the job. Fehr replaced him as the executive director of the union and ten years later was one of the most powerful labor leaders in the country, also the highest paid with an annual salary of approximately $1.5 million.

"When we're on a plane," said Lauren Rich, an assistant union counsel, "I watch the movie. Don reads about string theory in *Scientific American.*"

The Messersmith decision was among the union's major victories but the struggle with the owners continued. Unable to reach accord on a new Basic Agreement, the owners refused to open the spring training camps. At this point more than 300 players, following Messersmith's lead, had not signed their 1976 contracts. An economist, not an anarchist, Miller realized the danger: a large supply of free agents would depress, not increase salaries. Oakland's Charlie Finley appeared to be the only owner who understood the market. The more free agents, the lower the price.

To prevent swamping the market, Miller agreed to negotiate modification. But there was a problem. If he diluted Seitz, he said, a player or players could sue him and the Players Association for bargaining away their newly-won rights. Miller knew no player would sue. A master of public relations, he milked this scenario to the press.

It came down to this: Did the players want freedom of movement or to maximize their earnings? Money won. Miller and his executive board decided the ideal compromise was for free agency to kick in after six years of major league service. Not only would it limit the supply, but a six-year man, on the open market, would command the most interest; he would be near or at the peak of his career.

The owners' lockout continued. Bill Veeck, the maverick owner of the Chicago White Sox, protested and indicated he would open shop.

Said Veeck, who above all else enjoyed tweaking his fellow-moguls: "They have stuck their heads in the sand. Sometimes it seems to me that Marvin Miller is the only one who makes sense. He can't negotiate away the court's decision. If you were a player, would you let him?"

American League president Lee MacPhail hurried to Chicago and warned Veeck that the White Sox would be fined, for what one newspaper estimated at $500,000.

"The idea of playing baseball and negotiating at the same time is not desirable," MacPhail said. But the White Sox would be allowed to open, provided only minor league players were in uniform. Veeck opened with twenty-five players: twenty-four farmhands and veteran outfielder Cleon Jones, a free agent trying to make a comeback.

"I quit like a dog and it grieves me," Veeck told Tom Fitzpatrick of the *Chicago Sun-Times*. "I am turning tail and running but this is not an unconditional surrender. I'm complying with the letter of the rules, not the spirit."

A week later, Ted Turner of the Atlanta Braves, then a rookie owner, opened the gates, with nine minor leaguers reporting. The White Sox and Braves played two exhibition games but no major leaguers participated.

On March 14, Kuhn told the Associated Press, "The season will not be delayed. This has been a frustrating time for all of us. My job is to keep these guys meeting."

Three days later, on St. Patrick's Day, Kuhn, in his most statesmanlike decision, announced:

"It is now vital that spring training get under way without further delay. While nobody is more disappointed than I that we do not have solid progress to a final agreement, the fans are the most important people around and their interests now become paramount. Opening the camps and starting the season on time is what they want."

And that is what happened, although it wasn't until July 12, that a new Basic Agreement was in place:

• Any player with at least six years of major league service may, following the conclusion of the championship season, become a free agent by notifying his club in writing.

• Players with unsigned [renewed] contracts in 1976 to become free agents after the 1976 season; players with unsigned contracts in 1977 to become free agents after the 1977 season; players with multiyear contracts to become free agents at the end of the next regular season, if they don't sign a new contract prior to that time.

Gussie Busch, the 77-year-old autocrat who owned the St. Louis Cardinals, was critical of the settlement. So were Finley, McHale, Calvin Griffith of the Minnesota Twins, and Jerold Hoffberger of the Baltimore Orioles.

"We've been kicked in the teeth," Busch said. "It's our own fault and we're going to pay for it."

Did they ever. Player salaries exploded. The average player salary in 1974 was $41,000; 20 years later it was $1.2 million, an increase of 2,800 percent.

Free agency wasn't the only engine that drove the players to unexpected riches. There also was the twin motor of salary arbitration, which went into effect prior to the 1974 season. Initially, it seemed to be a harmless procedure.

Any player with three or more years of big league experience, dissatisfied with the club's salary offer, was eligible. It was a simple process. The player and management submitted sealed bids, the players' salary request versus the club offer. It was an either/or proposition, popular in settling municipal contracts. The arbitrator had to choose one or the other. Comparative salaries were included in the equation. For example, if Yankee owner George Steinbrenner had money to burn, and paid a slugging outfielder $100,000, the other owners, regardless of their revenue stream, had to match this wage if a player in their employ had similar stats and service time.

The ability to pay was not a consideration.

Worse for the owners, an arbitration award was for one year, only for the season ahead. Once eligible and if the player was not hooked into a multiyear contract, he could take his club to arbitration for three years, until he qualified for free agency.

In 1974, in the first battalion of 497 eligibles, fifty-three applied for arbitration but only twenty-nine went the distance. Most of the grievances, at that time and later, were settled by compromise prior to the hearing, some in the hallways outside the hearing chamber. The first case was pitcher Dick Woodson of the Minnesota Twins. Woodson requested $30,000. The Twins offered $22,000. Woodson won the $8,000 difference. Larry Hisle, an outfielder also with the Twins, was next. Hisle came in at $28,500. Again the Twins offered $22,000. Hisle won.

The aggregate loss for the clubs was $135,000, little more than tip money. There were thirteen player "winners," sixteen "losers." The next year the owners won ten out of sixteen at less than half the cost,

$52,500. But arbitration numbers are deceiving; 99 percent of the players who file come out ahead. If the clubs play low-ball, they are certain losers. To win, they must come close to matching the request. Also, the players' salaries constantly escalate.

Knowing the club's offer will be realistic, some players shoot for the moon; even if they "lose" they will be amply rewarded. Relief pitcher Bruce Sutter of the Cubs, in 1980, was an excellent example. The Cubs offered Sutter $350,000, a $200,000 boost. Jim Bronner, Sutter's agent, aimed for the stars. Sutter was coming off a Cy Young Award-winning season. Bronner filed for $700,000. The arbitrator, who later admitted he was a Cub fan, decided for Sutter. The $700,000 was the largest arbitration award to that time, the $350,000 a record for the winning spread; and the increase of $550,000 the largest overall, one season arbitration gain.

The arbitrators are drawn by lot. Some didn't know much baseball. Dick Moss recalled a hearing when both sides invoked the names of current and past players. "The arbitrator constantly interrupted," Moss recalled, "and said, 'Hold it a minute, how do you spell his name?' When Babe Ruth was mentioned, he said. 'Now, that's a name I recognize.'" It was his first and last case.

The possibility of salary arbitration was first suggested by Philip K. Wrigley, the altruistic and longtime caretaker of the Chicago Cubs. In 1957, testifying before a congressional committee on the "Study of Monopoly Power," Wrigley said:

"As far as arbitration goes, I think if you had a means of arbitrating [player] salaries you might as well have a commission to set all salaries, because I think they would all be arbitrated and that probably would be a good thing for baseball."

Sixteen years later, when Miller proposed salary arbitration, only Finley of Oakland and Dick Meyer of the St. Louis Cardinals opposed.

"I contacted every owner personally or by telephone," Finley recalled. "I told them, one and all, the evils of arbitration. They all listened attentively and thanked me for taking the time to call them. If I had been a betting man, I would have bet all the tea in China at least eighteen teams would vote against arbitration but when it came to a vote only the St. Louis Cardinals and Oakland A's voted against it. They didn't like or trust me. At that time my club was doing too much winning."

Following a two-year moratorium, arbitration resumed in 1977, after the Messersmith decision. Free agency now began pulling the salary wagon. Because of the arbitrators' instruction on comparative salaries and the million-dollar free agent signings, compensations soared across the board, a windfall for the players, and as Finley had predicted, an economic "evil" for the owners.

Pitcher Fernando Valenzuela of the Los Angeles Dodgers, in 1983, was the first to win a $1 million contract at the arbitration window. Nine years later Ruben Sierra of the Texas Rangers scaled the $5 million plateau; the Rangers had offered $3.8 million. In 1994, pitcher Jack McDowell of the Chicago White Sox was the new leader at $5.3 million.

McDowell filed during each of his three years of eligibility. His 1991 wage was $175,000, low for a player of his ability. McDowell asked for $2.3 million in 1992. The Sox came in at $1.6 million. McDowell "lost" but nonetheless won an 814 percent increase. The next year, when an arbitrator ruled in his favor, his salary jumped to $4 million. When he tried a third time, he lost and had to accept the club offer of $5.3 million. His cumulative three-year arbitration gain resulted in an incredible salary boost of 2,929 percent.

As salaries soared, so did the owners' displeasure. There had been scattered criticism of Kuhn in the executive wing, much of which was hidden from the press. But in the spring of 1975, Finley, his longtime antagonist, publicly revealed a "Dump Bowie" movement had begun. The Commissioner was entering the final month of his term. Under baseball rules, his contract can be considered for renewal between six and fifteen months before expiration.

Arrayed against Kuhn were Finley, Baltimore owner Jerry Hoffberger, Brad Corbett of Texas, and George Steinbrenner of the Yankees whom Kuhn had suspended for two years following his conviction for illegal contributions to the 1972 political campaigns, a federal offense. Technically, Steinbrenner was not allowed to vote. The Yankees were represented by Pat Cunningham, a New York politician. But Steinbrenner was behind the curtain, making the call. Only four votes were needed to unseat a commissioner, providing they were from the same league.

Steinbrenner pleaded innocence. "I would never vote against the Commissioner because of anything he did within his authority," Steinbrenner insisted. "People seem to think the Yankees' vote against him is because of my suspension but that is not true."

The rebellion surfaced at the owners' annual summer meeting in Milwaukee, on July 25, 1975, the day after the All Star Game. The American League revealed the vote against Kuhn was 8–4, one short of renewal. The National League, which had voted 11–1 for Kuhn (Ray Kroc of San Diego was the dissenter), hurried to the Commissioner's defense, with the claim that they were nothing more than straw votes. A formal vote could be taken only at a joint meeting of both leagues.

While Finley and Hoffberger were asleep in their suites at the Pfister Hotel, Walter O'Malley of the Dodgers and John Galbreath of the Pirates, along with several of their American League brothers, were making midnight telephone calls to Corbett and Steinbrenner.

The joint meeting was held at nine o'clock the next morning. After Kuhn was asked to leave the room, the owners extended Kuhn's contract for a second seven-year term. The American League approved 10–2, the National 12–0.

When he was called back into the meeting room, Kuhn was given a standing ovation, with Finley and Hoffberger joining in the applause. His term now extended through 1983, Kuhn told his minions:

"Thank you, gentlemen, especially those who voted for me. It's too bad it took so long but it's not surprising considering the quality of the opposition."

At a press conference that followed immediately, Kuhn told newsmen:

"Frankly, I was so disturbed, I was on the verge of telling them to take the job. I am human. But when so many men whom I respect said, 'We really want you,' I stuck it out."

Finley and a half dozen owners were in attendance. As Kuhn was finishing, Finley walked to the front of the room and said he wanted to issue a statement.

Replied Kuhn sharply, his voice trembling in anger, "Charlie, you may leave my room!"

Reporters followed Finley into an adjacent chamber. Finley admitted he had voted against Kuhn and said he had no malice to the twenty-two owners who supported the Commissioner.

"I would say the Commissioner hasn't been in baseball long enough," Finley said. "When you're in baseball, you realize you win a few and lose a few. And when you lose, you have to lose as graciously as when you win."

It was a tuneup for the main event five months later, the Finley versus Kuhn trial, baseball's most dazzling courtroom theatrical since the Black Sox scandal.

# 14 BOWIE KUHN
## PART IV

G entlemen, I am going to resist the temptation to open this trial by saying, 'Play ball.' I had many suggestions to do that but I won't. I am ready to proceed."

*Charles O. Finley* v. *Bowie Kuhn* et al., had begun in the crowded United States Courthouse in Chicago on December 16, 1976, the Honorable Frank J. McGarr of the U.S. District Court for the Northern District of Illinois presiding.

Attorney Neil Papiano, representing Finley:

"Your honor, the evidence will show that the sales of outfielder Joe Rudi and pitcher Rollie Fingers to the Boston Red Sox, and Vida Blue to the New York Yankees were, in fact, consummated without any rule violation. There was no dispute between the teams involved, or between any other teams in baseball with regard to these player sales. There was no moral turpitude problem involved, and there was no dishonesty.

"The evidence will also show that under those circumstances there is no authority whatsoever for the defendant, Bowie Kuhn, to induce the breach of these substantial contracts, and for the only

170

reason being what he unilaterally believed to be, as he termed, acting in the 'best interests of baseball.'"

On June 15, the last day of the trading deadline, Finley sold three
of his best Oakland players for an aggregate of $3.5 million, easily
the largest one-day player sale in baseball history. Rudi and Fingers
went to the Red Sox for $1 million each, Blue to the Yankees for
$1.5 million.

Finley was unloading. On April 2, just before opening day, he
traded two of his holdouts, outfielder Reggie Jackson and pitcher
Ken Holtzman, to the Baltimore Orioles. Both had been principal
contributors to Oakland's remarkable run of three consecutive world
championships, a dynasty that crumbled in the wake of the
Messersmith decision.

The bonds were loosening. On March 10, the traditional date
when the clubs automatically renewed contracts, 193 players were
unsigned and, in effect, playing out their options. On May 15 the
number had dwindled to sixty-two. Finley was the leader with six,
all front-liners, potential free agents who, at the end of the season,
could make a new connection without compensation from the
acquiring club to the player's former team.

Frantic, Finley began burning up the telephone wires. On June 15,
the final day of the trading deadline, he had a blockbuster. Rudi,
Fingers, and Blue had been sold for a total of $3.5 million, a mid-
night fire sale without precedent. Rudi and Fingers were among the
thirty-eight unsigned players eligible for free agency. Blue was not
among them. Finley, earlier in the day, had locked him into a three-
year contract.

In marched emperor Bowie Kent Kuhn. Invoking his "best interests" powers, he nullified the sales. Kuhn's principal objection, in
the beginning, was that the deals would upset "competitive balance." Later, the complaint grew: Finley was cannibalizing his

club—instead of the $3.5 million in cash, the exchange should have included some players, young prospects, an indication Finley was intending to rebuild.

Finley sued Kuhn for $10 million in damages. Named as codefendants were the American and National leagues, the major leagues' Executive Council, and the Red Sox and Yankees. Finley contended no rule had been violated, that Kuhn had deprived him of his rightful money, had acted in malice, in an "arbitrary, capricious and unreasonable manner," and tried to "injure, discredit, defame, vex, annoy and ultimately to compel the plaintiff to leave baseball."

Kuhn and Finley had been feuding for years. Kuhn fined Finley twice in 1972, first $500 after Finley had told him to "go to hell" for siding with Blue in a salary dispute, and $5,000 for giving his players illegal bonuses during the World Series. And another $7,000 the following year when he tried to put second baseman Mike Andrews on the disabled list after Andrews had committed two errors in the World Series. Finley repeatedly responded with invective, often describing Kuhn as the "village idiot," which he later expanded to the "nation's idiot."

By a 21–3 vote, the owners indemnified their Commissioner for personal liability. Against were Gussie Busch of the St. Louis Cardinals, Jerry Hoffberger of Baltimore, and Finley. It was an unusual twist. Win or lose, Finley was on the hook for one-twenty-fourth of Kuhn's court costs. Twenty-two people testified, fifteen called by Kuhn's attorneys, seven by Finley's. The litigation ran fifteen trial days.

American League president Lee MacPhail, a hostile witness, was summoned by Papiano on the first day:

Q: Did you give Commissioner Kuhn any advice as to whether or not he should take any action?

A: Yes, I advised him he should not take action. I urged that the sales should not be stopped, that they be approved.

Q: What were your reasons?

A: No specific baseball rules had been broken. At the time it appeared the American League pennant race would not be affected too much as a result of the assignments.

Q: Did Chub Feeney, the president of the National League, agree with your position?

A: Yes.

Q: Up until the time of June 15, 1976, do you know of any ceiling on the amount of money that could be paid by one major league team to another?

A: No.

Q: In your many years of experience has there ever been a custom and practice in baseball that the Commissioner decides on matters of competitive balance?

A: I don't remember of a prior case where he took action to preserve competitive balance.

Q: With respect to competitive balance, what has been Oakland's performance in the past ten years?

A: They probably have a better record than any club in baseball. They won the World Series in each of the last three years and five consecutive divisional championships.

Q: Is it good for one team to be as dominant as Oakland has been?

A: The ideal situation would be to spread the championships around a little bit.

"Competitive balance" was a mythic phrase created for the occasion. In a deposition taken on Finley's behalf, Bill DeWitt, a longtime baseball executive, dismissed it as philosophical nonsense:

"It would be an ideal arrangement if you could have all the clubs handicapped like they handicap horse races so that everybody would be figured to win the pennant. It would create more fan interest and would be more of a financial gain to the owners and players, but it doesn't work that way. There's no such thing as competitive balance. It's dog eat dog."

DeWitt also told of the days when he owned the St. Louis Browns, who were in a constant financial bind. One of his early sales was Vern Stephens and Jack Kramer to the Red Sox. Joe Cronin, who had preceded MacPhail as the American League president, was then the front office boss of the Red Sox.

Q: Did Mr. Cronin ever say anything to the effect that this was a bad thing he was doing?

A: The only thing he said was, "Why didn't you do it last year when I was manager so I could have a good ballclub?"

DeWitt, from 1947–50, also unloaded Ellis Kinder to Boston, Bob Muncrief and Walt Judnich to the Yankees, Billy Hitchcock to Boston, Johnny Berardino to Cleveland, Nelson Potter to Philadelphia, Sam Zoldak to Cleveland, Sam Dente to Washington, Al "Zeke" Zarilla to Boston, Bob Dillinger and Paul Lehner to Philadelphia, Jerry Priddy to Detroit, and Tom Ferrick and Joe Ostrowski to the Yankees.

"Money was the important thing," DeWitt said. "We were doing, you might say, a wholesale business, trying to pay off a $1.3 million debt."

Q: Was there ever any question in your mind that you had a right to make these sales?

A: No, and there were no objections. They were all approved and promulgated as all deals are.

Calvin Griffith, chairman of the Minnesota Twins, insisted he had advised Finley to restructure his deals. Like Finley, Griffith was a shrewd and penurious operator. On June 2, two weeks earlier, he had traded Bert Blyleven, his unsigned star pitcher, and infielder Danny Thompson to the Texas Rangers for $250,000 and four obscure players. Griffith testified for the defense.

Q: Did you have any conversations with Mr. Finley shortly before the attempted sales of Blue, Rudi and Fingers?

A: Yes, I did. A day or two before the trading deadline, he called me and asked if I had five and a half million dollars to buy all of his unsigned players. I said, "Charlie, you must be full of you know what. They're not worth it." I said, "Charlie, what's on your mind?" And he said "I'm going to sell them."

I told him, "Don't be a goddam fool. If you sell them without getting other ballplayers, you're making the biggest mistake in the world. Go ahead and trade them but get other players in return."

Q: Did you state your reasons?

A: I said, "It would weaken the other teams in the East. If you sell those three outstanding ballplayers to Boston and New York, the other four clubs in the section may have to go bankrupt. You can't hurt people like that in this game of baseball."

Three American League general managers didn't share Griffith's concern but were more interested in strengthening their clubs, all in the Eastern Division. Jim Campbell of Detroit, Dick O'Connell of Boston, and Gabe Paul of the Yankees were Finley's customers.

"Mr. Jim Campbell, would you please take the witness stand."

Q: Mr. Campbell, would you describe the circumstances of your negotiations with Mr. Finley?

A: Charlie called me Monday night, on June 14, and said, "I've got meat for sale. I'm selling my ballplayers who are playing out their options. I'm asking a million dollars for these specific contracts." And he named them off—Rudi, Fingers, Blue, Baylor and Campaneris. He mentioned $500,000 for Sal Bando.

I said, "Charlie, you've got to be kidding." He said, "No, I'm not kidding. There are clubs interested." He mentioned the Yankees being interested in Campaneris and Boston was interested in Rudi and Fingers. And then he said, "If you want to get in on the action, call me tomorrow morning or I'll call you."

Q: That was June 15th?

A: Yes. Charlie called me about 9:30 in the morning and again wanted to know if I had any interest. And I said, "Is the price still a million dollars? And if it is, I'm interested in Vida Blue." And I told him, "Charlie, before I call Mr. Fetzer [John Fetzer, owner of the Detroit Tigers] I want to make sure I'm not getting into a bidding contest." He said, "That's the price. I'll get back to you."

So I called Mr. Fetzer and he asked, "Do you suppose Charlie is trying to get us in a bidding contest?" And I said, "No, I don't. The man told me he would not do this. This was the price." And Mr. Fetzer said, "Well, we need a pitcher. If you recommend it, I'd say yes, go ahead."

Q: Did Mr. Fetzer ask if Blue had been signed to a contract?

A: Yes, that was one stipulation. When I called Charlie back I told him he had to deliver Blue with a signed contract. And I said, "The price is a million dollars, right?" He assured me that was the price and I said, "Sign Blue and we've got a deal." I called Rick Ferrell, our No. 1 scout, and Alex Kellem, our comptroller, into the office. We went over the whole thing. I was very careful about it because, frankly, I'd never paid a million dollars for a contract.

At that point I felt we had a deal for Vida Blue—if he could be signed. About three o'clock in the afternoon, Red Sox general manager Dick O'Connell called me and said, 'I hear you got Vida Blue.' I said. 'I wish Charlie would call me. I've been waiting to hear from him.' I was pacing around the office, and so about five o'clock in the afternoon I called Charlie myself.

And he said, "Jim, he's gone. Vida Blue is gone. That's all I can tell you."

I said, "Charlie, explain it." And he said, "I can't. The phone's ringing. I'll get back to you."

And that night they announced the deals, Vida Blue to the Yankees and Rudi and Fingers to the Red Sox.

I never heard another word from Charlie until Monday morning. He starts out, "Hi, Baldy, are you upset with me?"

I said, "You're damn right I am. You used me to get yourself another $500,000."

He said when he was talking to me on the phone, Gabe Paul was in his office. And, according to Charlie, Gabe wanted to get in on it. Charlie said he threw out a ridiculous figure, a million and a half dollars, and Gabe took it.

He said, "Now, Jim, what would you have done? I'm under financial duress. I can get another half million dollars."

I said, "'What would I have done? I'd have kept my damn word.' And I slammed the phone down."

John Fetzer, chairman and president of the Detroit Tigers, a leading member of the Executive Council, baseball's most powerful body, and according to John Gaherin, the owners' longtime labor negotiator, was the most influential owner in the American League. "Fetzer and Walter O'Malley ran baseball," Gaherin said. "At joint meetings O'Malley would pass a note to Fetzer, and Fetzer would respond by saying 'If you put it into a motion, I'll second it.'"

Q: Mr. Fetzer, in making the million dollar offer for Vida Blue, did you think you were violating any rules?

A: No, absolutely not. Our ballclub had finished last two years in a row and we were desperate for pitching help. We were actually going with about a one and a half man pitching staff. Jim Campbell and I had talked consistently about what we could do to acquire more pitching. At that time I told him, "I don't care what you have to do to get it, but get more pitching."

Later, he said "I've just made a great addition to our pitching staff." I asked who it was and he said, "Vida Blue." I said "That's great, that's wonderful. What's the price tag?" And he said "A million dollars." That was shocking to me, the fellow certainly isn't worth that kind of money. Campbell said the price of baseball talent is going up. He strongly recommended I approve this transaction.

So, I said, "Okay, if that's the way you feel about it, go ahead." But I didn't really like the smell of it.

Q: Did you think you were acting in the best interests of baseball?

A: No

Q: Did you, during a conference call, advise Mr. Kuhn to hold a hearing and protect his flank?

A: Yes.

Q: Did you think Mr. Kuhn felt that he had to find out whether or not he had the powers to do these things?

A: I don't know whether he subjectively said that; that was a reaction of mine at the time.

Q: Did you recommend that he not disapprove the sales but issue a strong statement for the future regarding such sales?

A: As I recall, I advised him to issue a strong statement of condemnation but I think I also said it would be very helpful if rules and regulations pertaining to such matters could be more importantly understood by the parties of the league and possibly that might be one of the methods of procedure.

Q: You recommended this so that everybody would know with respect to assignments what they could and couldn't do?

A: Yes, I did.

Q: But prior to June 15, 1976, had you ever received notice of any kind from any commissioner that a sale or trade of a player, which was within all of baseball's rules and followed all the custom and practice, would be disapproved?

A: No.

Dick O'Connell of the Red Sox:

Q: Mr. O'Connell, could you tell us of your dealings with Mr. Finley?

A: He called me and said, "This is Charlie's meat market. I have several good pieces of meat for sale and the price is a million dollars apiece." He named the players. After several more phone calls the Boston club agreed to buy Rudi and Fingers, each of them for $1 million.

Q: Did either of you say anything during these conversations to the effect that the assignments were subject to the approval of the Commissioner?

A: No.

Q: At the time you consummated the purchase of Rudi and Fingers, did you believe that your action was not in the best interests of baseball?

A: I thought it was in the best interests of the Boston club. That's all I was worried about.

Q: Did you conceive that the Commissioner might disapprove the sales?

A: Never entered my mind.

Q: Following Mr. Kuhn's decision, did you make this public statement: "We went by the baseball rules. How he can go against us is incomprehensible?"

A: I no doubt said that.

Q: Do you recall Mr. Yawkey [owner Tom Yawkey of the Red Sox] saying, "I don't know what the hell the Commissioner is basing his ruling on?"

A: I think I also have a recollection of that. What his exact words were, I still don't know because he was not in the ballpark at that time. He was in the hospital.

A veteran baseball writer, Fred Lieb, testified for Kuhn. The 89-year-old Lieb had remarkable recall. He began covering baseball in New York in 1911, nine years before Judge Landis's election, and in the previous quarter century had authored dozens of highly-regarded baseball books, most of them team histories. Because of his longevity he was summoned by the defense as the ultimate expert on interpreting the commissioner's "best interests" powers.

Q: Mr. Lieb, over the years, did you have occasion to talk baseball with Commissioner Landis?

A: Yes. We got quite intimate. When they were in New York, I invited the Judge and his wife to several shows. One, *The Earl Carroll Vanities*, was quite amusing because at that time they were beginning to get a little daring in the theater, and there was a nude who clung to the pendulum of a clock that swung back and forth. And where we were sitting there were merry-go-rounds and each had a single girl in it with her bare breasts just swirling around.

Judge McGarr: You have gotten into the only area more interesting than baseball. Go ahead.

A: Will Rogers was the head of *The Vanities* that year and chided the Judge about a game that was called because of darkness at 4:30 in the afternoon. So after the show I asked the Judge—I always called him Squire because that was what his wife called him—and I said, "How did you like the show?" He said, "Oh, fine. Will Rogers was just grand. I didn't mind him kidding me. Maybe I had it coming."

Then I asked Mrs. Landis what she thought of the show. And she said, "Well, Will Rogers was very funny but I would have preferred that the young ladies had worn a little more underwear."

A succession of owners and executives testified that Kuhn had unlimited power and that he was correct in nullifying the sales:

Walter O'Malley, Los Angeles; Ewing Kauffman, Kansas City; Ed
Fitzgerald, Milwaukee; Buzzie Bavasi, San Diego; John McHale,
Montreal; and former league presidents Warren Giles and Joe
Cronin, both recently retired.

Jerry Hoffberger of Baltimore, Finley's co-conspirator in the
aborted "Dump Bowie" movement, disagreed.

Q: Mr. Hoffberger, have you ever been notified by any commissioner that he felt he could prevent an assignment made within the
major league rules?

A: No.

Q: Have you ever been notified by any commissioner that he felt
he could act in whatever manner he determined, to maintain competitive balance between teams?

A: No.

Q: Has it been your experience that the "best interests" clause is
limited to acts of dishonesty, moral turpitude, or misconduct?

A: I always felt that is exactly why the clause is there and assumed
those reasons would be the only real reasons for the commissioner
acting under those rights.

Q: Does the commissioner have the power to deprive owners of
any of their property rights?

A: No.


Philip K. Wrigley, the longtime owner of the Chicago Cubs, had a
foot in each corner.

Q: There was a quote in the *Chicago Tribune* in which you reportedly said, "I don't see why the sales weren't approved. They were
according to the rules and regulations. I don't understand how the
Commissioner got mixed up in this in the first place."

A: I did say I didn't know how the Commissioner got into the act.
I very frankly said I thought the Commissioner made the wrong

decision. I also told the reporter I did not question the Commissioner's authority.

Q: Did Mr. Kuhn call you regarding your opinion?

A: He called after he had made his decision and said, "I understand you disagree with my opinion." I said, "Yes." I thought he had exceeded his authority. And then he said, "Are you questioning the Commissioner's authority?" I said, "No, I'm a member of the National League."

Q: Even if he decides it is in the best interest of baseball, can he determine who should be the stronger and who should be the weaker?

A: No.


Walter O'Malley was the most influential owner of the time and had sat on the Executive Council during the terms of four consecutive commissioners. It was widely held that Kuhn seldom made a significant decision without O'Malley's approval. "Walter O'Malley is the true commissioner of baseball, not Bowie Kuhn," insisted Bill Veeck. "Kuhn does what he is told."

Marvin Miller of the Players Association said he couldn't understand the furor. "Selling players for cash has been going on for decades. People have short memories. Connie Mack, in two different decades, dismantled his teams when he sold players for cash. People also forget that Babe Ruth was acquired by the Yankees for cash."

Miller believed the Finley sales were unshakable evidence of a player's value. If the Red Sox, for example, paid Finley $1 million for Rudi, they would be willing to deal directly with Rudi and give him an identical sum were he a free agent, in salary or as a signing bonus. The difference was that an owner would not be compensated.

Peter Bleakley, Kuhn's lead attorney, demonstrated that O'Malley, unlike Finley, had refused to bite the poisoned apple. O'Malley was then operating the Dodgers in Brooklyn, long before he struck gold in California.

Q: In 1953, did you receive a large cash offer for some of your star players?

A: You are referring, I take it, to the Bob Carpenter offer?

Q: Yes. Would you describe the Carpenter offer?

A: Mr. Carpenter owned the Philadelphia club in the National League. He knew I needed money and told me he was about to make the biggest offer ever made in the history of baseball. I became very attentive. He offered $650,000 for Roy Campanella, Duke Snider, and Gil Hodges, any two of them, and in addition would transfer five of his minor league players to the Brooklyn organization.

I had to chew on it. We had financial problems. The mortgage was due. Certain taxes had not been paid on the real estate. We very desperately needed money.

Buzzie Bavasi [then the Dodgers' general manager], when he heard about the amount, his eyes opened and he said, "What are you going to do about it?" I told him I would go up the street to the Brooklyn Trust Company, and see what sort of loan I can arrange. And if I can borrow money to solve our financial problems, that would be helpful in making the decision. I hocked everything I owned but it worked out all right. I told Mr. Carpenter I was flattered and intrigued by his offer but under no circumstances would I make the deal because I'd be breaking up our team.

Q: Is it important to have a strong commissioner?

A: My opinion is that we need a strong commissioner and that we would not be a self-disciplined, self-governed sport if we did not have one. We probably would be under a state or a federal athletic commission and that would be horrible.

Papiano, in a vigorous cross-examination, deflated the O'Malley balloon.

Q: Mr. O'Malley, you have stated that you thought the fans were the important reason for the refusal to allow the sales to go through, or that was one of your reasons, wasn't it?

A: Yes, I have very positive feelings about our responsibilities to the fans and this would have been a fraud on the fans to break up that team in the middle of the season.

Q: So, it would have been a fraud on the fans to move three players?

A: Whether it is one, three or ten. This particular transaction, in my thinking at the time, was that it would have been a fraud on the fans, on the public.

Q: Did you think it was a fraud on the fans when you moved your entire team from Brooklyn?

A: The Commissioner could have stopped it and we would have been bound by his decision.

Q: With respect to the commissioner's authority, is it within his authority or power to determine which team should be strengthened or which team should not be strengthened?

A: No, of course not. But I think he would have human feelings on it and I think he's got the power. But I doubt if any commissioner would be indiscreet enough to get into an act such as you're suggesting.

Finley's testimony consumed parts of two days. Initially, he said, he had tried for a straight one-for-one exchange. Rudi was offered to the Yankees for Thurman Munson, to Milwaukee for Darrell Porter, to Boston for Fred Lynn, to Texas for Jeff Burroughs, and to California for Frank Tanana. According to Finley, Bill Veeck of the Chicago White Sox and Brad Corbett of Texas were also trying to buy his stars minutes before the deadline. Veeck was interested in third baseman Sal Bando, Corbett in outfielder Don Baylor.

Q: What would happen if your unsigned players played out their options? Would Oakland get any compensation for the money they had invested in these players?

A: Nothing at all.

Q: When you first came into baseball as an owner and general manager, what was your understanding with respect to how you would go about making trades and sales?

A: It was a very simple understanding. If I cared to sell a ballplayer or buy a ballplayer, it was my prerogative, and by the same token if I wished to trade a player for a player, players and cash, any combination that I wished, I could make it, and the only thing that was necessary was once the deal was made between the two clubs, that each club would decide who would make out the official papers to be forwarded to the American League office and the Commissioner's office.

Q: Had you made sales and trades in reliance upon that understanding during the term you were in baseball?

A: Yes, for seventeen years.

Q: Prior to June 1976, had you received any notice in any fashion of a change in policy in relation to sales or trades as they are related to players who were playing out their options?

A: No.

Q: Did you, at the time of your sales, have any reason to believe that they were adverse to the integrity of the game of baseball?

A: Not at all.

Q: Did you follow the rules in making these sales?

A: One hundred percent.

Q: To your knowledge, during the time you have been in baseball, has any commissioner disapproved any sale or trade of any magnitude, or at any time, which was in accordance with the rules of baseball?

A: Not at all, not one.

Q: In your view are there any circumstances under which the commissioner could prevent an owner from selling his entire team for cash?

A: Not at all.

Q: Even if the owner intended to take the money and move to Brazil and reside there for the rest of his life?

A: I think that would be the owner's prerogative, to do whatever he wanted to do with his assets.

Q: When the Commissioner told you he was holding up the sales, did you tell him what you intended to do with the money you were receiving?

A: That was one of the most important things I brought to his attention. I told him I planned to use the money to sign young players and participate in the reentry draft of free agents.

Like Finley, Kuhn was on the stand for parts of two days.

Q: Is there any objective standard by which the term "the best interest of baseball" can be judged or determined?

A: I don't think it was intended to have objective standards. There are no standards, certainly when you try to evaluate what is in the best interest of baseball. You think of integrity and public confidence and the image of the game. You think of all those things. But I think in creating that concept in the Major League Agreement, the clubs were intending to give the commissioner very broad, very inclusive problems to deal with as they developed.

One of the things I must tell you that one has to wrestle with when he's commissioner of baseball, is the very breadth of those powers. They're awesome powers and one has got to use them with a kind of sensible and rational restraint that is necessary on the one hand, but on the other hand, they must be used in a way which will promote this game, and that encompasses so many things that if I tried to enumerate them I simply would not be able to cover them all. It's meant to very broad.

Judge McGarr: Before we go on, let me ask you a question, just to clear the air. I assume when you say you exercised your authority under the "best interests" clause, that you would agree with me, and I'm merely trying to sharpen this issue, there was no question of rules violations in these transactions in your mind?

A: That's correct.

McGarr: And there was no question, aside from the issue of the integrity of baseball, of moral turpitude on the part of any of the individuals involved?

A: That is correct.

Q (by Papiano): Is there any way that any owner, player or anyone else in baseball can determine the limits of your power?

A: I don't think there is any precise way. It's like the Chancellor's foot; its length is what he finds it to be, given the equities of the situation.

Q: Did you have any complaints from any of the clubs in either league about the sales of Rudi, Fingers and Blue?

A: I had no club call me and initiate a complaint.

Q: Isn't it true that Baltimore was the major competitor of New York and Boston in the Eastern Division?

A: I would say so.

Q: You didn't receive any complaint from Baltimore about upsetting competitive balance, did you?

A: I did not.

Q: Do you maintain a file on the ability of various players?

A: No.

Q: Is there any way for you tell how good a player is going to be for the remainder of the season, or for the next season?

A: I have to use my judgment.

Q: Do you have any scouting files as to the relative ability of the players?

A: No.

Q: Do you have any files as to how a particular player would fit into a particular team?

A: No.

Q: How do you define competitive balance, Mr. Kuhn?

A: In general, I would say competitive balance in professional baseball means having the maximum number of teams in competition for divisional championships, pennants and world championships.

Q: Does it mean that one team should not be dominant in its division or league?

A: Yes, I would say so.

Q: Prior to 1976, wasn't Oakland dominant in its division?

A: Yes, and that's an example of our efforts to achieve competitive balance not working as well as they should.

The proceedings ended on January 13, 1977. Kuhn was the final witness. Judge McGarr, in closing, said:

"Thank you, gentlemen, it's been a very interesting trial. I've enjoyed it. It's drawn the biggest crowd this courtroom has ever seen. If we had either tickets or a popcorn concession, we could have cleaned up. I commend you on a job well done. I'll rule on it as quickly as I can."

Judge McGarr announced his decision two months later, on March 17. His ruling, in part:

"The fact that this case has commanded a great deal of attention in the vociferous world of baseball fans, and has provoked widespread and not always unemotional discussion, tends to obscure the relative simplicity of the legal issues involved. The case is not a

Finley-Kuhn popularity contest. Neither is it an appellate judicial review of Bowie Kuhn's actions. The question before the court is not whether Bowie Kuhn was wise to do what he did, but rather whether he had the authority."

Judge McGarr cited Article 1, Section 2 of the Major League Agreement:

"The functions of the Commissioner shall be as follows:

"(a) To investigate, either upon complaint or upon his own initiative, any act, transaction or practice charged, alleged or suspected to be detrimental to the best interests of the national game of baseball.

"(b) To determine, after investigation, what preventive, remedial or punitive action is appropriate in the premises, and to take such either against Major Leagues, Major League Clubs or individuals, as the case may be."

Also, he cited Article 7, Section 2:

"The Major Leagues and their constituent clubs severally agree to be bound by the decisions of the Commissioner, and the discipline imposed by him under the provisions of this Agreement, and severally waive such right of recourse to the courts as would otherwise have existed in their favor."

Judge McGarr continued:

"The questionable wisdom of this broad delegation of power is not before the court. What the parties intended is. And what the parties clearly intended was that the commissioner was to have jurisdiction to prevent any conduct destructive of the confidence of the public in the integrity of baseball. So broad and unfettered was his discretion intended to be that they provided no right of appeal, and even took the extreme step of foreclosing their own access to the courts.

"Accordingly, it is the judgment of this court that plaintiff Charles O. Finley & Co., Inc., has failed to sustain the allegations of its complaint, and the relief sought therein is denied. Judgment is consequently entered for defendant Bowie K. Kuhn."

Five days later, George Steinbrenner of the Yankees, in an interview with *The New York Times*, expressed second thoughts.

"I like the Commissioner," said Steinbrenner "but no one man should have the power the baseball constitution gives the Commissioner's office. It's too much power."

Many owners and high echelon executives silently agreed with Steinbrenner, including some who testified for Kuhn. Later, some of them admitted they had stretched the truth. "Sure, we lied," an owner told me a week later on the condition of anonymity. "We were codefendants. What did you expect us to do?"

At the time and for many years thereafter, the almost unanimous opinion among baseball insiders was that Finley had been bamboozled out of $3.5 million. He sold his club three years later to the Levi Strauss heirs for $12.7 million.

# BOWIE KUHN
## PART V

Having won in Chicago where Judge McGarr decided the commissioner's powers were absolute, a month later a Georgia federal judge, Newell Edenfield, sitting in Atlanta, came down with an opposite opinion after hearing a lesser challenge from Ted Turner, owner of the Atlanta Braves.

Like Finley, Turner was a maverick, in his rookie season as a mogul. Bowie Kuhn welcomed him with a one-year suspension and a $10,000 fine for "tampering" with Gary Matthews, a power-hitting outfielder. In addition, Kuhn ruled the Braves would be deprived of their first round choice in the impending summer draft of amateur free agents.

Kuhn announced this decision on January 2, in the midst of the Finley trial. This action was generally interpreted as an effort to demonstrate to Judge McGarr the constant vigilance and discipline required against errant owners. Turner was charged with "improper conduct" in his pursuit of Matthews, who was planning to file for free agency but was then still under contract to the San Francisco Giants.

During a World Series media party, Turner told San Francisco owner Bob Lurie, an indomitable Kuhn supporter, "No matter what you offer Matthews, I'll do better."

Judge Edenfield, genuinely beloved by his constituency, heard the case in two days, on April 28 and 29, and chided Judge McGarr for stretching the Finley proceedings to two weeks.

During Kuhn's testimony, Judge Edenfield asked the Commissioner if he had taken into consideration that Turner may have been drinking when he had spoken to Lurie.

Replied the schoolmaster, "A good deal of baseball business, wisely or unwisely, is carried on by people who have been drinking. If we had two sets of rules, the result would be a shambles."

The 38-year-old Turner insisted the "punishment doesn't fit the crime." Turner took the stand as his only witness. During the cross-examination by attorney Richard Wortheimer, Turner became angry with Wortheimer's questions and told him, "Keep that up and when this is over you'll get a knuckle sandwich."

Judge Edenfield, in his May 19 decision, ruled that Kuhn had the authority to fine and suspend an owner but was out of bounds in trying to strip the Braves of a draft choice because there was no such provision in the Major League Agreement.

Judge Edenfield, who often flavored his decisions with colorful language, wrote:

"The whole case was one in which a casual observer might say was a comedy of errors . . . an Indian massacre in which the Braves took nary a scalp but lived to see their own dangling from the lodgepole of the Commissioner apparently only as a grisly warning to others."

Kuhn's attorneys hailed this as a "95 percent" victory. Judge Edenfield disagreed. In an interview with the *Chicago Sun-Times*, he said, "I went the other way from Judge McGarr. Commissioner Kuhn's got a lot more power than anyone I know, but it's not absolute."

Turner had the last word. "I'm never going to another baseball cocktail party in my life," he told Robert Markus of the *Chicago Tribune*. "I'm new in baseball, I didn't know all the rules. Couldn't they have taken me aside and told me that wasn't the way we do things here? They didn't have to grind me under their boot, like I was a draft dodger or up for manslaughter."

A week before Judge Edenfield's decision, when Turner's suspension was in abeyance, Turner provided some comic relief. Frustrated by the Braves' sixteen-game losing streak, he joined the club in Pittsburgh, suited up, and announced he had relieved field manager Dave Bristol whom he dispatched on a ten-day scouting mission.

A hands-on pioneer in the cable television industry, Turner said he wanted to manage the club because some fans had been asking why the Braves were losing. "I know we've had an unlucky string of injuries," Turner explained. "But I want to find out for myself."

Turner was the fifth owner without previous experience as a professional player to descend into the dugout. The others were Chris Von Der Ahe who managed the St. Louis Browns for parts of three seasons; Charlie Ebbets who managed 110 games and finished the 1898 season as the skipper of the Brooklyn Dodgers; Horace Fogel, who directed the New York Giants for 44 games in 1902; and Judge Emil Fuchs of the old Boston Braves, who spent the entire 1929 season managing his team. Short on funds, Fuchs replaced Rogers Hornsby prior to the season with the declaration, "I don't think we can do any worse." (And they didn't: The Braves won six games more than they had in 1928, improving to 56–98.)

The Atlanta slump continued. With Turner at the helm, the Braves lost to the Pirates, 2–1.

"I had the best seat in the house," Turner said after the game. "Managing isn't all that difficult. All you've got to do is score more runs than the other guy."

Kuhn held his tongue, deciding it was a league matter. The next morning National League president Chub Feeney benched Turner. Feeney also took the occasion to rebuke Turner for playing poker with his players.

"This means we have two classes of people in baseball—players and owners, and no fraternization," Turner told reporters. "Sure, I played cards with my players. I chased girls with them, too. You shouldn't be penalized for being friendly with people."

Finley couldn't resist. He called Turner and invited him to be his "guest" manager.

"Charlie said, it would help his gate," Turner reported. "But if I can't manage my own team, how can I manage his?"

When Turner appealed the Feeney decision, a reluctant Kuhn, weary of confrontations with Turner, entered the dispute. He upheld Feeney.

Three years earlier in another widely-publicized rhubarb involving home run king Hank Aaron, Kuhn had made a decision that was particularly unpopular in Atlanta.

Aaron had finished the 1973 season with 713 home runs, one short of Babe Ruth's career record. Bill Bartholomay, then the Atlanta owner—this was before his group sold to Turner—wanted Aaron to break the record at home, not on the road. The Braves were scheduled to open the season with a three-game series in Cincinnati. Bartholomay announced that Aaron would not play in Cincinnati. It would be an accommodation to the Atlanta fans, in addition to a windfall at the gate.

Kuhn contended the integrity of the game would be sacrificed. With Aaron out of the lineup, the Braves would not be giving their best efforts. The pursuit of individual records, however sacred, are secondary. Bartholomay was advised that failure to comply would necessitate the imposition of penalties.

Ordinarily a peaceable sort, Bartholomay described Kuhn's intervention as "unprecedented, an intrusion," and sent records to the
Commissioner's office that showed the Braves, against Cincinnati,
were at least as strong, if not stronger when Aaron was used only as
a pinch-hitter. Also, making out the lineup was the responsibility of
field manager Eddie Mathews and not within Kuhn's jurisdiction.

"Barring disability, I will expect the Braves to use Henry Aaron in
the opening series in Cincinnati," the Commissioner announced.

Most sportswriters sided with Kuhn and accused the Braves of
"commercialism." The erudite Leonard Koppett supported Bartholomay and asked, "If Kuhn orders Aaron to play the first three games in
Cincinnati, would he also 'order' him to hit a home run? And if Aaron
does not hit a home run, will he then be suspected of giving less than
his best?"

The question became moot. Aaron responded with a home run
over the left field fence, on his first swing off Jack Billingham, the
Cincinnati starter. Aaron was hitless in two subsequent at bats,
didn't play in the second game, and was 0 for 3 in the series finale.
He broke Ruth's record in the Atlanta home opener the next night,
connecting off the Dodgers' Al Downing before a record crowd of
53,775.

The Commissioner, accompanied by his wife, Luisa, witnessed
Aaron's record-tying home run in Cincinnati but did not make the
trip to Atlanta. As Kuhn explained later, "Having seen Aaron hit
Number 714, I felt no obligation to follow him day by day until Number 715 came along."

Aaron considered it a snub. It was many years before he forgave him.

In 1980, when Aaron was to be honored at a banquet for providing the most memorable baseball moment of the '70s, he refused to
attend after learning Kuhn would be making the trophy presenta-

tion. "What am I supposed to do?" Aaron said. "Scratch my head and forget what happened in 1974?"

Kuhn also ran afoul of two other former superstars. In 1979, following an announcement that Willie Mays had signed a 10-year contract with a gambling casino in Atlantic City, the Commissioner tried to dissuade him. Kuhn telegrammed:

"While I can appreciate the motivation leading you to this association, it has long been my view that such associations by people in our game are inconsistent with its best interests. Accordingly, I must request that you promptly disassociate yourself from the New York Mets. I hope you will elect to continue with the Mets."

Mays insisted he would not be directly involved with the casino's gambling operation: his duties were promotional, visiting children in hospitals, general "community work," and participating in golf outings. His contract with Bally International was for $100,000 a year, twice his pay with the Mets.

"I've been a model for baseball for twenty-two years," Mays replied. "But now I have to think primarily of my family."

Three years later, in an identical situation, Kuhn also gave Mickey Mantle the pink slip. Mantle, a $100,000 spring training coach with the Yankees, had agreed to work for the Claridge Hotel and Casino, also in Atlantic City. "I told Mickey I had no choice," Kuhn said in a prepared statement. "Baseball and casino employment are inconsistent."

"I wasn't doing that much in baseball, anyway," Mantle said. "I don't have any hard feelings toward the Commissioner. But he should understand that I'm not going to be standing in front of the hotel saying, 'Come in and gamble.'"

Kuhn's puritanical views were put to a vote only once. Following the same principle, he blocked the impending 1980 sale of the White Sox to Edward J. DeBartolo, Sr., 69, a multimillionaire whose privately held corporation reportedly owned 49 percent of the nation's shopping malls as well as banks and hotels. DeBartolo's fortune was estimated at $500 million.

DeBartolo's empire also included ownership, in full or in part, of three thoroughbred racetracks. Kuhn's objection was twofold. He didn't approve of DeBartolo's turf connections; also he was against absentee ownership. DeBartolo's home was in Youngstown, Ohio.

A comment DeBartolo had made earlier about his desire to put a big league franchise in New Orleans prompted additional fears that he might try to move the White Sox. In response, DeBartolo offered a $5 million indemnity against any transfer of the club out of Chicago. "If that isn't enough," DeBartolo said, "I'll make it $20 million."

Bill Veeck, a longtime Kuhn antagonist who had accepted DeBartolo's $20 million purchase, reacted with outrage. Veeck pointed out that five club owners were headquartered in cities other than where their franchise was located, and that George Steinbrenner of the Yankees and the Galbreath family in Pittsburgh, were up to their hip boots in the horse racing business. Concurrently, Kuhn was not challenging the impending sale of the Seattle Mariners to George Argyros, a resident of faraway Newport Beach, California, who also owned horses.

By a vote of 8–6, two short of acceptance, the American League owners rejected DeBartolo's bid on October 24, during a meeting in Chicago. A month later DeBartolo, in a letter to Kuhn, said he would sell his racetracks "in the shortest possible time, even if it means a loss." He also vowed to spend at least 20 percent of his time in Chicago.

As he had done in nullifying the Finley player sales, the all-knowing czar went into left field and looked into his crystal ball. Groping, he emerged with an unprecedented requirement for ownership: the degree of commitment.

In a reply to DeBartolo's letter, Kuhn wrote:

"As I have stated to your representatives on several occasions, I fully concur with the league regarding the problems presented by your application. Local ownership and racetrack operations were two of these.

"In addition, there are the complications of a busy man like yourself with nationwide business interests being able to devote the necessary time to the resuscitation of the White Sox franchise. While I have no question you would do the best you can, it still leaves to a matter of judgment whether the commitment would be sufficient."

A second and final vote was taken on December 11, at the Winter Meetings in Dallas. DeBartolo was a decisive loser; eleven of the fourteen clubs voted against him. It was a triumph for Kuhn but not without nasty implications. Kuhn was accused of an anti-Italian bias and, worse, the suspicion that the rejection indicated that DeBartolo had sinister business partners.

Having buried Veeck's preferred buyer, the Commissioner and the American League were susceptible to Veeck's threat of litigation. Nick Kladis, a member of the White Sox board, said Kuhn would be sued for triple damages, $60 million, if the club couldn't be sold, pronto! This was not a problem. Kuhn's buyer was in the wings.

Four weeks later the purchase was consummated by a group headed by Jerry Reinsdorf and Eddie Einhorn which matched the DeBartolo offer. Reinsdorf, a Brooklyn native, had grown roots in the Chicago area after he had graduated from Northwestern University twenty years earlier. Coaching Reinsdorf, advising him daily how to put his group together for certain approval, was Bud Selig of the Milwaukee Brewers, a staunch Kuhn supporter. Six days later, on January 14, 1981, Argyros bought the Seattle Mariners.

The DeBartolo rejection was never satisfactorily explained publicly, beyond the limp complaint of absentee ownership and his turf

connections. Many years later, Clark Griffith, who had been an executive with the Minnesota Twins, said the third strike against
DeBartolo was that Kuhn's investigators reported he was a high
stakes gambler.

Whatever, some owners were convinced that Kuhn, ostensibly
shooting at DeBartolo, was aiming at Veeck. Had DeBartolo been
approved, Veeck would have remained with the White Sox in an
advisory capacity. Looking ahead, Kuhn wanted a buyer who would
be a companionable ally, ready and eager to pledge unswerving
devotion, especially when the Commissioner's contract would be up
for renewal. Reinsdorf was the better fit. Like many men in power,
Kuhn was uneasy and constantly counting the votes. He could be
unseated by a thin one-fourth minority in either league.

The rebellion began that summer after a fifty-day players' strike:
712 games were canceled, the middle-third of the 1981 season. It was
the longest stoppage, to that time, in baseball history.

In previous negotiations, Kuhn had been an active and beneficial
participant. In 1969 he helped resolve a pension dispute and, in
1976, to the dismay of many owners, some of whom never forgave
him, ordered them to lift their spring training lockout. On both occasions he was lauded for his "patriotism." Even Miller publicly credited him with an assist.

Contrary to his oft-stated dictum, "power unused is valueless,"
Kuhn was a mere spectator during the 1981 shutdown.

The dispute was over compensation for free agents. Kuhn realized
the importance of this issue and later insisted that because he had
suasion over the owners only, he didn't attempt to coerce them into
avoiding a strike at all costs because he had no authority to order the
Players Association to do the same.

He was publicly silenced in May during a judicial hearing in
Rochester, New York. The players had sought an injunction to

prevent the owners from implementing their compensation proposal. In a successful effort to deny the injunction, management attorneys testified that labor disputes were not within the commissioner's purview, that this authority was solely invested in the owners' Player Relations Committee, a separate corporation which was management's exclusive bargaining agent with the union.

It was a weak argument. The PRC had been formed in 1967, during Eckert's term, in an effort to isolate the commissioner, to prevent his intervention. During the previous eleven years of his administration, Kuhn never acknowledged the quarantine and had functioned in the capacity of paterfamilias—father of the baseball family, a neutral force who could administer in the best interests of the fan. Kuhn's sudden withdrawal was among his biggest mistakes.

The 1981 strike was a holdover from the previous year when both sides were unable to complete settlement on a new four-year Basic Agreement, the collective contract that binds the owners and players together. Compensation for free agents was left unresolved. A 1980 Memorandum of Agreement was approved with the condition that the compensation problem would be tabled and settled separately.

When the Messersmith decision had gone into effect four years earlier, the only compensation a team losing a player to free agency received from the signing team was a choice in the June draft of amateur high school and college players. The owners maintained that this was not an adequate return. On an average, only 8 percent of these players surfaced to the big leagues. To soften the loss of a free agent, they demanded that the acquiring club yield a professional player in the exchange.

Miller argued this subverted free agency; it was not designed as a "trade" and would severely reduce the bargaining strength and mobility of a player eligible to make a new connection.

The Memorandum of Agreement forestalled the threat of a player strike. Included was the stipulation that if the parties couldn't agree, management had the right to announce during the period of February 16–19, 1981, that it would put its compensation proposal into effect for the coming season. The union, if dissatisfied, was entitled to serve notice by March 1 that it planned to strike, the walkout to begin no later than June 1.

The Players Association filed an unfair practice charge with the National Labor Relations Board on May 7, after management implemented its compensation proposal. On May 27, three days before the strike deadline, the NLRB upheld the union's request. The NLRB would seek a temporary restraining order to delay the stoppage.

On June 6, while awaiting a court decision, Miller countered with a "pool" proposal. Instead of direct compensation from the signing club, each major league team would be allowed to protect an as yet undetermined number of players and all remaining talent would be placed in a vast pool. Compensation players would be selected from this pool.

Four days later Judge Henry Werker of the U.S. District Court in Manhattan, sitting in Rochester, denied the injunction. Miller responded by distributing a strike memorandum to the players:

"As directed by the executive board's unanimous decision, no games will be played on Friday, June 12, or thereafter until a settlement is reached and approved by the players."

Peace came seven weeks later, on July 31, almost immediately after the owners had received their final strike insurance payments. To protect themselves in the event of a shutdown, they had taken out $50 million in strike insurance at a cost of $2.2 million, a small price considering the odds. Most of it was placed through Lloyds of London, obviously a baseball innocent.

In addition, the owners had squirreled $10 to $15 million in a mutual assistance fund that had been created two years earlier. Each franchise was assessed 2 percent of its gate receipts. Because of this foresight, several of the small-market clubs suffered little, if any, financial damage.

Crowed Calvin Griffith, the parsimonious owner of the Minnesota Twins, "I think we came out ahead."

The players were the clear winners. Miller's request for a compensation pool was granted. The owners agreed to a complex procedure for so-called Type A and B players, determined by a statistical formula. Basically, a team could protect only twenty-four players in its entire organization. All the other players were dumped into a pool, available to the clubs losing players through free agency. The owners also agreed to credit the players with full service time during the strike.

Kuhn was the biggest loser. Several owners, who as always, wanted it both ways, expressed displeasure that the Commissioner was not openly involved in helping settle the strike. During the playoffs and World Series, a succession of published reports indicated that the Commissioner's support was dwindling.

The rebellion broke into the open in mid-December during the Winter Meetings in Hollywood, Florida, with the disclosure that nine owners had signed a letter calling for Kuhn's resignation. The letter was shredded but there seemed to be no question about the identity of the signatories:

Gussie Busch, Jr., St. Louis; William Williams, Cincinnati; John McMullen, Houston; Ballard Smith, San Diego; Nelson Doubleday, New York Mets; George Steinbrenner, New York Yankees; Edward Bennett Williams, Baltimore; Eddie Chiles, Texas; and George Argyros, Seattle.

Reinsdorf of the White Sox twice was invited to join the revolt but declined. His debt to Kuhn for the White Sox franchise had been paid.

The drama had opened several weeks earlier with a top-secret meeting of the nine rebels at the Grand Hyatt in New York City. A one-page document urging Kuhn to resign was drafted and signed. Three owners were designated as postmen. Copies were to be simultaneously hand-delivered to Kuhn, as he sat peaceably at his desk in New York; to owner John Fetzer in Detroit; and to the Pirates' Dan Galbreath in either Pittsburgh or at his home in Columbus, Ohio. Fetzer and Galbreath were members of the Executive Council, Kuhn's advisory body.

At the eleventh hour, the rebels had second thoughts. The plan was changed. Delivery was delayed. It was then agreed delivery would be made at a specially arranged luncheon on December 10, in the midst of the Winter Meetings. By the time the luncheon was held—Fetzer was present but not Galbreath—the rebels had blown their cover. Milton Richman of United Press International broke the story.

At 2:30 the next morning, the phone rang in room 738 at the headquarter Diplomat Hotel.

"Ballard, is it true nine clubs are against renewal?" the Dodgers' Peter O'Malley asked Ballard Smith of the San Diego Padres.

As his late father had done six years before in Milwaukee, Peter O'Malley sounded the alarm. In less than an hour, the principal Kuhn loyalists assembled in the suite of American League president Lee MacPhail to devise a strategy.

Selig, as always, was the first to answer the summons. Bill Giles, recently christened by Kuhn as the owner of the Philadelphia Phillies, came on the run. Giles, whose father, Warren, had been National League president for eighteen years, was at a hotel a half-mile away. Also in attendance were John McHale of Montreal, Bob Lurie of San Francisco, and National League president Chub Feeney. Galbreath couldn't be reached. Fetzer was given a pass.

"Mr. Fetzer is 82 years old," Selig said. "And out of the normal course of decency you don't wake up an 82-year-old man at three o'clock in the morning."

The factions met head-to-head, in midmorning, at a regularly-scheduled National League meeting. Lurie asked Lou Susman about the letter. Susman, a young St. Louis attorney, was leading the mutiny. Handsome, vigorous and an excellent tennis player, Susman looked like an advertisement out of *Gentleman's Quarterly*. He was Busch's consigliere, constantly at his side. Some owners believed Susman also had his own agenda. For whatever reasons, he had a strong dislike for Kuhn.

"What the hell are we supposed to do?" Lurie shouted. "Sign it in blood!"

Susman pulled a sheet of paper from his attaché case, held it aloft, and announced, "Gentlemen, if it will make you more comfortable, I'll tear it up."

The evidence, torn in shreds, fluttered to the mahogany conference table.

"Mr. Susman tore it up in front of everybody," reported Andrew McKenna, president of the Chicago Cubs who sat on the board of a dozen Chicago area corporations. "I've seen that trick before. He said it was the letter but it could have been a blank piece of paper."

The anti-Kuhn forces, if they held, had more than enough votes to prevent Kuhn from a third term. One-fourth of the owners in either league, four in the twelve-team National League or five in the fourteen-team American League, was sufficient. Six of the signatories were from the National League. Kuhn was devastated, especially after learning that two of these clubs, St. Louis and Cincinnati, both held by hard-core conservatives and previously supportive, were calling for his ouster.

Some of the owners had personal vendettas. John McMullen of

Houston, for example, was angry because Kuhn had ignored him at a banquet. McMullen's primary complaint was that some owners were "in" the mainstream, appointed to committees, and others were "out." It was an accurate observation. From the beginning, Kuhn had cultivated the owners whom he perceived as the most influential.

Considering his political acumen, it was a remarkable blunder. Kuhn had forgotten that every owner, despite his degree of influence, had a vote. Kuhn immediately reduced the ranks of the dissidents by appointing Edward Bennett Williams and Ballard Smith to the Executive Council. Once on the inside, they switched camps and pledged fealty to the czar.

According to the rules, a commissioner's renewal could be voted on fifteen months prior to the expiration of his term. Kuhn still had twenty months to go. His termination date was August 13, 1983. With time on their side, the loyalists refused to yield. Six months later, during a two-day joint meeting, held on June 14 and 15, 1982 in Chicago, Kuhn's reelection was not on the agenda. Peace seem to be restored. But more than likely neither side was certain it had enough votes. Revenue sharing and restructuring were the principal topics. Kuhn described it as the most "constructive meeting in my thirteen or fourteen years as Commissioner." He was in complete accord with the proposed changes, which he said, "would significantly strengthen the Commissioner's office."

Kuhn and his followers were dreaming. The next joint meeting was held on August 18. Eager to end the Kuhn stalemate, a compromise was approved: A Chief Operating Officer, Business Affairs (acronym COOBA) would be hired, a co-Commissioner who would oversee network television contracts, marketing, promotion, films, licensing, long-range planning, revenue sharing, and office administration. His annual salary would be $300,000—$100,000 more than Kuhn's wage.

This prompted one of Kuhn's aides to comment "It looks like the party is over for us."

But the COOBA proposal included a sweetener. If Kuhn was willing to accept this solution, he would be extended for four more years, including the year remaining on his contract. Hanging in, aware his survival was now linked to the COOBA, Kuhn fudged and said, "There is room for both a chief executive officer [the Commissioner] and for a chief operating officer [the COOBA]."

The COOBA proposal, with Kuhn riding shotgun, was put to a vote on November 1, in Chicago, and failed to draw the necessary three-fourths majority. The American League approved 11–3. But the vote in the National League was 7–5, two short of the requirement. Opposing were Atlanta, Cincinnati, Houston, New York, and St. Louis in the National League, and Texas, Seattle, and possibly the Yankees in the American.

Kuhn expressed amusement and some satisfaction that the combined vote was 18–8 in his favor. "After fourteen years, I got 70 percent of the vote," he said. "In anywhere but baseball that's a landslide."

A good soldier, Kuhn immediately announced he would be willing to serve out his term and also cautioned against a COOBA which, he said "would diminish the office of the commissioner by turning it into a 'dual' situation."

Kuhn was now a lame-duck czar but the infighting continued for sixteen more months. Bud Selig, appointed chairman of the Search Committee, fiddled in the belief that, in time, Kuhn would be resurrected, reelected for a third term. Selig listed Kuhn among the candidates. The quest proceeded at a funereal pace, two steps forward, one backward.

Finally, Selig, forced to look elsewhere, found his man. The new czar was elected on March 3, 1984, with the understanding that he would not take office until October 1. Kuhn agreed to stay on in an interim capacity for the next seven months, or until his successor was available.

"Bowie deserves a lot of credit. He rode the tiger for fifteen years," Lou Hoynes, the former National League attorney, said years later.

In retrospect, Kuhn's reign, despite the union gains, appeared to be an era of unprecedented affluence. Attendance records were broken nine times. The annual network television revenue increased twelve-fold, from $15.5 million to $183 million. The average player salary in this same period, from 1969 through 1984, multiplied by thirteen times, from $24,909 to $329,408. Nonetheless, some owners, as they often do, insisted the industry was in financial distress, insisted a businessman was needed at the top.

Peter V. Ueberroth, who was to be both a curse and a blessing, was about to mount the throne.

# 16 PETER UEBERROTH
## PART I

U
nlike any commissioner since Judge Landis, Peter Victor
Ueberroth, from the beginning, made it clear he was not
working for the owners. The way he saw it—and he told
them more than once—they were working for him. Privately, he
expressed disdain for the lot of them with the exception of Bob
Lurie of San Francisco, a golf companion who had put his name in
nomination. The owners were "stupid," Ueberroth insisted, for
awarding their players long-term multimillion dollar contracts.

Ueberroth, 47, showed them how to increase revenues while
simultaneously lowering player costs. The solution was simple: Do
not enter into bidding wars for free agents. Grateful, they followed
his instructions. To their surprise and subsequent dismay, the
Players Association accused them of collusion. They were guilty, as
charged. An arbitrator clubbed them with a $280 million fine, the
biggest single penalty in history of sports.

Ueberroth was late in arriving—he was elected baseball's sixth
commissioner seven months before he took office—and yet he was
early in departing. In June of 1988, a year and a half before his con-

tract expired, he announced he would not accept another five-year term. It was not a tearful farewell.

Still, the owners profited from the experience. Ueberroth demonstrated the economic value of corporate sponsorship, which he had learned from his previous assignment as president of the Organizing Committee for the Los Angeles Summer Olympics. Starting from nil in 1985, he increased the owners' annual licensing and merchandising income to $36 million during his four and a half year term. But the Olympic flame, not baseball, is Ueberroth's legacy.

He had orchestrated an opening Olympic pageant of unprecedented proportions and crossed the finish line with a $215 million surplus, a remarkable windfall considering his predecessors almost always had a deficit. He was, and remains today, sports' all-time marketing champion.

To induce him to come aboard, the owners agreed to several significant concessions. They dumped the COOBA proposal and recognized the commissioner as baseball's chief executive officer with all departments under his iron heel; reelection no longer would require a three-fourths majority, the rule that toppled Kuhn. Instead, a simple majority would be necessary, provided there was approval from at least five teams from each league. The owners also granted him the power to penalize clubs up to $250,000. The previous limit had been $5,000.

"He knew how badly we wanted him," Jerry Reinsdorf of the White Sox observed. "He would have been dumb if he hadn't demanded the right to dictate the terms. He is a man of affluence and didn't need the job."

A workaholic who captured the American dream, Ueberroth was born on September 2, 1937, in Evanston, Illinois, the second child of Victor and Laura Ueberroth. His mother died of leukemia when he was four. His father, a traveling salesman of aluminum products, was constantly relocating the family. After sojourns in Wisconsin, Iowa, and Pennsylvania, the family settled in Burlingame, California.

His father, "a tough taskmaster," kept a stack of newspapers and encyclopedias next to the family dinner table. Daily, he would quiz Peter, his older sister, Jill, and his stepbrother, John, on a variety of subjects.

"This inevitably led to heated discussions," Ueberroth recalled in his aptly-titled 1985 autobiography, *Made in America*, an account of his Olympic success. "We learned to articulate various points of view. On some occasions Dad would be the debater, on others the moderator. For someone with less than a high school education, his knowledge seemed endless. He insisted we pay attention to what was happening in the world."

Up at dawn, delivering newspapers, Ueberroth was self-supporting when he entered high school. In his sophomore year he moved away from home to live and work at Twelveacres, a nearby orphanage for children from broken homes. He earned $125 a month as its recreation director.

He played on the high school basketball, football, and swimming teams. Water polo was his best sport. He captained the water polo team in his freshman year at San Jose State, twice leading his conference in scoring. He entered the U.S. Olympic Trials for the 1956 Games but didn't make the first team. His nose, slightly off center, was broken seven times in water polo matches.

In 1959, the same year he was graduated from San Jose State, he married his college sweetheart, the former Virginia Mae Nicolau, the daughter of a Long Beach baker. A month later the couple moved to Hawaii, into a one-room apartment, so small, his wife later said, "We could stand in the center of the room and reach out and almost touch all four walls."

Ueberroth plunged into the travel business. In 1963, starting with

capital of $5,000 and one employee, he founded the First Travel
Corporation and built the company into a giant, the second largest
travel business in North America. When he sold the business in 1980
it had 1,500 employees and annual revenues of $300 million. He had
a simple business philosophy: "Always deal directly with the top
executive."

Ueberroth assumed his Olympic assignment with apprehension.
For the first time, the Olympics had to be privately funded. An
amendment to the Los Angeles charter prevented federal subsidies.
Worse, lotteries, a traditional and lucrative source of revenue, were
illegal in California. Ueberroth took office on April 1, 1979, without
employees and with a bank account of $100 of his own money.

Against the advice of his aides, he offered the Olympic television
rights through blind bids and landed a $225 million network contract.
The sale of foreign broadcast rights brought another $75 million. Cor-
porate sponsorships accounted for an additional $120 million.
Whereas the 1980 Winter Games in Lake Placid had attracted 381
corporate sponsors, Ueberroth reduced the number to thirty and
raised the minimum price to an unprecedented minimum of $4 mil-
lion. Coca Cola paid $12.6 million.

This was followed with an innovative 82-day relay of the Olympic
torch across the country with each participant or his sponsor donat-
ing $3,000 for the privilege of carrying the flame five-eighths of a
mile. An estimated forty million people turned out to watch the
torch pass by. The original purpose was to raise funds but there was
an enormous ripple effect. It rekindled patriotism and fueled enthusiasm for the Games. *Time* magazine named him Man of the Year for
1984. He received hundreds of letters urging him to run for
President of the United States.

Hired by baseball at an annual salary of $450,000, the owners
embraced him without equivocation despite his chilly persona and

aggressive and sometimes abrasive style. The only dissenter was Calvin Griffith, the Minnesota curmudgeon. When Detroit's John Fetzer was trying to persuade Griffith to support Ueberroth. Fetzer emphasized Ueberroth's success with the Olympics, Griffith replied:

"Success? Hell. Anybody could do that if you've got 10,000 people working for you, all of them working for nothing."

Imperious, often intimidating, fastidious, and with a strong sense of family priority, Ueberroth was in absolute control during his Olympic assignment. Nobody owned the Olympics. Baseball was different; twenty-six well-heeled individuals, or the corporations they represented, held title to the major league franchises.

Before ascending the throne, Ueberroth said, if elected, "My job would be to make the sport better, not only for the owners but for the players, managers, coaches, minor leaguers, and most important for the fans."

He was not the first commissioner to pledge allegiance to all, but it soon became apparent that he would rule without consultation. His first crisis surfaced on October 1, 1984, less than twenty-four hours after he had assumed command. Richie Phillips, general counsel for the sixty-member Major League Baseball Umpires Association, announced the umpires would strike the playoffs and World Series if they did not receive an additional $340,000 for their postseason work.

The umpires struck on the eve of the playoffs. Initially, Ueberroth assigned the league presidents to negotiate. When they were unable to settle, he took over. Agreement was reached prior to the World Series. He sided with the hired help. It was a bonanza for the umpires. He gave them a 100 percent boost in postseason compensation and annual individual salary increases of $5,000, a three-year package at the cost of an estimated $1.2 million. The owners were stunned but silent.

A hairy-chested lot, seldom sentimentally inclined, the umpires finally had found a champion. The next spring training, at an exhibition game in Phoenix, veteran American League umpire Joe Brinkman hurried to his side. Brinkman, who operates an umpires' school in Cocoa, Florida, presented the Commissioner with a photograph of "Ueberroth Hall," a classroom named in his honor.

"You did more for the umpires in four days than anybody did in a lifetime," Brinkman told him. "Now every young umpire coming through this school will know who Peter Ueberroth is."

Baseball's Robin Hood struck again less than a year later. After six months of inconclusive bargaining, the executive board of the Players Association, meeting in Chicago on July 15, 1985, set an August 6 strike date. The stalemate was caused by the players' request for an increase of the owners' annual pension payment from $15.5 million to $60 million. This would maintain the union's one-third traditional share of the network television revenue which had ballooned to $183 million annually.

With the strike deadline approaching, the four owners on the executive board of management's Player Relations Committee assembled in New York City: Bud Selig of Milwaukee; Edward Bennett Williams, Baltimore; John McMullen, Houston; and Peter O'Malley, Los Angeles. On August 4, two days after their arrival, both sides offered compromise proposals.

The owners modified their benefit plan contribution but linked it to a change in the players' eligibility requirement for salary arbitration, with the added provision that an arbitrator's award could not exceed 100 percent of the player's previous wage. This proposal, according to owner estimates, would have resulted in a minimum saving of $1 million for each club, approximately $25 million a year.

The union rejected this demand but agreed to accept less than one-third of the television revenue if the owners would put the difference into a fund to help the so-called "disadvantaged" clubs. This was an early attempt for revenue sharing among the clubs, an issue that lingered into the mid-1990s.

Union chief Don Fehr insisted revenue sharing would help solve the financial woes of the smaller market franchises. "One way to help these clubs is to redirect revenues," Fehr said. "We're saying don't do it with your money. Do it with the money the players believe is theirs."

When another meeting, on August 5, failed to break the stalemate, the players walked. A lengthy stoppage was anticipated and could have become a reality. There had been previous shutdowns over disputes of lesser consequence. But this time "Peter the Great" was in the tower. Above all, he didn't want his watch scarred by a players' strike. It wouldn't look good on his résumé.

In the early morning of August 7, the second day of the strike, Ueberroth entered the ring. Ignoring the owners' four-man PRC, heavy with hard-liners, he called American League president Lee MacPhail. MacPhail and Barry Rona, counsel for the PRC, were negotiating for the owners.

"I want you and Barry to settle this today," Ueberroth ordered.

At ten o'clock that morning the parties assembled at MacPhail's Manhattan apartment. Rona and Fehr met in one room. MacPhail and National League attorney Lou Hoynes waited in an adjoining room. A third room was occupied by Marvin Miller, the former union boss; Mark Belanger, a onetime slick fielding big league shortstop, now among Fehr's assistants; and player reps Kent Tekulve of the Pittsburgh Pirates and Buck Martinez of the Toronto Blue Jays.

When Ueberroth arrived at noon the deal had been made. The owners agreed to drop their request for an arbitration ceiling and increased their pension contribution to $25 million in 1984, to $33 million from 1985 through 1988 and to $39 million in 1989. The players, in turn, made a rare concession: the arbitration requirement would jump from two to three full years of major league service.

Delighted, Ueberroth jumped the gun. His office issued a press release at one o'clock, before the ink was dry, before the PRC had been told of the settlement. The clubs were advised to inform the players the strike had ended and should be on the field the next day. A press conference was scheduled for five o'clock but was delayed. The lawyers needed more time to put the agreement into contract language. The official announcement was made an hour before midnight.

The PRC board members were enraged. Houston's John McMullen, who twenty-four hours earlier had told reporters, "This time we're going to win," insisted the arbitration ceiling was crucial and should not have been abandoned. Privately, he told his fellow moguls, "We shouldn't wait. We should fire him right now."

Peter O'Malley, who in league meetings was constantly ragged by Ueberroth, departed quickly, his face tightened in an angry silence. In mid-afternoon, he was on a flight back to Los Angeles. The comparatively mild-mannered Selig was stunned and asked, "How could Peter do this without consulting us?"

Only Edward Bennett Williams, the famed Washington attorney, was smiling. Williams was for peace at all cost. His Baltimore club was in the midst of an exciting run for the American League pennant. Ailing and eager to host a World Series, Williams was lyrical in describing Ueberroth's intervention. Said Williams, citing Shakespeare's *Macbeth*: "Mr. Ueberroth has a presence that hung over the negotiations like the ghost of Banquo."

Union officials refused to acknowledge Ueberroth's role, claiming their expertise and negotiating skills were responsible for the settlement. But MacPhail and Rona, in separate interviews, acknowledged Ueberroth was responsible. MacPhail wasn't altogether pleased. The next day, Haywood Sullivan, president of the Red Sox, confessed,

"Lee MacPhail did a terrific job for us even if he got his legs cut out from under him."

Ueberroth demurred, refusing to acknowledge his participation was crucial. "I want you to know very clearly I had no role," Ueberroth told *The New York Times*. "It was done by the two teams headed by Don Fehr and Lee MacPhail."

Several days later, Ueberroth scheduled a joint owners' meeting, on August 29 in St. Louis for the purpose of ratification. "I didn't know there was anything to ratify," said Jerry Reinsdorf. "I thought Peter settled it."

Only the outspoken Eddie Chiles of the Texas Rangers voted against ratification.

"Privately, a lot of people are still angry with Ueberroth," a National League owner said at the time on the condition of anonymity. "But they feel there's no sense in getting into a big argument with him. If more owners had spoken up, I would have joined against him. But everybody laid down. You can say—and you'd be very accurate— that the owners have no guts."

Particularly galling to the owners was the accurate belief they had the players on the run. The players were split. Many of the veterans didn't have the stomach for a prolonged shutdown. Bob Boone and Don Baylor, longtime Players Association activists, publicly admitted the issues were not crucial.

"In the early days I never had a doubt we were on the right side," Boone said. "This time I have my doubts."

It was Fehr's first strike, his maiden voyage. On the first night, when he appeared at a crowded press conference, his voice wavered with uncertainty. Unlike Marvin Miller, who never moved unless he had an overwhelming 95 percent majority, it was obvious Fehr lacked the confidence he could keep the players together. Ueberroth took him off the hook.

The two-day walkout was a blip on Ueberroth's watch. A total of twenty-five games had been canceled, fourteen in the American League, eleven in the National. In reality, they were postponements. All were rescheduled. Five of the games were made up in double-headers when play resumed August 8.

The new Basic Agreement was for five years. Retirement benefits soared because of the 100 percent pension fund increase.

At age 62, a player with ten years of big league service would receive $91,000 annually as contrasted to the former maximum of $57,000 for a twenty-year man at age 65. Ten years later it reached the federal maximum of $115,000.

"We have a new nickname for Ueberroth," said Jerry Reinsdorf of the White Sox. "We call him 'The 800-pound Gorilla.'"

Why the 800-pound Gorilla?

"Because he takes whatever he wants."

Ueberroth likened his role to that of a shepherd, not a gorilla. "The owners operate like sheep," he insisted. "They always go in one direction or the other."

Ueberroth presented a considerably different image to the baseball writers. The day before the Winter Meetings in Houston, he arranged a media softball game. Athletic and with remarkably good speed, he stretched a single into a double in his first at bat. At the end of the game, he led the rush to the beer wagon.

From the beginning, Ueberroth understood the importance of a favorable press. During his first World Series, in 1984 in San Diego, Ueberroth hosted a huge gala at Balboa Park for club and local officials, advertisers, and the national media. A woman rushed to his side and, said, gushing, "Mr. Ueberroth, you have such wonderful charisma."

He pointed toward a baseball writer who was standing nearby and said to the newest worshipper, "I wish you'd tell him that."

As commissioner, he had suasion over the owners, not the Players Association, except in the rare instances of moral turpitude. By
the time he took over, Marvin Miller had retired as the executive
director of the players' union but was hovering as a consultant,
determined to keep his monument from crumbling. When Miller
vigorously opposed Ueberroth implementing a plan for drug testing,
not only did Ueberroth withdraw gracefully but rankled ownership
with words of praise for Miller.

"I think he's an honest, hard-working, dedicated man," Ueberroth
said. "And I think one day you'll see him in the baseball Hall of Fame."

Ueberroth never expressed such lofty thoughts for any of the
owners and in his inaugural address, at the 1984 Winter Meetings in
Houston, made it clear he was prepared to confront a weighty problem which Kuhn had repeatedly avoided: the linkage between the
four clubs affiliated with superstations that were saturating the market and infringing on the territorial rights of the individual clubs.

Worse, they were diminishing the audience and decreasing the
value of baseball's billion-dollar contracts with the over-the-air car-
riers, the National Broadcasting Company and the American
Broadcasting Company, which were rewarding each of the twenty-
six clubs with $7 million annually for exclusive national television
rights.

Ted Turner of the Atlanta Braves was the principal target. Turner's
holdings included the Turner Broadcasting System, which telecast
the Atlanta games through a network of cable systems. Also guilty,
but to a lesser degree, were the Chicago Cubs, the New York Mets,
and the New York Yankees. The TV profits enabled the Braves and
the Cubs, in particular, to pour huge sums into the signing of free
agent players, fueling the salary revolution.

A reporter said to Ueberroth, "This was your first speech and four
clubs are already against you."

"I'm not trying to make anybody angry," Ueberroth replied. "I'm trying to do what's fair."

Prior to the Winter Meetings, Ueberroth had also blocked a proposal by Edward Chiles, president of the Texas Rangers, to sell the Rangers' television rights and a 33 percent interest in the club to Gaylord Broadcasting, which also had superstation potential. A heavy majority of the owners were in vigorous support of Ueberroth on this issue; it had been lingering for years without resolution.

At Ueberroth's insistence, Turner agreed, in 1985, to an annual $10 million superstation tax which was remitted into a central fund, the money divided equally among all twenty-six clubs, including the Braves. Once this deal was struck, Ueberroth used it as leverage with the other offenders. The Cubs agreed to a $5 million penalty. Similar in concept to a cost-of-living increase, the tax escalated. By 1992, the pool had risen to $20 million.

It was a small beginning, the genesis of revenue sharing. But penalizing the clubs with direct superstation outlets didn't address the much bigger problem of containing player salaries. Ueberroth repeatedly advised the owners the only way to control costs was to curtail "wild spending" on free-agents.

His pleas went unheeded—until mid-October of 1985 when Lee MacPhail, soon to retire as the chairman of the owners' Player Relations Committee, issued a five-page report on the financial state of the game. Included was the remarkable revelation that the twenty-six clubs combined, were on the hook for $40 million to players who had been released or retired.

The Collusion Era was about to begin.

# 17 PETER UEBERROTH
## PART II

T he owners were ready to be galvanized. Some stood up and confessed their stupidity and pledged not to sign any more high-priced free agents. Later, it was likened to a revival meeting. But they were not in church. They were in the auditorium at the headquarters of Anheuser Busch, Inc., the owner of the St. Louis Cardinals. The date was October 22, 1985, the day before the Cardinals were to host the Kansas City Royals in Game 3 of the World Series.

Peter Ueberroth, baseball's high priest, told his flock he understood what was wrong with baseball economics. According to management figures, in the previous year, the owners had suffered an aggregate $40 million loss, their eleventh consecutive year of losses.

Ueberroth began:

"If I sat each of you down in front of a red button and a black button and I said, 'Push the red button and you'd win the World Series but lose $10 million. Push the black button and you would have a $4 million profit and you'd finish in the middle.'"

Ueberroth stood silent, a theatrical pause.

"You are so damned dumb. Most of you would push the red button."

Another pause.

"Look in the mirror and go out and spend big if you want, but don't go out there whining that someone made you do it."

He closed with a statement—later denied, "I know and you know what's wrong. You are smart businessmen. You all agree we have a problem. Go solve it."

According to John Helyar of the *Wall Street Journal*, the next afternoon player-agent Tom Reich met with Bill Lajoie, the general manager of the Detroit Tigers. Reich was anticipating concluding negotiations for a long-term, possibly a lifetime contract for Lance Parrish, the Tigers' all-star catcher who was a year away from free agency.

Lajoie was clearly uncomfortable.

"Look, I don't know how to tell you this," Lajoie said. "but we have reviewed this and decided the best we can offer is a two-year contract and not at the kind of money we've been talking about."

"Where did that bull come from?" Reich asked.

"We had some meetings and decided that these are the economics," Lajoie replied. "This is the best we can do."

Ten minutes later Reich had Parrish on the phone.

"Something's up," Reich told him.

Soon after, Reich wrote a warning memo to his other clients. They were in for a mean season.

The mean season lasted three years, from 1985 to 1988, and came to be known as the Collusion Era. It froze the free agent market and arrested baseball's salary spiral, fulfilling the hopes of Ueberroth and Lee MacPhail, a management lifer who soon was to retire as the chairman of the owners' policy-setting Player Relations Committee.

In a farewell memorandum, delivered at the St. Louis meeting, MacPhail advised the owners, possibly to their surprise, they were already on the hook for $40 million to players no longer active.

Instead of acquiring costly free agents, most of whom had peaked, MacPhail recommended they fill their rosters with younger players who could be signed at minimal salaries. He also urged the rosters be reduced from twenty-five to twenty-four players.

MacPhail's report included several performance tables, a survey of 104 position-players and 57 pitchers, which demonstrated that production diminished in correlation with the length of a player's contract. Players were also more prone to injury. Over the previous ten years the ratio of players on the disabled list had grown from 14 to 28 percent, days lost from 7 to 15 percent.

MacPhail concluded:

"Most important is that all clubs practice common–sense economic self-restraint. We must rely on the unilateral, self-imposed restraints of each individual club to do what experience and reasonable expectations indicate is in its own best interest. We must stop daydreaming that one free agent signing will bring a pennant. Somehow we must get our operation back to the point where a normal year for the average team at least results in a break-even situation, so that clubs are not led to make rash moves in the vain hope that they might bring a pennant and a resulting change in their financial position. This requires resistance to fan and media pressure and is not easy. On the other hand, the future health and stability of our game depend on your response to these problems."

Free agency has been the heart of the Basic Agreement, the collective contract that binds the owners and players together. For a players to qualify, six years or more of major league service is required. From the moment of its birth in 1977, it has been a gold mine for the uniformed personnel. When established players began marketing their skills, the frenzied competition between clubs for their services resembled an auction for the crown jewels.

Twenty players were in the first wave, plus aging sluggers Willie

McCovey and Nate Colbert, both of whom had been given their unconditional release. In the beginning, and for eight or nine years beyond, it was known as the reentry draft because the players were absorbed back into the major league system. Each club, in inverse order of the previous year's standings, was permitted to acquire the negotiation rights to twelve players.

The first draft was held soon after the World Series, on November 4, 1977, in the Terrace Room of the Plaza Hotel in New York. Marvin Miller sat at a corner table monitoring the proceedings. The architect of the new order, Miller was apprehensive, fearful that the owners would find a way to subvert the process. But the owners reacted with enthusiasm. Miller expressed delight and complimented them for their good spirit in observing the letter of the law.

All of the clubs participated, with the exception of the Cincinnati Reds, who previously had announced they would abstain. Even Charlie Finley, who was the big loser (six of his players were on the block), claimed bargaining rights, which were without cost, to almost all of the free agents, none of whom he signed.

Finley also issued a warning to his fellow moguls. "Gentlemen, we're on our way to the poorhouse," he said. "We're going to go bankrupt."

Observed the parsimonious Calvin Griffith, chief executive officer of the Minnesota Twins: "Sports today are sick. If I'm going to stay in business, I'm going to need a rich partner."

Two days later, Bill Campbell, who had been a star relief pitcher with Minnesota, was the first free agent to make a new connection. Campbell signed a four-year $1 million contract with the Boston Red Sox, a bonanza; his 1976 wage was $23,000.

Not all of the free agents won a tenfold increase, as Campbell had done. But within the next three weeks, eleven more players, all front-liners and many of all-star caliber, agreed to million-dollar proposals, putting the torch to Miller's suspicions that the owners would conspire to keep the prices down. Reggie Jackson, who was among the Oakland alumni and the previous season had earned $165,000 won in arbitration, came away with the biggest haul: $3 million from the New York Yankees for five years.

The fringe players were also along for the ride. The 1976 average baseball salary for the 600-plus major leaguers was $51,501. The next year the average rose nearly 50 percent to $76,066. By 1980, it was $143,756, almost twice as much as it had been in 1977. It was $289,194 in 1983, more than double the 1980 average. In 1984, it was $329,408; twelve years later it had soared to $2.1 million.

Three years after implementation of the reentry draft, during the 1980 negotiations, the owners, in an effort to blunt the effects of the freedom riders, requested direct compensation to clubs losing a player. Instead of the original arrangement of yielding its first round choice in the annual summer draft of amateur players, the acquiring club would recompense the player's former team with a player from its twenty-five-man roster.

Direct compensation was the principal issue in the fifty-day 1981 strike, the longest stoppage until that time. Miller correctly contended a direct exchange would be the equivalent of a "forced trade" and would stifle movement. Miller responded with a successful counter proposal of indirect compensation: All of the clubs, after protecting sixteen players, would dump the rest of its players, including minor leaguers, into a general pool. For each departing free agent, the losing club could select a replacement from this huge vessel of more than 2,000 players. It was a crucial victory. The essential integrity of the new system was maintained.

The ripple effect of free agency was best explained by attorney Steve Fehr, who argued two cases before the U.S. Supreme Court, and won both, and is the outside counsel for the Players Association, headed by his older brother, Don:

"Baseball salaries are interdependent and collusion only works effectively if there are no exceptions. The objective is to reduce salaries and length of contractual commitments across the board. Thus, if the New York Yankees pay Jack Morris what he is asking, that affects what the Toronto Blue Jays must offer Jim Clancy, who is also a free agent, in order to re-sign him; and also affects what the Minnesota Twins must offer Frank Viola in salary arbitration; which in turn affects what the New York Mets must offer Dwight Gooden in salary arbitration; which in turn affects what the Boston Red Sox . . . and so on. The surest indicator of collusion is that the common goal can only be accomplished so pervasively if there are no deviations."

To guard against this possibility, the following sentence was added to Article XVIII (h) of the Basic Agreement:

"Players shall not act in concert with other players and clubs shall not act in concert with other clubs."

Remarkably, it was the owners, not the players, who requested this provision as protection against a repeat of what had happened in 1966 when Sandy Koufax and Don Drysdale, the stars of the Los Angeles Dodgers' pitching staff, in tandem, advised club officials that neither would sign without the other. Suddenly, the Dodgers had to please two to please one.

"It was a legitimate worry," Miller recalled many years later. "But I was going to give in only if it was a two-way street. They yielded instantly. It wasn't a big deal."

Players Association attorneys subsequently emphasized that the use of the words "act in concert" was deliberate. Other words such as "combine," "conspire," "agree," "consult," or "contract" were known to the draftsmen and could have been used. *Black's Law Dictionary* provides the following definitions:

"Concert. A person is deemed to act in concert when he acts with another to bring about some preconceived result.

"Concerted action (or plan). Action that has been planned, arranged, adjusted, agreed on and settled between parties acting together pursuant to some design or scheme."

Because the owners had acted in concert, with no deviations, the first boycott of free agents succeeded beyond Ueberroth's highest expectations. The final score of the 1985–86 season: of thirty-three free agents, twenty-nine went back to their old teams, having received no other offers. The four who moved on were marginal players whose former teams had shown no interest in re-signing them.

Only catcher Butch Wynegar, after he had re-signed with the Yankees, expressed sympathy for the owners. In what the *Chicago Tribune* described as the "surprising statement of the year," Wynegar said:

"Free agency is not what it used to be. I agree with the owners the salaries had to stop somewhere. The players are paid too much."

The 1985–86 free agents averaged a mere 5 percent salary increase. Two thirds got one-year contracts. Previously, in each year from 1976 to 1984, at least eleven reentry free agents had been awarded guaranteed contracts for three years or more, some for a term of five years or more. After the 1984 season, Ueberroth's first off-season as commissioner, the market was still ablaze. A majority of the free agents changed clubs; forty-seven players, some not eligible for free agency, were given long-term deals of three years or more.

And then the market evaporated.

Ueberroth denied the owners had colluded.

"They aren't capable of colluding," Ueberroth insisted. "They couldn't agree on what to have for breakfast."

Still, the inescapable conclusion was that the market had been rigged. In addition to Lance Parrish of the Tigers, there were, at the least, three other quality free agents: catcher Carlton Fisk of the White Sox, premier relief pitcher Donnie Moore of the California Angels, and infielder Tony Bernazard of the Cleveland Indians.

Only Fisk got as much as a nibble from another team. George Steinbrenner of the Yankees admitted he made an offer for Fisk but it was withdrawn after he got a call from White Sox chairman Jerry Reinsdorf.

Clearly, the code was "You don't sign my players, I won't sign yours."

According to George Argyros, "It was the first time owners had information about other teams. We had heard about it but never knew about it in detail. Signing players to multi-year contracts is not fiscally responsible. . . The reality is that money doesn't necessarily buy a winner."

The second class of free agents may have been the best group in history up to that time, and included pitchers Jack Morris, Ron Guidry, Jim Clancy, Doyle Alexander, Bob Forsch, Bryn Smith, Atlee Hammaker, and Tommy John; catchers Lance Parrish, Bob Boone, Alan Ashby, and Rich Gedman; infielders Bob Horner, Willie Randolph, Ray Knight, Doug DeCinces, and Darrell Evans; and outfielders Andre Dawson, Tim Raines, and Brian Downing.

Dick Moss, previously counsel for the Players Association, was now a player agent, with a stable of more than a dozen million-dollar players. Among them was Jack Morris, then with the Detroit Tigers. In the eight-year period from 1979–86, Morris was baseball's leading starting pitcher.

Moss wrote to all the clubs, except Detroit, expressing Morris's interest in playing for that club. Weeks passed without a positive response. Moss then arranged appointments with four clubs Morris would most like to play for: the Minnesota Twins, the California Angels, the New York Yankees, and the Philadelphia Phillies. A coast-to-coast tour followed. The owners and/or general managers listened politely but there were no meaningful offers. Morris re-signed with Detroit.

The trials and tribulations of Andre Dawson, another of Moss's players, also demonstrated the barbed-wire boycott. Dawson had been a superstar with the Montreal Expos. He hit for both average and power and was outstanding defensively. Of the players I have known, I can think of only two who were a constant inspiration to their teammates: Mickey Mantle and Andre Dawson.

Dawson wanted to play on a natural grass field to alleviate the pressure that playing on an artificial surface put on his surgically repaired knees. Playing his home games on grass would lengthen his career. The Chicago Cubs expressed minor interest but didn't make an offer. With spring training underway, Moss took his client to the Cubs' spring camp in Mesa, Arizona.

They marched into the office of general manager Dallas Green. Green's secretary said he was unavailable. Moss left her with a blank contract. Dawson would sign for whatever Green believed was fair. For the next three days Dawson watched the Cub workouts. The writers on the Cub beat trumpeted Dawson's arrival. Photographs of Dawson frozen out and standing behind a chain-link fence ran in the Chicago papers.

Gleefully, Moss revealed his blank check offer.

"Yes, they gave us something," Green acknowledged. "But it wasn't really important."

Later, Moss testified:

"Green said to me, 'That was some p.r. campaign that you ran. I didn't like it at all. You put us in a position, you got everybody in Chicago excited; you got everybody on the team excited and there was no way we could say no.'"

In apology, Green wrote a letter to the Player Relations Committee and the league presidents: "I was not quite as prepared to respond or handle this type of proposal as I should have been."

Dawson agreed to Green's numbers—$500,000 for one year, with an additional $200,000 in incentive bonuses, which he earned—but nonetheless $500,000 less than Montreal's base offer of $1.2 million.

Dawson responded with a great season. He led the league in home runs (49), runs batted in (137), and total bases (353), and was a near-unanimous choice as the National League's Most Valuable Player.

But as John Helyar wrote in his excellent *Lords of the Realm*, "[Initially] it had been an almost accidental conspiracy. Everyone was cowed into not wanting to be the first to sign a free agent. Nobody did. And it got to be habit-forming. The feeling was, 'Hey, for the first time we acted smart. Why not keep it going?'"

A few owners, notably Peter O'Malley of the Dodgers, were uncomfortable. O'Malley later said, "[It was] the low point in baseball for me, by far." He had several sharp exchanges with Ueberroth. Edward Bennett Williams of Baltimore also questioned Ueberroth and the management lawyers, "Are you sure this is okay?"

The Players Association filed separate grievances, charging collusion, that the owners had acted in concert after the 1985 and 1986 seasons.

The heat was on, and suddenly the free agent market began to loosen. Of the seventy-six reentry free agents in the winter of 1987–88, fifteen had offers from more than one club other than their former club. Three players in this group, Jack Clark, Brett Butler, and David Palmer, switched clubs. Many of the others re-signed with their former clubs, some at significant salary increases.

Nonetheless, the union filed another grievance.

Arbitrator Thomas Roberts found the owners guilty on the first charge of collusion. Dismissed by the owners, Roberts was succeeded by George Nicolau who also decided for the players on counts two and three. The owners were fined a total of $280 million, easily the biggest single penalty in the history of sports. Even so, many insiders insisted that, by depressing salaries, they still showed a $200 million collusion profit.

Then came a knotty problem. How to disburse the $280 million?

The Players Association decided that each player, when making his appeal (or appeals), should send a certified check for $2,500. This fee would cover handling expenses and, more important, discourage minimal disputes. On March 11, 1991, in a widely published legal notice, the affected players were advised claims could be filed for:

1) Lost salary.

2) Lost special covenants, such as signing bonuses; performance and award bonuses; trade limitation provisions; and option buyouts.

3) Lost multiyear (or longer multiyear) contracts.

4) Lost contract extensions options exercised.

5) Lost employment.

6) Other non-salary claims, such as lost major league service, etc.

7) Interest, both pre-Settlement and post-Settlement.

8) All other claims for consequential damages, to the extent that such claims were or could have been brought under the Basic Agreement.

More than 800 players filed in excess of 3,000 claims. Many insisted they had suffered damages during each of the three years. The total damages sought for the first two years, according to a union attorney, was five times more than the money allotted for that period. One player asked for $25 million. Babe Dahlgren, the first baseman who had replaced Lou Gehrig when Gehrig's consecutive streak was broken, was among the claimants. Dahlgren, who had retired after the 1946 season, insisted he, too, had been the victim of collusion.

Ueberroth professed bewilderment.

"I never did anything wrong," he told National League attorney Lou Hoynes at lunch one day.

"Technically, you didn't," Hoynes said. "The clubs heard your words, but they also heard the music. It was martial music. They all fell into the beat."

In late June 1988, a year and a half before the expiration of his contract, Ueberroth announced he would not accept a second term.

"In this way," Ueberroth said, "my successor will benefit from a smooth transition during which we will work hand in hand to assure that the game is on solid footing. When I took over, baseball was not healthy financially. Now it is."

# 18 BART GIAMATTI
## PART I

I keep trying to remind people there are lots of ways to love base-ball. Some come to it through a love of statistics, or the smell of the glove, or just for something that their grandfather recited to them when they were very young. There are many routes to the kingdom of baseball."

So said A. Bartlett Giamatti, the seventh commissioner. The own-ers, by unanimous acclaim, gave him the keys to the kingdom at the age of 50. A Renaissance man weighted with nine doctorates, Giamatti was part fan, part scholar, part essayist-poet, and much admired. He had a brief rein, 154 days, only five months, and was the first commissioner since Judge Landis to die in office.

Death came on September 1, 1989, nine days after he had given Pete Rose a lifetime ban for allegedly gambling on baseball, a pun-ishment equivalent to baseball's death sentence. A former superstar and baseball's all-time hit leader, Rose refused to confess but signed a paper, "acknowledging the Commissioner has a factual basis to impose the penalty." Giamatti's action was consistent with his rigid belief: the commissioner's essential assignment is to maintain the integrity of the game.

Giamatti was a scholar, a distinguished man of letters, and for eight years the president of Yale University. Once, at an owners' meeting, he interrupted a discussion on superstations with the declaration: "What will come out of the welter and farrago of this remains to be seen."

He also had the common touch. "Bart was a people person," said Terry Tata, a veteran National League umpire. "I knew him for two and a half years and every time I was with him he made me feel ten feet tall. He was the most influential person I ever met."

Giamatti had a special kinship with the umpires who have a lonely life. They love company. But they are generally ignored and often demeaned by baseball's administrators. A prominent baseball attorney described them as having "the intelligence of truck drivers." Giamatti had them as dinner guests, visited with them in their dressing room at every opportunity, and recognized they, too, were keepers of the flame. More than that, they are without pomposity and pretension, and they could educate him about things he didn't know, information he would never find in a book.

"He swore in Italian," said umpire Frank Pulli, a fellow paisano, delighted with the discovery the boss was capable of descending from the ivory tower. On a dare, Pulli began addressing him with an effusive "Aaaangelllo." Said Pulli, "Bart loved it."

Giamatti could also curse in English. Often, when somebody crossed him or an owner come after him, Bart had a "great line," said Fay Vincent, Giamatti's deputy. "He'd say, 'Fuck him and the horse he rode in on.' If ladies were present, he'd shorten it to, 'And the horse he rode in on.'"

Giamatti was fascinated by the playing rules and constantly quizzing Eddie Vargo, his principal baseball guru. The son of a Pittsburgh bus driver and an amateur boxer in his youth, Vargo has the physique of a weight lifter. He umpired in the National League for twenty-four years and upon his retirement was appointed the league's umpire supervisor.

They were constant companions and always had connecting rooms in spring training. "We kept the door open," Vargo recalled. "Bart stayed up late. He loved to read novels. One night, when my lights were out, he yelled, 'Hey, Eddie are you awake?'

"'I'm awake, Bart.'

"'What's Rule 6.02?'

"Bart always wanted to know. He would spend endless hours going over the rules. One night, I think it was in '88, in New York, the night before a crew chief's meeting, I invited Augie Donatelli and Al Barlick to have dinner with us. This was after they had retired. Between the three of us we had almost 100 years of big league umpiring experience. We got to the restaurant at six o'clock. We were there past midnight, when they closed the place. Bart loved to listen to baseball stories."

Unlike his predecessors, Giamatti often attended meetings of the Rules Committee. Over the years the strike zone had been lowered, without sanction, from the armpits to just above the belt to the top of the knees, a significant change that was to the advantage of the hitters.

"That's where the conversation got long and interesting," Giamatti said. "All these baseball people standing up trying to figure out just where the armpits are exactly, even though no umpire was calling strikes there anymore. Then, because some people thought the American public was not ready to hear on television the 'nipple zone,' we decided to define the strike zone as the middle of the chest.

"Dr. Brown [president of the American League and a former player] was marvelous. Every time someone would propose an anatomically inoffensive term, like the breastbone, he would explain that wasn't where we wanted the strike zone to be. So we ended up with 'mid-chest to the knees,' first to avoid the specious argument about where armpits are and, second, by lowering the strike zone we hoped, in a paradox that ought not be beyond everyone's capacity to reason, to get umpires to focus on the high pitch more."

Just as he had listened to Dr. Brown, Giamatti, a pragmatist as well as an idealist, was attentive to the players. After watching a tape of a brawl between the Atlanta Braves and Cincinnati Reds, Giamatti fined Ozzie Virgil, the Braves' catcher, and followed with a letter of remonstration. Virgil responded with a call to the Commissioner's office and told Giamatti, "You've got this exactly wrong. You misunderstood what you saw. I swung my arm like that because I was trying to get their guy off the pile."

A few weeks later, in another melee, Virgil was clearly a peacemaker. Giamatti immediately telephoned Virgil with his compliments. "After that," Giamatti said, "Mr. Virgil and I became more than nodding acquaintances, and that was nice."

The chunky czar—five feet eight and 210 pounds, thirty pounds overweight—also gave an ear to the owners. He was not a lone-wolf executive as Ueberroth had been.

"Peter was very impatient and had a tendency to do things himself," observed Chicago White Sox chairman Jerry Reinsdorf. When Bart came along many owners had tired of Peter's one-man style. Bart got everybody involved. The wonderful thing about Bart is he knows what he knows and knows what he doesn't know."

Baseball administrators revealed Giamatti was considerably more direct and blunt in their private dealings than he was in his public pronouncements. A .400 hitter as a talker—"That's what I do best," he admitted—Giamatti usually tried to bench his oratorical style, developed in academia, at league meetings and in discourse with players and umpires.

"For being book smart, he had an awful lot of street smarts," echoed Whitey Herzog, the most successful field manager of the 1980s.

Giamatti wrote a handful of books and dozens of articles, many of them on baseball. His favorite player was pitcher Tom Seaver whom Giamatti saw as an Olympian, on and off the field. Among his essays, perhaps the most interesting was his recurring fascination on "home." What follows is a composite:

"What's home? Home is a longing for when you were happy because you were younger. At least you thought you were happier. Why isn't it fourth base? Leaving home and struggling to return is as ancient as Homer. Baseball is about going home and how hard it is to get there. Its wisdom says you can go home again but that you cannot stay. The journey must always start once more, the bat an oar over the shoulder, until there is an end to all this journeying.

"Innumerable are the dangers. Most efforts fail. In baseball, the journey begins at home, negotiates the twists and turns at first, and often founders far out at the edges of the ordered world at rocky second—the farthest point from home. Whoever remains out there is said to die on base. Home is finally beyond reach in a hostile world full of quirks and tricks and hostile folk."

A traditionalist, Giamatti expressed disdain for the antiseptic new circular stadiums, many which had been constructed in the '60s; the designated hitter, which upset the delicate balance between offense and defense; artificial turf which eliminated the bad bounce and the tricky hop; team mascots, ballgirls, domed stadiums and the huge video scoreboards that induce cheering.

"Why couldn't architects build ballparks with odd angles and uneven walls and irregular distances?" he asked. "It would elevate the strategy of the game. A stadium should be a box, not a saucer."

To him, Eden was Fenway Park in Boston or Wrigley Field in Chicago, both constructed prior to 1920, the major league's smallest and most ancient arenas.

Giamatti gloried in his assignment. During a lunch with David

Stern, the highly-acclaimed commissioner of the National Basketball Association, Stern tweaked him.

"All right, Bart," Stern said, "baseball is America's national pastime, but football is America's passion and basketball is America's game."

Chuckling, Giamatti replied, "I can live with that, David, as long as you understand that I have historical priority, and therefore I run the country."

"He would have made a great President," insisted Bruce Froemming, a veteran National League umpire. "The umpires would have campaigned for him. And he didn't go easy on us. He was a friend but he was tough. I've got an interview with him on my desk. He's talking about complaints he hears about the umpires. 'Hey,' he says, 'I love the umpires.'"

There was also affection at the top. Bud Selig of the Milwaukee Brewers, who had headed the Commissioners' Search Committee, was won over the first time they met and thereafter was unswerving in his admiration.

Giamatti had not been ill. He died suddenly of a heart attack. "I didn't just lose a friend," Selig said, "I lost a brother."

Selig has never forgotten their first meeting. Twelve years later he still knew the date—June 6, 1983. Selig had begun a week-long expedition, interviewing candidates to succeed Bowie Kuhn. Giamatti led the list. They had dinner at the Helmsley Palace Hotel in New York City and walked the streets well past midnight.

Several days later Selig sent a ten-page letter to the committee members, advising there was no need to continue the quest. He had found their man. But it was a troubled time for Giamatti. He was in the midst of settling an acrimonious strike of Yale employees. He had promised the Yale trustees he would finish his term. Unable to delay, the owners anointed Ueberroth.

Three years later, in 1986, Giamatti was ready. Chub Feeney, the longtime president of the National League, was retiring. Giamatti made the leap with the understanding he would succeed Ueberroth who was uneasy in the commissioner's chair. Most of Giamatti's Yale colleagues expressed dismay, unable to comprehend the allure. To the few who approved, Giamatti told them:

"I'm almost 50 years old and I have fallen in love. I'm running away with a beautiful redhead with flashing eyes whose name is baseball."

Angelo Bartlett Giamatti was born in Boston on April 4, 1938. He was raised a few blocks from Mount Holyoke College in Hadley, Massachusetts, the grandson of an immigrant laborer. Giamatti's father, Valentine, could not speak English when he entered the first grade, but was graduated from Yale with honors and became a professor of Romance languages and Italian literature, the foremost expert on the works of Dante.

Bart's mother, Mary Claybaugh Walton, met Valentine in 1933 in Florence, Italy, where he was studying, and she was taking her junior year abroad from Smith College. Her antecedents had been New England sea captains and shoe manufacturers.

"About the only thing to do in the summer," Giamatti told an interviewer "was ride my bike and listen to Boston Red Sox games on the radio. I was probably seven or eight years old when my father and uncle took me to my first baseball game. I'd been listening on the radio often enough, but going to Fenway Park, I was just astonished at the whole thing."

Bobby Doerr, a steady infielder, was his hero. Many years later when asked why he chose Bobby Doerr over Ted Williams, Giamatti said, "I could imagine myself playing second base but not hitting .400."

Giamatti's dream to join the Red Sox was shattered when he tried out for the South Hadley High School team. He didn't survive the final cut. "He played his heart out," coach Tom Landers recalled. "He was very enthusiastic and great to have around." Landers made him the team manager.

"Maybe I love baseball so much because I wasn't very good at it," Giamatti recalled. "My coach used to send me behind the backstop during the games to check on the umpires. I began watching the umpires at a very early age."

Encouraged by his parents, Giamatti displayed an aptitude for language and literature. He learned Italian from his father while still a child and often participated in weighty dinner table discussions. He completed his secondary education at the upscale Phillips Academy in Andover and entered Yale where he majored in English.

He received his bachelor's degree magna cum laude in 1960 and his doctorate in comparative literature in 1964. He moved on to two mostly dreary seasons at rival Princeton University where he taught literature. The Princeton University Press published his well-received doctorate dissertation, "Earthly Paradise and the Renaissance Epic."

Two years later he returned to the Yale bosom, which to him was rich with milk and honey. He joined the faculty as an assistant professor of English. More than likely, they were his happiest days in the so-called groves of academia. As a fledgling professor during the 1960s, he adopted the plumage of the counterculture: head crowned in a Red Sox cap, his clothes rumpled, with longish hair, a goatee and an unassuming manner. The students were enthralled with his charisma.

As Paul Gray wrote in *Egghead at the Plate*, his classrooms overflowed. "They enrolled in his courses and came out of them equally entranced by their teacher, but for radically different reasons. Bart expected them to actually read their assignments. He believed in grades, tough grades. He argued that being a civilized human being is not a matter of instinct but of unrelenting hard work and discipline. He is a person who holds and acts upon deep moral convictions." Advancement came rapidly. He was a full professor at 33. Seven years later, on July 1, 1978, he was elected the 19th president of Yale.

Chartered in 1701, Yale was still largely a depository for the well-born, an elegant bastion of erudition with ornate gates, moats and battlements, defined as a place where, "Under Almighty God, youth were to be trained for service to church and civil state." Giamatti was 40, Yale's youngest president in more than 200 years and the first of at least partial non-WASP ancestry.

He accepted with feigned reluctance and told reporters that his only ambition had been to become president of the American League, not of Yale.

As popular as he had been as a professor, he was as unpopular as an administrator, adrift in his new assignment as a fund-raiser and adjudicating labor-management disputes. Yale was heavily in debt, in a budget crisis, and bitterly engaged in a strike with two local unions representing 4,000 employees. There was also a retrenchment on student activities.

"Being president of a university is no way for an adult to make a living," he later wrote. "It is to hold a mid-nineteenth century ecclesiastical position on top of a late-twentieth century corporation. I learned that because the corporate world is interested only in quarterly results, it talks a great deal about long-range planning. We needed a corporate strategy, a corporate policy. I, of course, had no policies."

The *Yale Daily News* ragged the new "Dean of Discipline":

"Giamatti's administration is off to a miserable start. Rather than giving us control over our lives, or at least addressing concerns of students such as the crying need for a student center so we can make friends or any of the myriad of other injustices that riddle the fabric of the quality of life here, the new administration is insensitive and repressive and the future bodes awful."

As Yale's labor problems persisted, Giamatti's office was picketed by administrative assistants, clerical workers and blue-collar strikers bearing signs:

"BART, BART, HAVE A HEART!"

"BOOLA, BOOLA, WHERE'S OUR MOOLA?"

There were many other upsetting moments such as when several hundred protesters assembled in front of his house in a candlelight vigil, chanting: "Bart can't sleep because Yale is cheap!"

According to James Reston, Jr., in his wonderfully insightful 1991 dual biography of Giamatti and Pete Rose, Giamatti was longing for a more joyful pursuit:

"The travel, the begging for money from rich people, the sharp criticisms of his once-boon companions, had exacted a price. His health had suffered, as had his family life. At the age of 46, he was beginning to look twenty years older."

In January 1984, a year before the Yale strike was settled, Giamatti decided to resign, giving notice after the fifth year of what was intended to be an eight-year term.

Baseball came to the rescue. With Ueberroth still in office but packing for a hasty exit, Giamatti entered through a side door, and on June 9, 1986, was elected president of the National League. Peter O'Malley of the Los Angeles Dodgers was among his champions.

"Many people claim they love baseball," O'Malley said later "but Bart had respect as well as love. We were sold on his ability to communicate." Giamatti was given a salary of $200,000, same as the President of the United States. He took office on December 31, 1986, and served in this capacity for almost two and a half years.

Said a checkout girl at a New Haven supermarket to one of Bart's Yale colleagues, "I knew Giamatti would make it big some day."

I was not among the early worshippers, especially after he was quoted in the *Boston Herald* in an early August interview. In part:

"I like ballet, which is one of the reasons I like baseball. Or it might be that I like ballet because I like baseball. I'm really not sure which way it goes. I mean, watching Ozzie Smith and watching Baryshnikov to me are similar pleasures.

"Academics love baseball. Because of its history. Because it's susceptible to having a philosophy. Because it's been around a while. Because the game allows you to get inside it. It's susceptible to endless quantification. That accounts for the bifurcation I encountered in the academic community between people who thought becoming the National League president was absurd and those who thought it was splendid."

I responded with a small knock in my column in the *Chicago Tribune*:

"It is difficult to understand the National League owners' fascination with Giamatti other than wanting him to lead them in a Great Books course. I would rather see a former player or a general manager or an umpire take over for Feeny.

"The American League went that route with the appointment of Dr. Bobby Brown, a onetime infielder with the Yankees, and Brown has worked out exceptionally well. Even the AL umpires like and respected Brown, which is the ultimate compliment."

Roger Angell of the *New Yorker*, possibly the most erudite baseball Boswell since Father Chadwick, embraced the professor with a bear hug. In a lengthy article of approval titled "Celebration," Angell wrote: "Baseball, for all its ordered paths, is a game of constant surprises, but its choice of a bearded Ivy League scholar-prexy as the twelfth president of the senior circuit was a startler unmatched in the pastime since Al Weis' home run for the Mets in the fifth game of the 1969 World Series."

Kindred spirits, Giamatti told Angell:

"There are people who insist that my going from my old job to this one was as if I'd suddenly taken up being a dogsled driver or something, but I don't agree. Both jobs involve historically oriented, retrospective cultures, very slow to change. They're closed in—not hermetically, but they're very conscious within themselves of who you are and of the kind of apprenticeship it takes to become whatever you're going to be. They're medieval cultures. My friends say it tells a lot about me that I was drawn to such things. There's even more. You're administering nonprofit organizations—the league is nonprofit—which means you have to work by suasion. You have multiple constituencies, equally intent on collaborating and competing. The departments are the teams, of course, and the umpires are the deans. Guilds and chivalric codes—medieval!"

After a quiet first year in the National League, Giamatti made several controversial decisions in 1988. He gave Pete Rose, then the Cincinnati manager, a stiff thirty-day suspension and a record $10,000 fine for twice shoving umpire Dave Pallone during a heated game against the Mets on April 30.

In the top of the ninth, with the score tied at 5–5, Pallone called Mookie Wilson safe on a close play at first base that gave the Mets the lead. Raging, Rose pushed Pallone who countered by poking a finger in his face. With that, Rose gave Pallone a hard shove with his forearm. Pallone ejected him instantly and turned his back and began walking away when Rose shoved him from the rear a second time. The Cincinnati fans began rioting. Play didn't resume until fifteen minutes later, without Pallone.

Giamatti suspended the Dodgers' Pedro Guerrero for four days and fined him $1,000 for throwing his bat at David Cone after Cone had hit him with a pitch. He sat pitcher Jay Howell for two days following the discovery that Howell had pine tar on his glove in the third game of the playoffs.

Philadelphia pitcher Kevin Gross got ten days for implanting a wedge of sandpaper into the heel of his glove to scuff the ball and alter its flight. "I worked as hard on my response to the Kevin Gross appeal as I worked anything I did while I was at New Haven," Giamatti told Angell. "It was challenging to try to be clear about cheating and what it meant, and to be fair at the same time."

Curious, Angell exhumed Giamatti's opinion on the Gross appeal and concluded, "It's ten pages of resonant text shone forth like Cardozo:

". . . Unlike acts of impulse or violence, intended at the moment to vent frustration, acts of cheating are intended to alter the very conditions of play to favor one person. They are secretive, covert acts that strike at and seek to undermine the basic foundation of any contest declaring the winner—that all participants play under identical rules and conditions. Acts of cheating destroy that foundation and the faith in the game's integrity and fairness. Cheating is contrary to the whole purpose of playing to determine a winner fairly and cannot be simply contained; if the game is to flourish and engage public confidence, cheating must be clearly condemned with an eye to expunging it."

Baseball's Cardozo was warming up for the main event—the Pete Rose suspension.

# BART GIAMATTI
## PART II

*The matter of Mr. Rose is now closed. It will be debated and discussed. Let no one think that it did not hurt baseball. That hurt will pass, however, as the great glory of the game asserts itself and a resilient institution goes forward. Let it also be clear that no individual is superior to the game.*

—A. Bartlett Giamatti

Pete Rose had a distinguished 24-year playing career and at the finish had more hits, more games played, more times at bat, more singles, and more seasons with 200 or more hits than anyone in baseball history. In addition, he was the only player to have played more than 500 games at five positions—first, second, and third base, and left and right field. He was as popular a player as baseball has known.

He was also a compulsive gambler and made no secret of his affliction. He often was seen at racetracks and dog tracks, and along with millions of Americans, openly bet on football games. Like his relentless pursuit of Ty Cobb's seemingly unapproachable hit record, Rose's gambling was an obsession. Inevitably, he became involved with a succession of unsavory characters and was heavily in their

debt. The same week he broke Cobb's record, he accepted a cocaine
dealer's $17,000 loan.

Peter Ueberroth, on February 20, 1989, in his final month as commissioner, summoned Rose to his office. "We have heard about your
gambling," Ueberroth told him. "We have only one purpose here. We
don't want to hear about your betting on football or basketball. Did
you or did you not bet on baseball?"

Rose and his attorneys danced around the maypole. Rose denied he
had bet on baseball or that he had a problem with bookies. When an
inquiring reporter called and asked about the meeting, Ueberroth kissed
it off: there was nothing ominous and there would not be a follow-up.

Several days later, having returned to the Reds' spring training
camp in Plant City, Florida, Rose was interviewed by Tim Sullivan of
the *Cincinnati Enquirer*.

"Don't you think players are tempted to bet on baseball because
they know more than the average person?" Sullivan asked.

"No, you can't do that," replied Rose who was beginning his third
full season as the Cincinnati manager. "That's asking for trouble.
There wouldn't be anybody you could trust. No way. I mean, you're
asking to get a new job. You'd have to be the dumbest son of a bitch
in the world to do that. You have to uphold the laws of gambling on
baseball because baseball has integrity."

Giamatti, then the National League president and marking time
for Ueberroth's departure, was also aware of the necessity of maintaining baseball's integrity. After discussing the apparent problem
with Fay Vincent, his future deputy, Giamatti decided an investigation was appropriate.

Vincent recommended the hiring of an outsider and knew the
man for the job: John Dowd, a Washington attorney then with the
firm of Heron, Burchette, Ruckert and Rothwell. Dowd had been a
prosecutor with the U.S. Justice Department and headed a successful

probe of mobsters and their financial irregularities. He had also investigated Clarence Kelly, then the director of the FBI, on charges of accepting improper gifts.

A former Marine Corps captain, Dowd had a deserved reputation as a bulldog investigator, skillful in extracting information and zealous in his pursuit of the quarry. Vincent told Giamatti: "When Dowd sees evil, the gloves come off. If he went after the Pope, he'd bring him down." Dowd accepted the assignment on February 23, 1989, five weeks before Giamatti succeeded Ueberroth.

Baseball Rule 21(d), set in large type and posted in all major and minor league clubhouses, states with stark finality:

"Any player, umpire or club or league official or employee, who shall bet any sum whatsoever upon any baseball game in connection with which the bettor has no duty to perform, shall be declared ineligible for one year.

"Any player, umpire or club or league official or employee, who shall bet any sum whatsoever on any baseball game in which the bettor has a duty to perform shall be declared permanently ineligible."

At the conclusion of his investigation, Dowd released a 225-page report, along with seven volumes of depositions, statements and exhibits, which laid out in detail—and with what seemed to be overwhelming corroboration—that Rose, while playing and managing the Cincinnati Reds, had bet on baseball and on his own team. Dowd's findings were based on interviews, depositions, a taped telephone conversation, telephone and bank records, canceled checks and betting slips stolen from Rose's home, identified by an expert as being in Rose's handwriting. The betting sheets contained a listing of major league games, including Cincinnati games, with the final scores.

The report further stated that in an effort to conceal his gambling, Rose used as many as five intermediaries and that in one three-month period he was $400,000 in debt. In a sworn deposition given to Dowd, Rose denied having been in debt from gambling losses, with the claim he "owes nobody nothing."

The Dowd report emphasized that debt leads to obligation which leads to corruption and quoted Rose acknowledging under oath that on one occasion, a bookie had threatened, in Rose's words, "to burn my house down and break my kid's legs if I didn't pay him."

Perhaps the most damaging evidence against Rose was a summary of telephone calls from Paul Janszen, who was placing Rose's bets, to bookmakers: from Janszen to Rose's home and to Rose's clubhouse office; to Rose's hotel room when the club was on the road; from Rose to Janszen; and to sports' services, either from Rose or his associates, for the latest game-scores.

A daily chronology of the telephone traffic, from April 8, 1987, through July 5, 1987, consumed seventy-two pages of the 225-page report. For example, from April 8 through April 30, a period of twenty-three days, and typical of the constant communication, there was a total of 278 calls, most of them less than two minutes in duration.

A typical entry:

"June 1, 1987.

"The Reds played the Cardinals in Cincinnati at 7:35 PM and lost 9–6 in 10 innings. Telephone records indicate Paul Janszen called Pete Rose's home at 12:31 PM. The call lasted one minute. Janszen called Pete Rose's home at 1:29 PM. The call lasted two minutes. Janszen called Ron Peters at 5:57 PM. The call lasted one minute.

"Janszen called Pete Rose's home at 5:58 PM. The call lasted two minutes. Janszen called Peters at 6:36 PM. The call lasted four minutes. Janszen called Pete Rose at the Reds' clubhouse at 6:45 PM. The call lasted one and a half minutes. Janszen called the sports line at 8:28 PM. The call lasted one minute. Between 8:42 PM and 11:30 PM, Janszen called the sports line five times.

"According to Peters' records, Rose bet $2,000 each on the Reds,

Cleveland, Toronto, the Yankees, Kansas City, the Dodgers and Philadelphia. He won one and lost six bets."

The sequence of the calls, Dowd observed, "[Is] consistent with the writer/agent calling the bookmaker to get the line, then calling the bettor to give him the line and get the wagers. The writer/agent then calls back to relay the wagers he just accepted from the bettor."

Janszen and Ron Peters, the principal accusers, testified that they placed bets for Rose. Peters was a bookmaker. He accepted some of the bets but also laid some off with other bookmakers. Janszen and Peters agreed Rose bet on the Reds but always to win, never to lose.

Janszen was a bodybuilder, six feet three and a muscular 300 pounds. He had served four months for tax evasion and later was convicted of dealing drugs. For several years, he apparently was Rose's closest confidante. Janszen sometimes traveled with the Reds, who more often than not paid his expenses, and with his girl friend, Danita Marcum, was a guest at the house Rose rented during spring training.

Peters, in his deposition, described Marcum: "She's a blonde, she's, you know, built. She's got a nice body." Marcum was also among Rose's runners and testified that she occasionally placed bets for Rose.

Dowd: Did you bet on the Cincinnati Reds at the request of Pete Rose?

Marcum: Yes.

Dowd: While he was manager of the Cincinnati Reds baseball team?

Marcum: Yes, he did.

Dowd: Is there any question in your mind about that?

Marcum: No.

Peters owned a restaurant in Franklin, Ohio, and was awaiting sentencing on charges of cocaine trafficking. Peters and Janszen were not friends. Working with federal drug agents in July 1988, Janszen, wearing a hidden microphone, bought an ounce of cocaine from Peters which led to a guilty plea by Peters and a two-year prison term.

Peters said he broke from Rose when Rose owed him $34,000. Janszen had an identical grievance. Janszen insisted Rose owed him $44,000. In an effort to collect, Janszen met with Reuven Katz, Rose's principal attorney and financial advisor, who had the power of attorney to sign checks from Rose's personal account. Janszen said he needed the money to hire a lawyer to defend him on a drug charge brought by the FBI. If he wasn't recompensed, Janszen threatened to expose Rose. In an unsuccessful attempt to appease him, Katz gave him a check for $10,000.

To the end, Rose insisted he had never bet baseball. When advised, Janszen and Peters and a half dozen of his other associates had testified to the contrary, Rose said:

"Those guys could have had a quintet in the last three months. Because they're all singing. They're all singing a lot. They have to sing or they'll be in Sing Sing."

Dowd assured Peters that if he talked, he would do whatever possible to have his sentence lightened. And so a five-paragraph letter, crafted by Dowd and bearing Giamatti's signature, the equivalent of the Good Housekeeping Seal of Approval, was dispatched to the sentencing jurist, Carl Rubin, the Cheif Judge of the U.S. District Court for the Southern District of Ohio. Rubin had an iron reputation: When it came to sentencing he would not be swayed by anyone not directly involved in the investigation.

The letter stated that Peters's testimony had provided baseball with "significant and truthful cooperation."

Giamatti regarded it as a routine request and described his own action as nothing more than a "human reproductive xerographer." He said he "simply wanted to communicate to the judge that this man had been forthcoming and cooperative."

The controversial letter, dated April 18, 1989, in full:

"I am advised that Ron Peters will appear before you shortly to enter a plea of guilty to two felonies and to receive his sentence.

"It is my purpose to bring to your attention the significant and truthful cooperation Mr. Peters has provided to my special counsel who is conducting the investigation into allegations concerning the conduct and activities of Pete Rose, the manager of the Cincinnati baseball club.

"Mr. Peters has been readily available at all times and has provided critical sworn testimony about Mr. Rose and his associates. In addition, Mr. Peters has probative documentary evidence to support his testimony and the testimony of others. Based upon other information in our possession, I am satisfied Mr. Peters has been candid, forthright and truthful.

"In view of the confidential nature of my inquiry, I would respectfully request this letter to remain under the Court's seal until the completion of my inquiry.

"Thank you for your consideration of this letter on behalf of Mr. Peters."

Most judges would have dismissed it as an inconsequential intrusion. Rubin regarded it as an affront and outrage. The mistake was that Dowd, not Giamatti, should have signed the letter. It gave Rose's attorneys the ammunition they needed: Giamatti had prejudged Rose and was not capable of an impartial hearing.

Judge Rubin was a die-hard Cincinnati baseball fan. Rose was in his pantheon. Judge Rubin was not involved in the baseball investigation and could have remained silent. Instead, he called Reuven Katz. They had been friends since they were boys, "friends for sixty years," Judge Rubin told the *Cincinnati Post*. Two days later the letter and Judge Rubin's angry reaction appeared in the Cincinnati newspapers.

"I don't want to get into an imbroglio involving Rose," Judge
Rubin was quoted as saying. "But there is evidence here, in my opinion, of a vendetta against him."

Katz responded with the claim that Giamatti could not be allowed
to be "the judge, jury and appellate court." On June 19, a week
before Giamatti was scheduled to open his hearing, Rose's legal team
filed suit against the Commissioner in Ohio State Court, major league
baseball and the Cincinnati club, charging that Giamatti should be
replaced by "an impartial decision-maker" because of his "displayed
bias and outrageous conduct."

Judge Robert Nadel, in an extraordinary, nationally televised
Sunday court proceeding, restrained baseball from moving against
Rose. It was a shameless hometown decision by Nadel, who was up
for reelection. Many of Nadel's colleagues said his decision was without basis; he was prematurely intervening with an incomplete
administrative proceeding. Nadel, himself, confirmed this observation with the acknowledgment he was entering "uncharted" legal
territory.

Judge William Matthews, in a diplomatic statement, told the
*Cincinnati Post* that Nadel had a "tough decision to make with the
hometown crowd watching."

Nadel read from a copy of the letter when he announced his decision in a crowded courtroom. The *Chicago Tribune* reported that the
ruling was "heard in a circus atmosphere as reporters elbowed for
position in the courtroom and the hallways . . . a Rose supporter
stood on the outside steps wearing a leather football helmet, waving
a baseball glove and bat, and carrying a sign: "There's nothing
wrong with an honest bet."

Suddenly, the controversy changed course. It was now a personal
duel between Giamatti, who loved the rules, and Rose, who loved to
break them. According to the baseball rules, supported by the com-

missioner's "best interest" powers, Giamatti could have suspended Rose without a hearing. But he wanted to give Rose his day in court.

For the next four months, with a case founded almost entirely on Giamatti's letter, Rose's attorneys were able to neutralize the Commissioner. Giamatti's attempt to summon Rose for a hearing were repeatedly blocked. Confronted with the lengthening stalemate, Rose's attorneys began discussing the possibility of a settlement with the condition there would be no admission by Rose that he had bet on baseball.

On August 24, 1989, six months after the investigation had begun, Giamatti exiled Rose from baseball. The suspension was announced at a midmorning news conference at the New York Hilton and was carried live on national television. Copies of a five-page document, titled "Agreement and Resolution," signed the day before by Giamatti and Rose, were distributed to the media.

"The banishment for life of Peter Rose from baseball is the sad end of a sorry episode," Giamatti said, reading from a prepared statement. "One of the game's greatest players has engaged in a variety of acts which have stained the game, and he must now live with the consequences of those acts. Let it also be clear that no individual is superior to the game. I will be told I am an idealist. I hope so. I will continue to locate ideals I hold for myself and for my country in the national game, as well as in other of our national institutions. The matter of Mr. Rose is now closed."

In addition to declaring Rose permanently ineligible, the document "acknowledges that the Commissioner has treated him fairly" and "Rose will conclude these proceedings before the Commissioner without a hearing and the Commissioner will not make any formal findings or determinations on any matter including without limitation the allegation that Peter Edward Rose bet on any major league baseball games."

The agreement further stipulated that counsel for Rose had taken steps to dismiss a civil suit against Giamatti, and that Rose "acknowledges that the Commissioner has a factual basis to impose the penalty provided herein and agrees not to challenge that penalty in court or otherwise."

Within minutes, Giamatti purposely broke his part of the bargain. During a press conference that followed, Giamatti responded to a query as to whether he believed Rose had bet on baseball.

"In the absence of a hearing and therefore in the absence of any evidence to the contrary," Giamatti said, "I am confronted by the factual record of the Dowd report. And on the basis of that, yes, I have concluded that he bet on baseball."

And, he was asked, on the Cincinnati Reds?

"Yes," Giamatti replied.

And about the possibility of reinstatement?

"Is there a deal, a secret number? No. There is a standing rule on the subject."

The rule to which Giamatti referred is 15(c) which states: "No application for reinstatement from the Ineligible List may be made until lapse of one year from the date of placement on the Ineligible List."

Rose responded with a press conference in Cincinnati, also nationally televised.

"As you can imagine it's a very sad day," Rose said, his voice wavering. "I've been in baseball for three decades, and to think I'm going to be out of baseball for a very short period of time hurts . . . I've made some mistakes, and I'm being punished for those mistakes. However, the settlement is fair. Especially in the wording that says there's no finding that I bet on baseball . . . Regardless of what the Commissioner said today, I did not bet on baseball."

Asked if he expected to be in reinstated, Rose replied, "Absolutely, without a doubt."

He would apply for reinstatement as soon as the rules permit. As for his gambling habits, he insisted: "I don't think I have a gambling problem—not at all. I won't be seeking help of any kind."

A reporter asked, "If you are innocent why did you agree to this?"

Rose was silent for several seconds and then stepped aside. Reuven Katz answered for him. In a carefully worded response, Katz said Rose had confessed certain indiscretions in his meeting with Dowd such as betting with bookmakers and consorting with felons that are in violation of Rule 21(f) that says: "Conduct not in the best interests of baseball—whatever that conduct may be—is subject to penalty, including permanent ineligibility."

For Rose, the Commissioner's decision terminated his tenure as the manager of the Reds. He was also barred from any activities association with professional baseball, including visiting clubhouses or a playing field participating in old-timers games, and from accepting any position. He was the fifteenth man placed on the permanently ineligible roll since the Office of Commissioner was established in 1920.

Giamatti died nine days later, on September 1, 1989, of a massive heart attack at his vacation home at Edgartown, Massachusetts on the island of Martha's Vineyard. He was 51, only three years older than Rose.

Giamatti's wife, the former Toni Smith whom he had met in a drama class at Yale, and their son Paul, one of three grown children, found him unconscious and in full cardiac arrest in midafternoon. Efforts to revive him were unsuccessful. He had the shortest reign, five months, of any commissioner.

There was an enormous outpouring of affection. Memorial services were held at Yale and at Carnegie Hall. On the Yale campus, a black granite bench was dedicated in his memory, only the fourth memorial to a Yale figure in the university's history. The inscription was a quote from Giamatti: "A liberal education is at the heart of a civil society, and at the heart of a liberal education is the act of teaching."

Pete Rose was convicted on two counts of income tax evasion on July 29, 1990, and served five months in a federal minimum-security prison at Marion, Illinois. He was also fined $50,000 and ordered to pay $366,042 in back taxes. On February 8, 1991, in anticipation of his first year on the ballot, the directors of the Hall of Fame changed the rules for election so that any player on the Ineligible List could not be a considered for the Cooperstown shrine. Rose received forty-one write-in votes in 1992; by 1995 the number had diminished to fifteen.

# FAY VINCENT 20

Fay Vincent was the last of the big-foot commissioners. He was elected on September 13, 1989, two weeks after the death of his good friend, Bart Giamatti. Vincent signed on with the naive notion he would ladle justice in equal portion to all: fans, players, umpires, and owners. He departed with a scowl and the knowledge he was beholden only to the owners. When he refused to acquiesce, they not only forced his resignation but virtually abolished the office in favor of a chairman of the board.

With the exception of Judge Landis, who inherited the Black Sox scandal, none of Vincent's predecessors was confronted with as many difficulties in his maiden season: An earthquake in the San Francisco Bay area halted the World Series for ten days; a thirty-two day spring training lockout, imposed by management, delayed the opening of the 1990 season; and a seemingly endless investigation into the alleged improprieties of George Steinbrenner, the general partner of the New York Yankees, who was given a stiff two-year suspension.

"Fay Vincent really had a baptism by fire," said Fred Wilpon, co-owner and president of the New York Mets and a Vincent loyalist to the finish. "He had to deal with more serious problems in his first few months than other commissioners have dealt with in a full term of office."

It was a perilous journey throughout. Vincent contributed to the turmoil with the insistence that he adjudicate all significant disputes, some of which should have been handled by the league presidents. National League president Bill White appeared to be in almost constant contention with the eighth commissioner. Dr. Bobby Brown, the American League president who rarely expressed displeasure, also registered concern with what may have been an unprecedented letter of complaint.

Otherwise, it was an exhilarating ride. A genuine fan, Vincent was constantly touring the ballparks. It was his greatest pleasure. He signed autographs and spoke to everyone: players, the managers and coaches, umpires, club officials, and writers. He kept a daily journal and may have been the most accessible of all commissioners. He ate hot dogs in the second inning, ice cream in the sixth. And he understood the game.

"In the early innings," he said, "there are two things I concentrate on—the pitchers and the umpires. The first inning is the toughest for a pitcher, so I study his control. I watch the umpires to get a fix on their strike zone. Important considerations as the game progresses."

Like Giamatti, he was thrilled when introduced to his boyhood heroes. He asked Joe DiMaggio who was the toughest pitcher he ever faced, how he guessed what pitch was coming, how he hit the knuckleball. The Hall of Fame ceremonies in Cooperstown were heaven. He presided at the dinner on the eve of the inductions, then sat, until midnight, in the rocking chairs on the circular back porch at the Otesaga Hotel, smoking long cigars and engaging the dozens of returning diamond immortals. The delight was mutual. They, too, were pleased in making his acquaintance.

"Fay really enjoyed being Commissioner," said Richard Levin, baseball's public relations director.

Francis Thomas Vincent, Jr., of Irish-American descent, was the best athlete to occupy the throne. He was born in Waterbury, Connecticut, on May 29, 1938, the son of Francis Thomas Vincent, who had been a telephone company employee, and the former Alice Lynch, a kindergarten teacher. He inherited his love for sports from his father who had captained the Yale football team. The elder Vincent was also a professional football official and umpired amateur baseball games until the age of 76, two years before his death.

When Vincent was five his family moved to New Haven. He went to grammar school in the nearby town of Hamden. For his preparatory education, he attended the Hotchkiss School in Lakeville where he was the star guard and captain of the football team.

"He was a moose of a guy, 6 foot three and 240 pounds, with short legs and big shoulders," recalled his Hotchkiss teammate William H.T. "Bucky" Bush, the younger brother of President George Bush. "Half the plays we ran were behind Vincent. He was so strong he could take out two men."

When they were 18, Vincent and Bucky Bush drove to Texas to work as roughnecks in George Bush's oil fields. They shared a one-room apartment. Bucky Bush, who later became an investment banker in St. Louis, recalled that the other roughnecks were in awe of Vincent. Said Bush: "Fay's IQ was higher than the rest of them combined."

Following his graduation from Hotchkiss, Vincent enrolled at Williams College in Williamstown, Massachusetts. In his freshman year he suffered a crippling back injury that altered the course of his life. It occurred when his roommate, as a prank, locked him in their fourth-floor dormitory room. To get to the next room, Vincent climbed out the window onto an icy ledge. He slipped and fell. Two vertebrae were crushed, his spine severely damaged and his legs partially paralyzed.

Surgeons rebuilt the broken vertebrae with bone from his hip but expressed doubt he would ever walk again. During his first year of recuperation, he watched all the Yankees games on television. "And if the game was rained out, I'd be very sad," he told interviewer Roger Cohen.

Vincent learned how to walk with a cane. But he never regained full strength of his legs. He has been philosophical about his terrible misfortune. "When I got hurt I was really a jock," he said. "That was a big part of my life. Then I became more interested in academic and intellectual things. I've always thought getting hurt may have pushed me in a direction that was better in the long-term."

He finished four years of the Williams curriculum in three. Graduating cum laude in 1960, Vincent planned to become a Jesuit priest but abandoned that hope when he was told his disability would prevent him from celebrating Mass. Instead, he entered the Yale Law School, which granted him an LLB degree in 1963. For the next fifteen years, he was a corporate attorney in New York and Washington. In early 1978, he joined the U.S. Securities and Exchange Commission. Unhappy in this assignment, he resigned six months later and accepted an offer from Herbert A. Allen, a friend from Williams College, whose family controlled Columbia Pictures. In the wake of a scandal, Allen needed "someone with impeccable integrity."

"I was in law enforcement on Friday," Vincent recalled, "and on Monday I was running a worldwide entertainment business." In 1982, after Coca Cola purchased Columbia Pictures, he was appointed chairman of the board and a vice president of Coca Cola, a position that offered lucrative stock options. When he departed in 1988, he was a multimillionaire.

Vincent and Giamatti had met at a party before a Yale-Princeton football game in 1979. Vincent referred to it as a "magical" occasion.

They discussed the possibility of working together. This became a reality when Giamatti was elected commissioner. Giamatti created the position of deputy commissioner and put Vincent in charge of broadcasting, special events, corporate sponsorship, licensing, and publishing.

"I could think of nothing better than to get up in the morning and work for Bart and baseball," Vincent said. "To me that was very close to nirvana."

Nirvana was a taunting and uncontrollable mistress. A month into his term, Vincent was confronted with his first crisis. The Bay Area was rocked by a major earthquake on Tuesday, October 17, 1989, at 5:04 PM Pacific Daylight Time, thirty minutes before the San Francisco Giants and the Oakland Athletics were to meet in Candlestick Park in Game 3 of the World Series before a sellout crowd of 62,000.

The quake centered sixty miles south of San Francisco, registered 7.1 on the Richter scale, shook the stadium for fifteen to twenty seconds, and cut off the power supply. An auxiliary press box that hung from under the roof along the third base line began swaying. The next day local engineers said that if the quake had lasted ten seconds longer, the press box would have torn loose and fallen on the thousands of fans below.

Once the vibrations ceased, many in the crowd, unaware of the devastation caused elsewhere, began chanting: "Play ball." A half hour later, after being told that power could not be restored, Vincent called the game off. The damage to the Bay Area was estimated at more than a billion dollars. A section of the upper deck of the Bay Bridge, the major link between San Francisco and Oakland, dropped onto the lower level. A mile and a half stretch of the Nimitz Freeway collapsed, crushing cars and trucks below. The fatality count for the entire area was sixty-seven.

Less than twenty-four hours later, the city still without power, Vincent held an eerie candlelight press conference at the St. Francis Hotel in San Francisco. Having met with stadium engineers, with representatives of both leagues, both teams, officials of the Players Association, and with civic officials, Vincent announced that the Series—which he described as "our modest little sporting event"— would be postponed for at least a week.

The ten-day postponement was the longest in Series history and the first ever for anything other than inclement weather. Through it all, Vincent was lauded for his common sense and obvious concern for the citizens in this time of crisis. At his suggestion, the major league clubs voted to contribute $100,000 each into a relief fund.

"If ever the business of fun and games was put in the proper perspective, Vincent did it," Hal Bodley wrote in *USA Today*. It was the high point of Vincent's reign. The earthquake gave him a national identity and, in retrospect, a new level of confidence. Unfortunately, it also gave him an exaggerated sense of his power. As author John Helyar observed, "It was the beginning of the transformation of his role. He started looking for issues."

He didn't have to look far. He dismissed Barry Rona, who for more than a decade, had been effective as the owners' point man in negotiations with the players' union—an experienced and wise head at the bargaining table. Simultaneously, Vincent appointed Steve Greenberg, a Los Angeles attorney, as his deputy. The son of Hall of Fame slugger Hank Greenberg, Steve had studied English literature at the foot of Giamatti at Yale and to complete the bond, he was on the board of Hotchkiss.

More important, Greenberg had been a player agent and had a good relationship with Don Fehr, executive director of the Players Association. Vincent believed Greenberg's presence would enhance his standing and credibility with the union and that he would be in a stronger position to forge a peaceable settlement during the labor negotiations. It was an error in judgment. Fehr couldn't care less; his only concern was making the best possible deal for the players.

Vincent was aware he had been hired and was being paid by the owners. But he was determined he wouldn't toady to them and didn't want to be portrayed as a stodgy figurehead above the fray. Buoyed by his acclaim for his sensible handling of the earthquake disaster, he made the mistake of trying to mediate.

It was the usual acrimonious dispute. The major issues were the rules governing free agency and salary arbitration. Once coupled together, in 1989 they had driven player compensation beyond the $3 million plateau. Charles O'Connor of Washington, who, in effect, succeeded Rona, presented a new concept—a "Partnership Plan." The owners were willing to make available 48 percent of all gate receipts and national and local broadcasting revenues for player salaries and ancillary benefits. In exchange, they asked for a salary cap. As soon as a team reached the cap, it would be prohibited from signing any more free agents until its payroll dropped below the designated ceiling.

Another component provided for a pay-for-performance system to replace salary arbitration and would apply to players with less than six years of major league experience. These players would be grouped into two categories, their salaries determined by length of service and a statistical formula covering the previous two seasons. As in the past, when players reached the six-year level, they would become free agents.

Fehr correctly contended the cap was a veiled attempt to harness the free market system, which it was, and disagreed that a new system was necessary because some of the small-market franchises were in a severe financial bind. After nineteen fruitless bargaining sessions, Vincent, on February 19, 1990, chaired a joint meeting to brief the owners on the stalemated negotiations. It was then decided that lacking a settlement, the owners would not open the spring training camps.

Following a weekend break, negotiations resumed. For the first time, Vincent attended negotiation sessions and proposed several solutions, all rebuffed by Fehr. Aware that some owners, perhaps a majority, were angered by his intrusion, Vincent explained, "Faced with a season in jeopardy, it would be a big mistake if the Commissioner did not become involved."

Vincent had been reaching out to Fehr in private meetings. On February 15, management imposed its threatened spring training lockout. Some owners, Fred Wilpon of the New York Mets, Peter O'Malley of the Dodgers, and Eli Jacobs of Baltimore, urged Vincent to wangle a settlement whatever the cost. The majority expressed the opposite view and repeatedly told him to stop playing "Mr. Nice Guy." Vincent agreed. He would no longer participate. O'Connor would take over. "From now on," Vincent said, "I'm going to be known as the Conan the Commissioner."

On Thursday, March 8, after another inconclusive bargaining session, O'Connor told the members of the Player Relations Committee to play it cool: "If they try to call us over the weekend, don't respond. We'll wait until Monday or Tuesday and come back fresh."

On Saturday afternoon, O'Connor was with his son at Madison Square Garden watching a college basketball game. At half time a reporter approached and asked:

"What's Fay meeting with Don Fehr for?"

"He's not," O'Connor replied. "He's at his home in Greenwich."

"You're half right," the reporter said. "He's in Greenwich with Don Fehr."

Vincent was still trying to do good. But according to O'Connor and PRC chairman Bud Selig, his efforts for compromise was scuttling the owners' bargaining position. It was at that moment that the anti-Vincent faction began to grow. It also prompted the owners to consider supplemental legislation that would prevent the commissioner, any commissioner, from intervening in labor matters.

The lockout lasted thirty-two days, washed out most of spring training, and caused a one-week delay in the start of the 1990 regular season. In settling, both sides agreed to expand the rosters from twenty-five to twenty-seven players during the first three weeks of the season. At the suggestion of the Players Association, it was also decided that, in addition to make-up doubleheaders, three days would be added to the season so the full 162-game schedule could be completed.

Shorn of his powers during the labor struggles, Vincent picked his crown up from the floor and in the first week of June plunged into what should have been, at most, a minor hearing. Instead, it developed into a lengthy litigation that concluded with a strange two-year exile of George Steinbrenner, majority owner of the Yankees. Like Finley before him, who was unjustly penalized by Bowie Kuhn, Steinbrenner was a victim of his reputation. There was no crime.

The only explanation was that Vincent, overzealous, was pandering to the New York press which, regardless of the circumstances, portrayed King George as a menacing ogre. I am convinced that if the Yankees had been in contention, or near-contention, the New York baseball writers would have been busy chronicling the events on the field. But the Yankees were dull copy, in last place in the American League East. The only accessible avenue to lively reading was to assault the villainous owner.

The media shrill included the specious charge of mismanagement. Steinbrenner, in effect, was responsible for the decline of the Yankees. If poor management was a violation, Connie Mack, who was among baseball's most revered figures, would have been exiled to

Elba. Mack's Philadelphia Athletics finished last seventeen times. Philip Wrigley, the longtime overseer of the Chicago Cubs, would have suffered a similar fate, guilty of twenty consecutive seasons in the second division.

The source of the sordid allegations against Steinbrenner was Howard Spira, a small-time gambler with mob connections. Spira, later indicted in federal court on eight counts of attempted extortion, brought Steinbrenner potentially damaging information on Dave Winfield. An all-star outfielder, Winfield was a free agent following the 1980 season and had signed a ten-year contract with the Yankees for $22 million. As part of the deal, Steinbrenner was obligated to pay an additional $300,000 annually to the David M. Winfield Foundation, a nonprofit organization for the underprivileged.

Spira worked for the foundation in a nonpaying public relations position and claimed that Winfield and Al Frohman, Winfield's agent and principal gofer, who was also an officer of the foundation, had misused the charitable funds. This charge was later corroborated when, in a court settlement, Winfield paid $229,667 in delinquent contributions. Spira also insisted that Winfield had loaned him money to help him pay gambling debts and produced a copy of a check payable to him from Winfield for $15,000. Winfield acknowledged the loan but insisted he was unaware Spira was a gambler.

This was in December 1986, when Peter Ueberroth was still in office. Steinbrenner, who had been feuding with Winfield, alerted Ueberroth of the Spira allegations. In subsequent sworn testimony, Ueberroth conceded Steinbrenner had come to his office and had expressed concern about Winfield's association with a gambler.

According to a lengthy article in *Sports Illustrated*, which conducted its own investigation: "Ueberroth made Steinbrenner sound like the little boy who cried wolf, always coming to baseball with allegations that couldn't be corroborated. As a result, Ueberroth said, he assumed that any and all allegations raised by Steinbrenner were untrue.

"George regularly came to us with a litany of things that were wrong," a Ueberroth aide recalled. "'This guy's bad. This owner did this. This umpire's bad.' Frankly, looking back, maybe we did throw water on things that were important."

A cursory investigation followed. For the next two years there was no response. Steinbrenner interpreted the silence as an indication of approval, that the Commissioner's office was either covering up or had condoned Spira's relationship with Winfield.

According to Steinbrenner's attorneys, it was Spira who insisted he be interviewed:

"Spira appeared at the Commissioner's office [in February 1989] and demanded to be interviewed. The interview, conducted by Kevin Hallinan, baseball's director of security, was taped. The transcription ran 189 pages. Spira provided Hallinan with additional information concerning Winfield, the Winfield Foundation, and Frohman.

"Further, Spira told Hallinan that Steinbrenner had made no promises, and that Spira had intended to approach Steinbrenner and request $150,000, a job, and a place to live. Hallinan did not investigate the matter further.

"More importantly, neither Hallinan nor the Commissioner's office contacted Steinbrenner to advise him of this meeting—and most significantly, they did not inform Steinbrenner that if Spira asked for money, Steinbrenner should not give him any—even though the Commissioner's office knew that Spira was going to approach Steinbrenner and request money and a job."

In early June 1990, three and a half years after Steinbrenner had sounded the alarm, Vincent, who previously had described

Steinbrenner as a "blight on baseball," ordered a hearing. Vincent's action was in response to a three-page March 18 exposé in the *New York Daily News*, sold to the paper by Spira who revealed that Steinbrenner, six months earlier, had paid him $40,000. The article revealed the "bizarre and tangled relationship of two unlikely soul mates [Spira and Steinbrenner] sharing an obsession of making life miserable for Winfield."

Two days later, Vincent hired John Dowd, the bulldog Washington D.C. attorney who helped hang Pete Rose, to lead the investigation.

Steinbrenner's attorneys, from the beginning, were convinced the inquiry was biased. Roland Thau, a veteran public defender who briefly represented Spira in criminal proceedings, later testified that Dowd asked for his assistance—in Dowd's words—"to bring George down," a request made only four days after Dowd's appointment as Vincent's "special counsel."

For Steinbrenner, the road to justice was littered with what appeared to be unfair procedures. During the Vincent hearing, Steinbrenner was not permitted to present testimony from any witness other than himself; he had seven witnesses, he said, whose testimony would be crucial. Nor were his attorneys allowed to cross-examine any witness whatsoever.

Steinbrenner insisted he was a victim of extortion, that he had given Spira the $40,000 after Spira had told him he would go public with the allegation that Lou Piniella, the Yankees' field manager, along with other club employees, had been betting on baseball. In addition, Steinbrenner said Spira had been threatening him and his family.

In the end, Vincent pulled the "best interests" clause from his ample quiver, claiming that Steinbrenner's relationship with Spira and his eagerness to collect "dirt" on one of his players was detrimental to baseball. It was a curious judgment. Had Steinbrenner attempted to keep secret his connection with Spira, there would have been a basis for the charge. But Steinbrenner had come forward and requested Ueberroth's intervention almost four years earlier.

Vincent's hearing lasted only two days, July 5–6, 1990. On July 30, Steinbrenner was declared ineligible from baseball for two years, effective August 20, and ordered to withdraw as the Yankees' general partner.

Vincent's statement read, in part:

"Mr. Steinbrenner has accepted the opinions in my decision to the effect that his conduct violated Rule 21(f) of the Major League Agreement for conduct not in the best interests of baseball and will have no further involvement in the management of the New York Yankees or in the day-to-day operation of that club.

"Mr. Steinbrenner agrees that he is to be treated as if he had been placed on the permanent ineligible list subject to the following exceptions: 1) With my approval, he may be consulted and participate in major financial and business decisions of the New York club; 2) Commencing in the spring 1991 he may seek my approval in writing to attend a limited number of major league games.

"By accepting these sanctions, Mr. Steinbrenner has agreed he will not litigate or challenge the decision or these sanctions and that he will not institute litigation as a result of any decision I might make arising out of this agreement or these sanctions."

The absence of the word *suspension* was significant. Had he been suspended, Steinbrenner feared it would discredit and possibly force him to resign from his position as a vice president of the United States Olympic Committee. This was crucial to him; he took great pride in his Olympic activities. Also, he didn't have to sell his majority interest in the team. Control of the Yankees would remain within his family. After Steinbrenner's oldest son, Hank, declined, Robert

Nederlander of Cleveland, a longtime Yankee investor, was named the general partner.

Word of Vincent's decision quickly reached Yankee Stadium, where the Yankees were playing Detroit. The crowd of 24,037 greeted the verdict with a two-minute standing ovation for Vincent—in effect, boos for Steinbrenner. But there was no cheering in baseball's executive suite.

The comment of Gabe Paul, a baseball lifer who had been among Steinbrenner's Yankees associates, was typical.

Said Paul: "He was like a man who was pinched for speeding and convicted of murder."

Observed Jack Gould, a vice president of the Chicago White Sox:

"We don't know what the crime is. Maybe Steinbrenner is guilty and did something awful. I wish someone would tell us what it was."

Steinbrenner was "paroled" two and a half years later, at 12:01 AM on March 1, 1993, and immediately went on the air on WFAN, New York City's all-sports radio station which welcomed him with the playing of "Hail to the Chief." It was a glorious homecoming. The Yankee employees, players included, wore stickers which read "The Boss is Back." *Sports Illustrated* had Steinbrenner on the cover, astride a white horse and outfitted in a Napoleon costume. The Boss was returning from Elba.

Vincent was not on the welcoming committee. He had resigned under pressure six months earlier.

# ALLAN "BUD" SELIG 21

I nto the valley of death rode Allan H. "Bud" Selig, who had been on the phone for twenty-three years, canvassing every square foot of baseball's problems, particularly at the executive level. He had been the quintessential insider. Nobody had matched his devotion, serving on all of the owners' committees, big and small, some of them for two and three terms.

He had purchased 2,000 shares when the Milwaukee Braves went public in 1963: $24,000 for a 1 percent stake. Two years later, when the Braves were under new management, they were uprooted and transplanted to Atlanta. Distraught, Selig dedicated himself—no, more than that, he dedicated his life—to the quest of obtaining a replacement franchise for Milwaukee.

It was a four-year quest. On April 1, 1970, one week before the season began, Selig and Milwaukee were awarded the Seattle Pilots, an American League expansion team that had gone bankrupt after one year of operation. The price, set by a federal bankruptcy judge in Seattle, was $11 million.

Selig was 31, the youngest major league owner. At the time of Fay

Vincent's departure, he had been in baseball for almost a quarter of a century and was chairman of the Executive Council, the game's most powerful body. As such, he was second in command. The owners elected him commissioner pro tem without dispute. Remarkably, he has continued as an interim czar for more than five years, longer than the combined reign of his two predecessors.

Selig rules by consensus. Unlike Bowie Kuhn, who cultivated only the owners he believed to be the most influential, Selig never made such a grievous mistake. Selig is aware that each owner, including those not politically inclined, had a vote that could be used against him. Selig did not have a pecking order. He had telephone time for all.

Said Bob Quinn, a vice president of the San Francisco Giants, a second generation baseball executive with a good grasp of present and former times: "He has no hidden agendas. He knows the owners have twenty-eight diverse personalities and twenty-eight different agendas. He has been a master puppeteer in keeping everybody happy."

Quinn made this observation during the 1994–1995 players' strike, 232 days, the longest stoppage in American professional sports, which included cancellation of the 1994 playoffs and the World Series. The Series shutdown scarred Selig's reign; most fans have never forgiven him. As he later insisted, he was the messenger. All but two owners were in support. Though Selig made the call, Don Fehr, head of the Players Association, should have shouldered at least half the blame. The players were on strike, not the owners.

Testifying before a congressional committee on April 2, 1981, Stan Kasten, president of the Atlanta Braves, described Selig as a "true American success story."

Born on July 10, 1934, in Milwaukee, into a comfortable Jewish household, Selig attended public school. He graduated from Washington High School in 1952 and from the University of Wisconsin three years later, with a major in American history and political science. He served two years in the Army, inducted the day Don Larsen pitched his perfect World Series game. After a two-year hitch, he returned to civilian life and went to work for his father, Ben, who had established an automobile dealership in suburban West Allis.

Early on, beginning in fourth or fifth grade, he exhibited all the signs of the incurable sports fan. He scoured the sports sections and read all the sports biographies and team histories in the school library. Joe DiMaggio, the legendary Yankee Clipper, was his hero. His ambition of playing big-time baseball was shattered in an American Legion game when he was hit by a pitch, on either the shoulder or the head—he can't remember which. He never played organized sports again.

His mother, Marie, a Milwaukee school teacher who was an ardent fan, kindled his interest in baseball. She hauled her sons, Bud and Jerry, to old Borchert Field, home of the minor league Brewers. She taught them how to keep a box score, how to compute batting and earned run averages, and the cardinal baseball sin of being thrown out at third base for the third out.

One summer, when Selig was 12 or 13, in reward for his good schoolwork, his mother took him on a train trip to New York City. There were three major league teams in New York at that time. They went to a game every day. "It was more than just enjoyable," Selig recalled. "It was paradise."

Tall and spare (he still rides a stationary bicycle 45 minutes each morning) Selig married Donna Chaimson, a storekeeper's daughter from Northern Wisconsin, when he was 22. They were divorced in 1975, nineteen years later primarily, she said, because she had been ignored; his love for baseball left little time for her. Selig remarried less than two years later, in 1977, to Sue Lappins, who had been a real estate broker. She attends almost all of the Brewers' home games. He has two daughters from his first wife, Sari Markenson who works in her father's auto leasing firm, and Wendy Selig-Prieb, an attorney who has been operating the Brewers since his election as the interim commissioner. Her husband, Laurel Prieb, is the club's vice president of corporate affairs.

Of all the commissioners, Selig has been the busiest. His mission was to bring baseball into the twenty-first century, with a hard-core minority not eager to make the leap. Still, Selig's term has been marked with a succession of unprecedented accomplishments: dividing each league from two to three divisions, giving birth to the wild card in postseason play; inter–league play; awarding expansion franchises to Phoenix and Tampa; the elimination of the failed Baseball Network television experiment; and a new Basic Agreement, the collective contract that binds the owners and players' union together.

Labor peace was achieved at a terrible cost for both sides. In retrospect, a players' strike was inevitable and had been building since negotiations had reopened on the Basic Agreement in December 1992, a year prior to its expiration. Yet, throughout 1993, there was almost no bargaining. Concerned that the owners might implement unilateral changes after the expiration of the Basic Agreement, union chief Donald Fehr warned of a player strike in 1994.

On February 17, 1994, back at the bargaining table, the owners linked their demands to include a salary cap and revenue sharing. In June, they agreed to split all revenues with the players, 50-50, including licensing money, with a guarantee of $1 billion for player salaries. In exchange, the owners asked for a cap and the elimination of salary arbitration but were agreeable to lowering the free agency requirement from six to four years of major league service with the provision that a player's existing club could match any offer until he had six full seasons of service.

There were subsequent adjustments, most of which were not acceptable. The owners, for example, agreed to take the salary cap off the table and replace it with a team luxury tax; in essence, it would have had a similar, if not identical effect, of curbing player salaries. On July 28, the union's executive board, by unanimous acclaim, set an August 12 strike date. Selig responded with a "tentative" September 9 deadline for canceling the remainder of the season.

Five days later, on September 14, America groaned as Selig dropped the other shoe at a press conference at Milwaukee's County Stadium. His patience and the 1994 season had come to an end. It was the first time the championship season had been aborted since 1918, during World War I, but even then there was a World Series.

"I had a sick feeling inside," Selig recalled years later. "I thought of all the World Series I had seen, beginning with the Cubs and Detroit in '45. But I don't look at it that I canceled the Series. I had called Don Fehr a few days before. I said, 'Don, we need to talk about the World Series.' The television networks were on me. They would have had to rearrange their programming. The advertisers, our sponsors, were calling. We had tickets to print. And Don said, 'We're not even close.'"

A resolution favoring cancellation was signed by the owners, with two abstentions, Peter Angelos of Baltimore and Marge Schott of Cincinnati. The feisty son of Greek immigrants whose fifteen-person purchase group had paid a record $173 million for the Orioles a year earlier, Angelos had been urging the owners to settle at any price.

"We've given in twenty times in a row," Schott told newsmen. "You can't lose all the time. The players don't like what's going on. But they're a union and they have to stick together." She also complained that Reds fans had been refunding a lot of 1995 season ticket orders. She recommended the World Series be played with replacement players who could be brought up from the minor leagues.

It was the eighth stoppage in the past twenty-two years. The Players Association was undefeated, seven victories and one small loss not of major consequence. During Ueberroth's term, the players approved raising salary arbitration eligibility from two to three years of service. Given this history, the players were confident the war would last only two weeks, and that the owners, as in the past, would collapse within a fortnight. They were wrong. Selig kept them united.

The dispute was costly for both sides. The loss to the owners was originally estimated at $900 million, but this deficit was reduced to $376 million as a result of savings in player and administrative salaries, ballpark maintenance, and other miscellaneous expenses.

The players lost 29 percent of their pay, $350 million, because of the cancellation of the final fifty-two days of the 183-day season. Also sacrificed were the many suddenly unreachable statistical bonuses measured by performance over a full season. The playoff and World Series shares that would have accrued to the 200 participants in the postseason were also lost, plus the fame and glory, crucial to even the most hardened professionals.

The superstars were the biggest losers. Bobby Bonilla of the New York Mets led in lost wages: $1.8 million. Others who surrendered more than $1.5 million were Joe Carter and Roberto Alomar of Toronto; Rafael Palmeiro and Cal Ripken, Jr. of Baltimore; and Jack McDowell of the White Sox. For players earning the $109,000 minimum, it was $30,992. Some of their losses were softened by a union war chest, collected for several years in anticipation of a shutdown.

To keep the players from bolting, Fehr scheduled nine regional "informational" meetings, including two pit stops in Latin America. Fehr explained that the owners were intent on fixing salaries. There were occasional dissenting murmurs. At the Chicago meeting, relief pitcher Randy Myers, the Cubs' player rep, told Joey Reaves and Paul Sullivan of the *Chicago Tribune*, "It's a situation where quite frankly a lot of players are disgusted."

So were the fans. Prior to the shutdown and the cancellation of 669 games, it had been an unusually exciting season. Tony Gwynn of the San Diego Padres was batting .394 and was in a position to become the first .400 hitter since Ted Williams in 1941. Matt Williams of the San Francisco Giants, with 43 home runs, and Ken Griffey, Jr., of the Seattle Mariners, with 40, were challenging Roger Maris's one-season record. Other sluggers with 35 or more home runs were Jeff Bagwell, Houston, 39; Frank Thomas, White Sox, 38; Barry Bonds, San Francisco, 37; and Albert Belle, Cleveland, 36.

"We were having one of our greatest seasons and shot ourselves in the foot," said White Sox chairman Jerry Reinsdorf.

Ozzie Guillen, the veteran White Sox shortstop, was among the players who were never wholly in support of the strike. After he had returned to his home in Venezuela, Guillen said the shutdown mystified the Latin American fans.

"Its kind of weird," Guillen reported. "It's a shock down here. I know how the Venezuelan people, the Latin American people, feel about baseball. I try to hide. All they ask about is the strike. They can't understand it. Really, it's a shock, not only in the States but all over the world."

In a television interview in Houston, pitcher Greg Swindell of the Astros, said he was ready to bolt; "I've got house payments, I've got ex-wife payments, I've got a five-year-old, a three-year-old. I have very few friends in baseball that I'm close and personal with. If the time comes and things happen, they can think what they want."

Barry Bonds, the San Francisco Giants' superstar, went to court to have his monthly family support payments cut in half, from $15,000 to $7,500. San Mateo County Commissioner George Taylor granted the request. When in court, Taylor asked Bonds for his autograph. Following a public outrage, Taylor reversed his decision and withdrew from the case. Bonds lost on appeal.

Despite the many indications of player unrest—probably 50 percent or more were against the strike—Fehr was masterful in holding them together. The owners also remained united but bickered among themselves in regard to revenue sharing. All of the small and many of the middle-market clubs were gung-ho for freebies. The major market clubs, except Reinsdorf, were not eager to subsidize the clubs at the bottom of the economic pole.

The pivotal meeting began a year before the player walkout, on August 10, 1993, at the swank American Club in Kohler, Wisconsin, about fifty miles north of Milwaukee. Dick Ravitch, the owners' lead negotiator, presided. Time was running out. Ravitch explained the necessity of finalizing a revenue-sharing procedure he could present to the players so that a salary cap could be adopted.

"We're going to stay here till the finish, until we come to a deal," Ravitch said.

The owners assembled at noon in the Appley Theater Building. The doors opened for a midafternoon snack and again at 7 PM when a platoon of waiters wheeled in their dinner.

Tom Hardicourt of the *Milwaukee Journal Sentinel*, aware that the owners were divided into two camps, made the most telling comment; "The dinner menu is lobster thermidor for the big-market operators. And the small-market guys are saying 'Give us some of your lobster and we'll give you half of our ham sandwich.'"

It was an accurate observation. The next day, the big-market owners separated themselves from the ham-and-eggers. They walked out and rented a room in a building 300 yards away. Emissaries hurried back and forth to report the latest developments. Reinsdorf and Stanton Cook of the Cubs were the main couriers.

Like Bill Bartholomay before him, Haywood Sullivan, president of the wealthy Boston Red Sox, said, "The guy we need is Arnold Schwarzenegger. We need someone to break some heads."

The meetings ended in stalemate, but with some movement. Reinsdorf and Cook of Selig's "Great Lakes Gang" had convinced Wayne Huizenga of Florida and Jerry McMorris of Colorado to abandon the big-market coalition. But there was no similar progress with the Players Association, and so on December 23, 1994, the owners declared an impasse and announced that they would implement their final offer, which included a cap and the elimination of salary arbitration. The players appealed to the National Labor Relations Board.

The NLRB sided with the union. On March 31, 1995, U.S. District Judge Sonia Sotomayor, presiding in the same Manhattan courtroom where Curt Flood made his unsuccessful 1970 attempt for free agency, ruled against the owners. No, that isn't quite correct. She savaged them in her twenty-minute opinion and ordered them to continue bargaining and reinstate the conditions of the expired Basic Agreement. If there was to be a 1995 season without a new deal, the previous collective contract would be in force. Immediately, Fehr announced the players were no longer on strike.

By this time, President Bill Clinton, having dispatched a so-called super-mediator, William J. Usery, Jr., to intervene, was on the White House porch, pleading, "America has been living far too long without baseball. It's time for this strike to end."

Usery, a former secretary of labor who had been successful in mediating many labor disputes, had a good reputation with the Washington D.C. press. In Washington, he seldom met with reporters more than twice a week. This strike was different. In order to feed the goat, a platoon of elite baseball writers, faced with daily deadlines, was constantly on his ass.

Worse for Usery, they had been at the rat hole for several years and were not easily bullshitted. They knew all the participants, from both factions, and understood the issues as well as he did. They also stayed at the same hotel, ate in the same dining room, and swam in the same pool. There was no escape. His only consolation was his huge fee, assumed equally by both sides, reportedly $30,000 a week, plus expenses for himself and his staff.

One afternoon, at the Landsdowne Conference Resort, fifteen minutes from Dulles International Airport, when negotiations were at a standstill, Usery told management representatives, "Settlement is in sight. The union wants to make a deal."

"You know that's not true," an owner insisted.

"I know it," Usery replied. "But I'm a mediator. I'm supposed to say things like that."

Throughout the debate, Reinsdorf was portrayed as the "big foot" among the owners. Having temporarily broken with Selig, Reinsdorf had absented himself from the fray. Fehr, nonetheless, repeatedly fingered Reinsdorf as Enemy No.1. In a subsequent negotiation session in Rye Brook, New York, when Fehr reiterated this view, John Harrington of Boston, president of the PRC, got up from the table, opened a window, and shouted into an empty parking lot, "Jerry! C'mon up here!"

The gap widened, especially after the owners revealed that they would open the 1995 spring training camps with replacement players; if necessary, they would also be employed during the season. Angelos, an attorney who had made his fortune representing unions, dissented and insisted if replacement players were used, the damage "would be immeasurable."

John Franco of the Mets, a veteran relief pitcher, vowed to go after the strikebreakers with his fists. Scott Kaminiecki of the Yankees said he would throw at the heads of the batters who crossed the picket lines. Bobby Bonilla, the Mets' player representative, carried it one step further: "Anyone crossing the picket lines will end up in the East River."

A total of seventeen replacement players who participated in spring training exhibitions eventually appeared in major league games. Ron Rightnowar, a pitcher with Selig's Brewers, was the first, working two and one-third innings of relief against Texas on May 20, 1995. The second was Ron Mahay, a 24-year-old center fielder with the Boston Red Sox who appeared the next day.

"No one on the team spoke to me the first two days," Mahay told an interviewer. "I knew it was going to happen." Player rep Mike Greenwell, a veteran outfielder who was the Boston player rep, broke the ice on the day Mahay was in the starting lineup for the first time. Mahay went 2 for 5 and brought the Fenway Park crowd to its feet after his first hit and again when he made a diving catch.

When pitcher Rick Reed was recalled by the Cincinnati Reds, his new teammates argued about how they should treat him. Initially, it was suggested that he should be assigned to a locker next to the toilet. Outfielder Deion Sanders said they should lay off, that they didn't know what Reed's reasons were for breaking ranks.

Reed was a 29-year-old journeyman who had had a 9–15 won-loss record with three big league teams since his 1988 debut with Pittsburgh. According to a story in *Sports Illustrated*, his mother was a diabetic who needed money for medicine. The car she drove had one door held on by a rope. With his spring training salary, Reed bought her a new car.

There is no accurate count of the number of replacement players signed by the big league clubs. More than likely it was in excess of 600. Many of the clubs refused requests from the press for their names. In anticipation of reprisals, some general managers kept their best prospects out of harm's way and used only players, who according to scouting reports, did not have a big league future.

Wondering when it would ever end and now confronted with the possibility that the 1995 season would be washed out, the players and owners, on April 5, approved a tentative agreement to begin play on April 25, three weeks after the scheduled openers had been canceled. The schedule was then reduced from 162 to 144 games. Because of the delay, the players were docked 11 percent of their pay, bringing their combined loss since, since August 12 of the previous year, to 40 percent of a seasonal salary.

The season was played without interruption, but it wasn't until November 26, eight months later, that a lasting peace was achieved. The new contract was for four years, expiring on October 31, 2000. Still standing, at the finish line, were Selig and Fehr, along with Randy Levine, a twelfth hour replacement for Dick Ravitch, who had been management's chief negotiator since the Basic Agreement was opened. Like Ravitch, Levine had a long record of success with New York City labor unions.

According to John Harrington, the burly Ravitch, who had a thick neck and raspy voice, was dismissed because "he didn't play well on television." Ravitch couldn't control his shirt tail and was constantly tugging at his drooping pants. Had he worn suspenders, as I often suggested, he may not have lost his $750,000 post, the highest executive salary of the time, $100,000 more than Vincent's commissioner wage.

Levine arrived with an excellent record as a negotiator. Still, he was a baseball rookie and benefitted by the presence of holdover Rob Manfred. A Washington D.C.–based labor specialist with Morgan, Lewis and Bockius, Manfred had been at the table for sixteen years without interruption. He knew the territory, and equally important, had mastered the low profile essential to survival.

As the struggle continued, I was reminded of an anecdote relayed by John Gaherin, who had been management's first negotiator and

Marvin Miller's original opponent in the early days of the Players Association.

"Nearing the finish, the principal negotiators met privately," Gaherin said. "And one said to the other, 'If you save my face, I'll save your ass.'"

As they always do, both sides claimed victory, but Fehr and the players were the clear winners. They gave up nothing of consequence. The owners walked away without a salary cap, without a significant adjustment in salary arbitration, and agreeing to an increase in the minimum salary. It was chump change, from $150,000 in '97, to $170,000 in '98, to $200,000 in '99.

The final agreement included an unprecedented player concession in the form of a payroll tax. They agreed to pay the equivalent of 2.5 percent of their 1996 and 1997 salaries into a newly-created fund to promote baseball, here and abroad, and to supplement the clubs' revenue sharing program. The two-year payout was approximately $40 million.

Two other taxes were also approved:

The first was a so-called luxury tax paid by the five clubs with the highest player payrolls. It was a complex procedure but, simply put, the tax rate was 35 percent on team payrolls in excess of $55 million, the proceeds distributed to the small-market clubs. The union argued it would inhibit owner-spending, but it was a needless concern. The superstar salaries continued to soar, to $10 million in 1997 and to $11 million the following year.

The second tax—the most significant change of all—was revenue sharing, also designed to give distressed clubs some financial relief and, hence, a better opportunity to compete. It was manna from heaven. In 1996, for example, Detroit received the largest payment, $5.5 million. Pittsburgh was next with a $5.4 million grant, followed by Montreal, at $5.1 million; Kansas City, at $4.9 million; Minnesota, at $4.6 million; and Oakland and Milwaukee, at $4.4 million each. The Yankees paid the most, $7.3 million.

Revenue sharing was among Selig's major triumphs. Said Selig: "Four or five years ago everyone said it was impossible."

Part of the new deal included a two-year experiment of limited interleague play. It was successful, another feather in Selig's commissioner cap. His winning streak ended in 1997 when he tried for severe realignment. The majority opposed. For the first time Selig didn't rule by consensus.

Like Fay Vincent before him, Selig wanted the teams to be grouped according to their geographical location. His original plan, if adopted, would have resulted in the movement of fifteen franchises, some from the American League to the National and vice versa. Defeated, he offered a more modest proposal that would affect only six or seven changes. Defeated again. At the finish there was only one move: Selig's Milwaukee Brewers from the American to the National League.

While this was going on, there was the quadrennial debate on the election of a commissioner. Bowie Kuhn, the former czar, urged that both sides, players and owners, have an equal voice in the selection. This possibility, Kuhn said, had often been mentioned during his term:

"If you popped it at them right now neither side would be close to agreeing but I guess the owners would be closer to agreeing."

Former big league pitcher Jim Bunning seconded Kuhn. Now a Kentucky congressman in the U.S. House of Representatives, Bunning in his Hall of Fame induction speech said, "Hire a commissioner by mutual agreement."

It was nonsense. Bob Feller, the legendary pitcher, said neither Kuhn nor Bunning were realistic: "If a commissioner is elected by both sides, the office is eroded. Don Fehr loses clout and so does Bud Selig. I don't see that happening."

Marvin Miller, who had built the union into a powerhouse, was more specific.

"The concept of a mutual commissioner indicates no understanding of the labor-management relationship," Miller said. "It's a conflict of interests when you say 'We should have someone represent both sides.' The owners have every right to hire somebody, pay him, tell him his duties and responsibilities, and fire him when they believe he has been unsatisfactory. What is fraudulent is when people are told the commissioner represents both sides."

As Selig continued to operate out of Milwaukee, the commissioner's New York office was without leadership. This was corrected on July 22, 1997, when Paul Beeston of the Toronto Blue Jays moved to New York as baseball's president and chief operating officer, in charge of the various departments such as marketing, licensing, broadcasting, special events, legal, etc.

Two months later, Beeston began urging the owners to elect Selig as baseball's full-time commissioner. By this time, Selig's interim term was entering its sixth year.

# 22 EPILOGUE

There is a reluctance to rank the commissioners because they reigned in different times and were confronted with different problems. Judge Landis, for example, ruled with an iron fist, permissable three-quarters of a century ago when the players were without recourse. Today, the Players Association would run him off the track.

Still, I have come to some conclusions. Contrarian that I am, the two commissioners who had the worst public images and were the most pilloried by the press, were (and are) the best: Ford Frick, who was in office fourteen years, two full terms; and Bud Selig, currently in his sixth season as the so-called acting commissioner.

Frick is best known for often saying "This is a league matter," which at the time was interpreted as a weakness; he failed to take action. In my view, this indicated he had an excellent understanding of the assignment. He didn't interfere in lesser matters that should have been decided at a lower level. Also, he seldom, if ever, fed his ego and refused to bang the drum on his own behalf.

Buzzie Bavasi, the longtime general manager of the Brooklyn and Los Angeles Dodgers, who was among Frick's contemporaries concured: "We'd go to an owners' meeting," Bavasi recalled. "Ford would say, 'You have an investment. I don't. You should make the rules. That's fine with me. But you're going to have to live by them. And when you don't, I'll step in.'"

Unlike Frick, who was chastised as a do-nothing czar, Selig's term has included a succession of significant changes: dividing the league into three divisions which created a "wild card"; interleague play, first proposed seventy-five years earlier; and revenue sharing which helped sustain the small-market franchises. That he pulled down the 1994 World Series was a necessity. The fans are still booing him. What they have forgotten is that the players were on strike. Selig had no other option.

Landis was a bigoted curmudgeon whose predjudices, at that time, were generally acceptable. His best decision was his first: the lifetime suspension of the eight White Sox players who were in on the infamous 1919 World Series fix. Thereafter, Landis seemed to rule by whim. He was the "Great Punisher." The more I learned about him, the more my admiration dwindled.

Happy Chandler did more for the players than any of the commissioners. Bowie Kuhn, as has been said, "rode the tiger for fifteen years." But Kuhn was handicapped as no commissioner before him. His term coincided with the arrival of Marvin Miller, the executive director of the Players Association who brought the players unexpected riches. Miller defeated Kuhn and the owners at every turn.

Peter Ueberroth, sixth in the succession, disliked the owners even more than they disliked him. But Ueberroth was a marketing genius and, more than anyone before or since, led them to financial success. Bart Giamatti was on the job for only five months, too brief for an assessment. Fay Vincent was dismissed principally for his naive belief that he also represented the players and that in times of crisis, the press would be his best ally. He was wrong on both counts. General Eckert, the "unknown soldier," was an aberration. He did the best he could.

288

# BIBLIOGRAPHY

Allen, Lee. *100 Years of Baseball*. New York: Bartholomew House, 1950.

———*The National League Story*. New York: Hill & Wang, 1961.

Allen, Maury. *You Could Look It Up: The Life Of Casey Stengel*. New York: Times Books, 1979.

Asinof, Eliot. *Eight Men Out: The Black Sox and the 1919 World Series*. New York: Holt Rinehart and Winston, 1963.

Creamer, Robert W. *Stengel: His Life and Times*. New York: Simon and Schuster, 1984.

Durocher, Leo and Ed Linn. *Nice Guys Finish Last*. New York: Simon and Schuster, 1975.

Flood, Curt and Richard Carter. *Curt Flood: The Way It Is*. New York: Trident Press, 1970.

Frick, Ford C. *Games, Asterisks and People: Memoirs of a Lucky Fan*. New York: Crown, 1973.

Giamatti, A. Bartlett. *The Time For Paradise: Americans and Their Games*. Fort Worth: Summit Books, 1989.

Holtzman, Jerome. *No Cheering in the Press Box*. New York: Holt Rinehart and Winston, 1973.

Kuhn, Bowie and Martin Appel. *Hardball: The Education of a Baseball Commissioner*. New York: Random House, 1987.

Mann, Arthur. *Baseball Confidential: Secret History of the War Among Chandler, Durocher, MacPhail and Rickey*. David McKay Co., 1951.

Reston, James, Jr. *Collision at Home Plate: the Lives of Pete Rose and Bart Giamatti*. Edward Burlingame Books, 1991.

Seymour, Harold, Dr. *Baseball: The Golden Age*. New York: Oxford University Press, 1971.

Spink, Taylor, J. G. *Judge Landis and Twenty-Five Years of Baseball*. New York: Thomas Crowell Co., 1947.

Trimble, Vance. *Heroes, Plain Folks and Skunks: The Life and Times of Happy Chandler*. Chicago: Bonus Books, 1989.

Ueberroth, Peter, Richard Levin and Amy Quinn. *Made in America: His Own Story*. New York: William Morrow, 1985.

Valerio, Anthony. *Bart: A Life of A. Bartlett Giamatti*. New York: Harcourt Brace Jovanovich, 1991.

Veeck, Bill and Ed Linn. *The Hustler's Handbook*. New York: Simon and Schuster, 1965.

———*Veeck—as in Wreck*. New York: Simon and Schuster, 1962.

Voight, David Q. *American Baseball: From Gentleman's Sport to the Commissioner System*. Norman: University of Oklahoma Press, 1966.

*Current Biography*

# INDEX